BRUCIE

THE LIFE. THE LAUGHTER. THE ENTERTAINER.

BRUCIE

A CELEBRATION OF SIR BRUCE FORSYTH 1928–2017

JULES STENSON

JOHN BLAKE

Published by John Blake Publishing Ltd,
3 Bramber Court, 2 Bramber Road,
London W14 9PB, England

www.johnblakebooks.com

www.facebook.com/johnblakebooks ▪
twitter.com/jblakebooks ▪

First published in paperback in 2013
This revised edition published in 2017

ISBN: 978 1 78219 463 7

British Library Cataloguing-in-Publication Data:

A catalogue record for this book is available from the British Library.

Design by www.envydesign.co.uk

Printed in Great Britain by CPI Group (UK) Ltd

1 3 5 7 9 10 8 6 4 2

Papers used by John Blake Publishing are natural, recyclable products made
from wood grown in sustainable forests. The manufacturing processes conform
to the environmental regulations of the country of origin.

Every attempt has been made to contact the relevant copyright-holders,
but some were unobtainable. We would be grateful if the appropriate people
could contact us.

John Blake Publishing is an imprint of Bonnier Publishing
www.bonnierpublishing.com

CONTENTS

INTRODUCTION

It was a fine way to bow out. Sir Bruce Forsyth died on the afternoon of 18 August, 2017, in bed at his Wentworth home next to his favourite golf course, surrounded by his beloved family. His health had deteriorated markedly in the weeks before and the cause of death was bronchial pneumonia.

Bruce was survived by his wife Lady Wilnelia Forsyth and his six children – daughters Debbie, Julie and Laura from his first marriage with Penny Calvert, Charlotte and Louisa with his second spouse Anthea Redfern and a son, JJ, with Wilnelia – as well as nine grandchildren and three great-grandchildren.

Bruce's long-time manager, Ian Wilson, released a statement on behalf of the family at 4.37pm saying: 'It is with great sadness that the Forsyth family announce that Sir Bruce passed away this afternoon, peacefully at his home surrounded by his wife, Wilnelia, and all his children.

'A couple of weeks ago, a friend visited him and asked him what he had been doing these last 18 months. With a twinkle in his eye, he responded, "I've been very, very busy ... being ill!" Unfortunately, not long after this, his health deteriorated and he contracted bronchial pneumonia.

'The family would like to express their thanks to the many people who have sent cards and letters to Bruce wishing him well over his long illness and know that they will share in part the great, great loss they feel.'

The great and good paid tribute to our greatest entertainer – the ultimate song and dance man who had tap danced his way into our hearts over an incredible career spanning more than 75 years. Prime Minister Theresa May tweeted: 'We have lost a national treasure. Like millions of others, for years I watched Sir Bruce dance, sing, joke & laugh. He will be sorely missed.'

One of his oldest friends, the veteran broadcaster and interviewer Sir Michael Parkinson, said: 'He loved being a star. He loved making people laugh. He loved entertaining people. All those clichés of that kind of era and that kind of life were true in his case. There wasn't a phoney part of him. He was true and true vaudeville like a stick of rock.

'The training he went through – that's all gone now. He's the last remaining survivor of it all. There was no-one quite like him. Never was, never will be.

'What made him great was his impeccable work rate and his determination not to ease into anything, to approach every show as if it were his first. I remember watching him thinking, "You crafty old sod, you make it look so easy." And yet of course he was working away to get it right. You can't be as good as that and take it for granted. He took it seriously, and that's why he lasted so long and became so good at it.'

Comedian Jimmy Tarbuck, another close personal friend who succeeded Bruce as host of *Sunday Night at the London Palladium*, said he was 'one of the most talented men this country has ever produced.'

Strictly Come Dancing bosses paid their own tribute to the star, saying the show's success was in part due to being 'fronted by a genuine legend of stage and screen'. His *Strictly* co-stars were heartbroken. Tess Daly, Bruce's co-host on *Strictly* from when the show first started in 2004, said: 'There are no words to describe how heartbroken I am to be told the saddest news, that my dear friend Sir Bruce Forsyth has passed away.

'From the moment we met, Bruce and I did nothing but laugh our way through a decade of working together on *Strictly Come Dancing* and I will never forget his generosity, his brilliant sense of humour and his drive to entertain the audiences he so loved.

'He was a gentleman and a true legend and I will miss him deeply. My heart goes out to Winnie [his wife], and his beautiful family at this sad time.'

Claudia Winkleman, who took over Bruce's role hosting the show with Tess, said: 'He was the King of TV, the Prince of performers and the most generous of people... all toe-tapping twinkle, all kindness, all love....'

Len Goodman, *Strictly*'s former head judge, said Forsyth was one of his heroes. 'He was so kind and encouraging to me, the other judges and all those involved in the show,' he said. 'I used to pop round to his dressing room and chat about stars he met. The truth is there was no one I mentioned he hadn't met.

'His work ethic, professionalism and charm will be with me forever. One of his catchphrases was "you're my favourite". Well, you were one of mine and the nation's favourites. Bruce, it was nice to see you, to see you nice.'

Former *Strictly* judge Arlene Phillips paid tribute, saying: 'Working with him on *Strictly* was personally a joy. His endless teasing of my judging style, particularly with strong sportsmen, was an ongoing joke. His enormous support after I was let go from the *Strictly* panel meant so much. He was a true national treasure and there will never be another like him. He will be missed by many generations.'

Sir Bruce, whose career spanned an astonishing eight decades following his first TV appearance as an 11-year-old in 1939, had not been seen in public since hosting *Strictly*'s Children In Need special in 2015.

He had announced that he was quitting *Strictly Come Dancing* a year before – on April 4 2014. He said it was the 'right time to step down from the rigours' of hosting the live show after 12 years at the helm.

'After 10 wonderful years and 11 series, I believe it is now the right time to step down from the rigours of presenting the *Strictly* live shows,' said Sir Bruce. He said that he would miss the show but would be 'watching intently'.

'I've always said that at the end of last series I was getting that feeling, 'Is this the time?',' Sir Bruce revealed to the BBC. 'I've just been on my three month break in the Caribbean, I've been thinking about it all the time. Live television takes its toll when you've been doing it for many years, it's a pressure thing. But I'm not retiring, that's the last thing in the world I want to do. This isn't Brucie walking into the sunset.'

Sir Bruce said phoning co-presenter Tess Daly to break the news had been 'like a boyfriend breaking up with his girl.'

'She was in tears and started me off a bit. It's sad, I've loved doing it,' he said. 'But there are times when you look at yourself in the mirror and say, "Should you be doing this any longer?" That was our biggest series last year that we've ever had so it's a high to go off on.'

Sir Bruce, who was knighted in 2011, missed a number of shows in his final series of *Strictly* due to illness. He quit the results show in 2010 and was replaced by Claudia Winkleman. The results show is recorded immediately after the live show on a Saturday.

In one of his last interviews, Sir Bruce admitted to the *Mail on Sunday* that he did not miss *Strictly*. 'I don't regret it, it was time to go,' he said. 'I never enjoyed it as much as people thought. The problem for me was that I didn't get to meet anyone in the show, nor really get to know anyone very well – not even backstage. And what I actually like is the interaction. It's what I do. I found *Strictly* very lonely.

'When I left I knew it was the right time. Leave it at the top. I just didn't want to do it anymore. It was the same with *The Generation Game*. I quit that show when we had 20 million viewers and people couldn't believe it.' When asked about his Saturday night viewing, the star said: 'I'll record *Strictly* but I like to take my wife out to dinner on a Saturday night like a normal person.'

His health suffered and he largely disappeared from public life. In October 2015 he suffered a fall at home which saw him rushed to hospital with minor concussion and cuts on his face. Further investigation uncovered an abdominal aortic aneurysm which required keyhole surgery.

Following surgery, he recorded a video message from his Surrey home after missing the show's 2015 Christmas special, which would be his last appearance on British TV. Holding his three-week-old granddaughter, he said: 'I can't tell you how disappointed I am not to be with you on this Christmas Day.

'Well, actually I can tell you. I'm absolutely gutted. 'I haven't quite got over my operation, which went very well by the way. But mind you, I was a bit worried when the surgeon stood over me and said, "I'll carve?"

'Anyway, that's enough of my rehearsed ad-libs. Thank you to all our stars and their professional partners for doing this special Christmas show. Remember you are all my favourites, and I haven't said that for a long, long time.

'I'll be thinking of you. Merry Christmas, Happy New Year and keep dancing!'

As the camera panned out to reveal the baby, the entertainer added with his trademark humour: 'I've been busy babysitting my new three-week-old granddaughter Anastasia Monroe, isn't she lovely? I hope she's got my chin.'

Sir Bruce, whose beloved catchphrases included 'Nice to see you, to see you nice', 'Give us a twirl' and 'Didn't he do well?', was desperate to return to television, but continued to battle poor health. He was left bedbound and had to cancel a string of public appearances. While recovering from keyhole surgery, he missed the funeral of close friend Ronnie Corbett in April 2016.

Then in February of 2017, six months before his death, the former *Sunday Night at the London Palladium* presenter was taken to hospital with a severe chest infection, spending five days in intensive care.

Brucie's wife of 34 years – ex-Miss World Lady Wilnelia – reported in May that he was doing 'much better' and had started 'walking around now'. In another interview she revealed that she prayed her husband would be able to perform again.

Lord Michael Grade, who visited the star just ten days before his death, said that while his body may have been 'frail', his mind remained 'sharp as a tack' in his final days.

The TV boss said: 'He'd been very ill. I went to his house and we spent the whole morning talking and reminiscing. He was laughing with me and his memory was phenomenal and the twinkle was in his eye, which is how I will always remember him.

'He was wonderfully amazed at how well he's done. He couldn't believe that he had lasted as long. He was very proud of the fact that he had been on so many hit shows. My heart goes out to Winnie and all the family. And to the nation who have lost their favourite and greatest ever entertainer.'

On the night of his death, the BBC pulled *The One Show* off air to broadcast a special hour-long tribute. The corporation's director general Tony Hall said Sir Bruce, who had a £17million fortune, was 'part of all of our lives and we'll miss him dearly'.

He added: 'Sir Bruce was one of the greatest entertainers our country has ever known. He has delighted millions of people and defined Saturday night television for decades. His warmth and wit were legendary.'

Sir Bruce, officially crowned the male TV entertainer with the longest career in the 2013 *Guinness Book of World Records*, had been open about his own mortality.

In one of his last interviews, he told *The Sun*: 'There's no getting away from it. When I look at all my friends that have gone – Eric Sykes, Frankie Howerd, Sammy Davis Jr – I know I'm on borrowed time.

'How I'm still here I just don't know. I don't know how, why or wherefore. But I'm not questioning it that much. The day will come and it could be tomorrow, who knows? It's no good saying it's never going to come. You've got to be able to accept it, so I'm conditioning myself so it's not going to be a big surprise. It will just be, "OK, time to go".

'When the time is up I'll be ready for it. I probably won't be very happy about it, but I'll know it's time to go.'

CHAPTER 1

FRED ASTAIRE
AND A FUR COAT

Bruce Forsyth was born lucky. He came into the world on 22 February 1928 – halfway between the First and the Second World Wars. It meant that he missed the killing fields of the Somme and was also too young to ever be called up to fight Hitler, being just a few months short of his 17th birthday when the Nazis were defeated. Not that Bruce ever saw himself as a fighter. Almost from the moment he took his first kick, he knew that he was destined for a career in show business. And that extraordinary career began when he was still just a boy.

Bruce began life as Bruce Forsyth-Johnson – the double-barrelled name came from the fashion of the day that when somebody married into a wealthy family, the two surnames were hyphenated. That is what happened on his father John's side of the family before Bruce was born. The future Mr

Showbiz grew up in Edmonton, north London – then quite a prosperous suburb of the capital, though it isn't as smart these days. Bruce's parents lived in the area all their lives. He was the youngest of three children – his sister Maisie was 10 years his elder and his brother John (as was common then, the family tradition was to call all first-born boys John) came five years later.

His father ran a garage business in a small alleyway that ran alongside the family home. As well as three pumps for the sale of petrol, mechanic John also bought, sold and repaired cars. Bruce's father was a workaholic who would never turn down a job as he tirelessly provided for his young family. With the garage right next to the family home, customers would be calling at all hours, even when the pumps were shut. Canny John never turned anyone away. This proud work ethic was instilled in all of his three children. It also gave the Forsyth-Johnsons a comfortable living, which would be considered solidly middle class these days. A key sign of their prosperity was the fact that they had a television as early as the late 1930s when few families could boast such luxury. The mass ownership of TVs didn't happen until the Queen's Coronation in 1953 when millions were sold.

Though never religious himself, Bruce's father and mother Florence were both members of The Salvation Army. Sundays were devoted to religion, with all the children attending as many as three Salvation Army meetings. John Senior played the euphonium and the cornet in the local Salvation Army band, as well as organising a boys' drum-and-fife band. Florence was a talented singer who was well known in the area for singing hymns each Sunday morning on Edmonton Green.

Bruce – also know as Bru or even Boo Boo by his devoted parents – was always a bit of a handful. As he himself admitted, 'I was a nightmare to control – a horrible, miserable, bossy child who always wanted my own way.' He would throw such uncontrollable tantrums when his parents left the house without him that they would have to secretly sneak their coats and bags into the car without eagle-eyed Boo Boo seeing. Maisie would be left to babysit while her poor harassed parents enjoyed a few hours away from the chaos.

Starting school, inevitably, proved to be a nightmare for a child with such an explosive temper. Bru cried so much on his first day that Florence was forced to take him home. The stubborn five-year-old then refused to return for several days before finally settling in. No academic high-flier, he was far happier on the football field where he attracted the nickname 'Spider Johnson' because of his snaking runs down the right wing.

Bruce's life was to change for ever on a trip to the Regal cinema in Edmonton as a six-year-old when he saw Fred Astaire and Ginger Rogers starring in the 1935 classic *Top Hat*. It featured two unforgettable songs by Irving Berlin, 'Top Hat, White Tie and Tails' and 'Cheek to Cheek', and was the most successful film in the Astaire and Rogers partnership. Bruce was captivated by Astaire – his boyhood hero – and would spend hours at home trying to mimic his best-known moves. He saw *Top Hat* at least four times in the space of a few weeks. 'I want to dance like Fred Astaire when I grow up,' he told his mother. And from that moment both his parents knew that their son would never be happy unless he was allowed to try his luck in show business.

For a father with an engineering background such as John Senior, this could have been a difficult decision to accept. But, in fact, both he and Florence could not have been more supportive of their hyperactive little Boo Boo. His father, in particular, wanted his youngest to aspire to a better and more comfortable life than the one he had endured. He once held up his hands to his boy – they were ingrained with years of black grime from the engines he tweaked daily. 'You don't want to end up with hands like these,' his father told him solemnly. Boo Boo knew this only too well – even at such a tender age. He said later, 'My head was always up in the air, show business, becoming a big star – that was the only thing I thought about.'

Other times Bruce would be at the theatre with his parents when a tap dancer would appear on stage. 'You're twice as good as him,' his proud father would tell the young Bruce, who, embarrassed that they would be overheard, would lovingly tell his dad to keep his voice down. John's encouragement had a purpose: he knew only the most determined dancers would ever make it to the top. If Bruce doubted his talent, others would too and he would be finished. It was a very American attitude – and a very unusual one for 1930s Britain. But it worked – one thing Bruce never lacked was self-belief and a lot of that was down to his doting dad.

Bruce knew that the key to achieving his dream wasn't just talent but good old-fashioned hard graft. He had natural dancing skills was abundance but, crucially, he was also dedicated enough to guarantee that he made the very best use of what God had given him.

Soon Bruce had converted his parents' front room into a

makeshift dance studio, rolling up the carpet so that he could imitate Fred Astaire's best moves on the red lino, which added a more authentic tap-dancing sound to his steps. Tireless Bruce would dance till he dropped – even venturing on top of the corrugated roofs of his dad's lock-up garages for some really ear-shattering routines. The easiest way to describe him was simple: he was the Billy Elliot of his day (but without the interfering dad who thought dancing was only for girls).

With young Bruce showing so much promise as a dancer, his parents quickly realised he would also need a little more finesse if he were ever to make it beyond performing in school productions. They began sending him to dancing lessons with a teacher called Tilly Vernon in Tottenham, a short bus ride away from his home. Bruce was the only boy in the class. He soon outgrew this tuition and found a more experienced teacher miles away in Brixton, a five-hour round trip right across London every Saturday. Bruce never missed a lesson – it was already something of an obsession with him.

Young Bruce – hyperactive from all that dancing – was a slip of a boy. Or as he described himself, 'a skinny little runt'. Florence, a talented seamstress, would make all the very girlie costumes – complete with sequins to make them glittery – he needed for regular tap-dancing competitions. Bruce received a fair amount of stick from other boys, who branded him a 'sissy'. No coward though, Bruce was brave enough to take on his tormentors and boasted of giving one particularly obnoxious lad a 'right pasting' after he underestimated young Boo Boo's prowess with his fists.

Aged just 10, Bruce made his first appearance on television. It was just a few weeks before the start of the Second World

War in 1939 when television was still in its infancy. *Come and be Televised* was a very early version of *The X Factor* – grown-ups and young performers such as Bruce performed their act for the presenter Jasmine Bligh. If she thought an act was good enough, it went straight on the show, broadcast from *Radiolympia*. This was where the BBC pioneered television broadcasting. The studios at Alexandra Palace, north London, were opened on 2 November 1936 and provided the world's first regular high-definition television. Its initial range was 35 miles – easily far enough to reach Bruce's family home in Edmonton.

Needless to say, Bruce breezed through his audition with a polished song-and-dance routine. An impressed Bligh asked Bruce to name his hero and his main ambition in life. Quick as a flash, he smiled and replied, 'I wanted to be a famous dancer like Fred Astaire and buy my mother a fur coat.'

Bligh loved his response, which was pure show business, and, laughing, told the young wannabe, 'All right then, do your song and dance for us.' Bruce remembered being terrified of the huge television camera capturing his every move. In fact, the whole experience was disconcerting. There was no audience, which Bruce had been used to and he had to create an atmosphere using his charisma and burgeoning professionalism. Somehow he did and his act was a success. His dad was working at the garage that Saturday morning but his proud mother was there to see Bruce light up the screen. Almost no one else was. Few homes in those days had a TV and Bruce had told no one about the audition. Sadly, no tape exists of Bruce's big debut.

Bruce left the studio walking on air. He was still not even in his teens, yet he'd already had his allotted 15 minutes of fame. But there was no way this determined young showman was going to settle for that. He already wanted to become one of the biggest stars in Britain.

Any chance of Bruce building on this early success was abruptly curtailed by the start of the Second World War. With bombs about to start dropping across the capital, it was considered far too dangerous for Bruce to stay in north London and he was evacuated to the Essex seaside resort of Clacton. Unlike other boys his age, Bruce was billeted to his new home on his own rather than as one of a pair. His brother and sister were deemed too old to leave the capital. Bruce, living with an elderly lady, was desperately lonely and the petulant boy whose tantrums when he didn't get his own way had caused his parents so much upset longed to return to Edmonton. Bombs or no bombs, there was no way he was staying on his own in miserable Clacton.

Just three days after his evacuation, John and Florence came to see their lonely little boy. He immediately parked himself in their car and refused to get out until they had taken him home. The rules stated that parents weren't obliged to evacuate their children. And when John saw a huge British warship moored near the end of the pier, he figured, not unreasonably, that his son was no safer next to an obvious bombing target like that than he was back in north London. 'Good God, he's nearer to the war than we are,' he told his wife. So Boo Boo got his wish and spent the rest of the war in the bosom of his family.

Bruce was a happy child of war. His schooling over the next three years – disrupted inevitably by the tumultuous events going on in mainland Europe – was practically non-existent. Instead, he kept busy performing in an amateur song-and-dance troupe set up by his mother to put on entertainment shows to raise money for the war effort. They performed all over London wherever they were wanted: in school halls, churches, even factories. Takings – around £75 a show – went straight into a 'Buy a Spitfire Fund'. As well as performing with a group, Bruce would do solo numbers and soon found that he was a natural at interacting with the enthusiastic wartime audiences. He would crack a joke – often at the expense of their straw-hatted female pianist – and they would be rolling in the aisles. Bruce was fast becoming not just a singer and a dancer, but an entertainer – an entertainer with a skill that would soon make him a fortune: how to work an audience.

These were hairy times for Bruce and his family. Edmonton was badly bombed – and the Forsyth-Johnsons had their own Anderson air-raid shelter in their back garden. Such was the relentless nature of the night-time Nazi blitzes that they often huddled together with other families in larger shelters in the local park. The war, to the teenage Bruce, was one big adventure. He would collect shrapnel that had fallen on to the roofs of his dad's garages the previous night. Anything with a number on it, particularly from a shot-down Messerschmitt fighter or Focke-Wulf bomber, was particularly prized.

Bruce left school at 14 – considered perfectly normal at that time. He had absolutely no qualifications and would be the first to admit that his best subject was bunking off. While most of his classmates began working in factories as part of the war effort, Bruce had a very different idea about how he could serve his country – by keeping everyone entertained on stage. By now, Bruce wasn't just an accomplished dancer and singer but also a talented pianist, and he was adding comedy to his act by doing impressions of the leading stars of the day. His parents, as ever, backed the move, telling their boy, 'Go for it, Bru.'

In those days, pupils were given a school-leaver's form – signed by the head and detailing their academic progress – to pass on to future employers. Bruce was summoned by his head and told his report wouldn't be good. Bruce wasn't the least bit worried – he knew academic qualifications would be of no use to him on the stage. With the irrepressible confidence of an adolescent who had never had a serious setback, he told the head, 'I'm going into a business, sir, where they go more by what they can see you do, rather than what you've done.' What business is that? Bruce was asked. 'Show business,' he replied. The head laughed and told him, 'Then you are going to need all the luck you can get. Off you go.'

Luck was again on Bruce's side at this time. Winston Churchill was acutely aware of the need to keep up morale at home as Britain was blitzed by the Nazis. That meant keeping all the theatres across the country – with as many as three or four in even the small cities – open to entertain the masses every night. Clearly, with so many performers fighting overseas, there was a shortage of acts, which created almost limitless opportunities for an ambitious teenager keen to take up any job offered to him, no matter how lowly or poorly paid. Bruce quickly showed, in the guise of his new act – dramatically entitled Boy Bruce, the Mighty Atom – that his confidence was not misplaced.

CHAPTER 2

THE MIGHTY ATOM BOMBS

Bruce Forsyth was hardly what you would call an overnight sensation. All the success he enjoyed over the years was founded on the years he spent toiling in small theatres across the country to often bored and inattentive audiences. It was here that he learned his craft and took the rough edges off an act that he was honest enough to admit was 'awe-inspiringly awful' at times. Mighty things from small beginnings grow. And this was certainly true of Bruce. For he started out as the smallest thing of all: an atom.

Yes, an atom. Or to give him his full name: Boy Bruce, the Mighty Atom. You have to admit, it does have a bit of a ring to it. What audience member isn't going to be at least a little bit intrigued about what this extraordinary act could involve? The idea for the name actually came from Bruce's parents. It was the dawn of a new scientific age and all the talk of the day was of molecules and atoms – and, at 14, Bruce was so young that it seemed particularly apt. Proud of his new moniker, Bruce announced his availability to the theatre world in an advert in *The Stage* newspaper, which simply said that he was 'Vacant for Everything'.

That vacancy was soon filled when Bruce landed his first stage role – bottom of the bill in a touring show starring The Great Marzo. He was so far down the running order in the programme notes that he was listed next to the wines and spirits available from the bar. The show had been put together by a London variety agent who Bruce had starting working for as an office boy in his first job since leaving school. This largely involved making the tea.

A week before the tour was due to start, the agent suffered serious cash-flow problems. He was so desperate that he ended up tapping up Bruce's ever-loyal parents for cash – without their help their son's debut was in jeopardy. They were asked to stump up £25 – not only a substantial sum in those days but a small fortune to a couple surviving on earnings from a modest garage business. The fact that they didn't hesitate in helping shows once again how determined they were to do everything they could to get their beloved youngest on the road to stardom. Bruce felt guilty that they were so out of pocket but, keen to further his career, he was just happy that the show would go ahead.

Bruce's first night was at the Theatre Royal in Bilston, near Wolverhampton – a complete dive of a venue that has long since been demolished. His act was hardly likely to go down in show-business history as one of the great debuts. It involved the teenage Bruce, dressed as a hotel page boy, opening a series of suitcases, playing an accordion and ukulele, and finishing off with a tap-dance. If it sounded like a dog's dinner, that's because it was. Bruce later admitted that it was 'truly dreadful'. Some of Bruce's excited relatives had made the long trip up to the Midlands to see him and they were so embarrassed by his performance that they skipped seeing him backstage afterwards. So yes, the Mighty Atom had bombed!

The show had a disastrous first week, with Bruce's share of the takings a paltry 13 shillings and 4 pence – not even enough to pay for his digs and his train fare home. This time, Bruce had to tap his parents for some money so that he could make the humiliating trip back to Edmonton. Such a disastrous baptism of fire has killed many fledgling show-business careers before they have even got started. But Bruce was made of sterner stuff. He knew that he had to improve fast but his boundless enthusiasm remained and he wasn't going to let one small setback put him off.

For the next few years Bruce continued to learn the ropes travelling around the country appearing in dingy theatres like the one in Bilston. This involved long train journeys, with Bruce still so small and skinny that he was able to curl up and go to sleep in the overhead luggage racks. Bruce also worked for the Red Cross, appearing at American army camps all over Britain. While he stayed in many pretty unseemly dumps, on some occasions the accommodation was far better and he would experience comfort like never before. He remembered staying in one Manchester hotel room that had its own telephone. 'What luxury for a fifteen-year-old,' Bruce recalled years later. 'I immediately phoned home and said this was the life for me.'

By the time the war ended, Bruce had formed a double act with Les Roy, a drummer and dancer. He celebrated Victory in Europe (VE) Day on 8 May 1945, while performing with Roy at the Whitehall Theatre, just down the road from 10 Downing Street in central London. He clambered on to the theatre roof to enjoy wonderful views of the dense crowds dancing in the streets on that sunny day in late spring as Prime Minister Winston Churchill declared that Germany had been defeated. He recalled the huge roar that went up at midnight when the 'official ceasefire' was declared – and the spectacular fireworks display next to Big Ben that followed. Some dancing girls were sunbathing topless on the same roof. Wary of getting strap marks, which didn't look good on stage, they used halfpennies and, in some cases, larger half-crowns to cover their nipples. Frisky Bruce didn't know which way to look!

Bruce had been a boy living and working in an adult's world. To survive he had to grow up fast. It was a pretty risqué environment for a lad brought up by two God-fearing Salvation Army followers, for whom any discussion of the birds and the bees was a complete taboo. 'Sex was never, ever discussed in our house,' Bruce said. 'I don't even think my parents knew that homosexuality existed.' Bruce was surrounded by gorgeous female dancers who wouldn't think twice about picking up men for sex at the digs shared by their teenage co-star. Bruce longed for a slice of the action but was way too young to ever get an invite to the party. As he complained later, 'My chief problem was I was the youngest in the troupe. Love and sex were all around but not for me, it seemed. And I hadn't got a clue how to change things. All the girls simply saw me as a kid, the baby of the show. They'd give me chocolate but nothing else!'

One night in Nottingham – famed for having the most beautiful girls in the country – Bruce's luck changed. After the last show of a week's cabaret at a dance hall, Bruce caught the eye of a petite beauty in high heels and asked her for the last waltz. They got on famously and she then allowed him to walk her home and invited him inside for a nightcap. As she took off her coat and they prepared for what would be Bruce's first night of sex, he spotted, to his horror, a picture of her baby boy on the mantelpiece and then, even worse, right next to it another of a man in a soldier's uniform. It was clearly her husband who was away serving in the war. Bruce was plagued by guilt, thinking, 'I shouldn't be here – this is all so wrong.' How was he going to get out of this sticky situation? He did what women have done for centuries and told his older suitor that he had a headache and needed an early night in his own bed!

Bruce did finally pop his cherry aged 19 while appearing in a show in Carlisle. It hadn't been doing well at the box office and half the cast was laid off just eight weeks into its four-month run. Those cast aside included Bruce and a pretty young dancing girl called Doris who he had taken a shine to. Bruce had longed to ask her out but was too shy to make the first move. However, with both of them out of a job and about to go their separate ways, Bruce knew this was his last chance. After their last show together, they went out for a few drinks. Bruce drove her back to her digs afterwards in his Austin Ten and they became very amorous in the car as they tearfully comforted each other over losing their jobs. One thing led to another and, rather magically, the fumbling young Bruce ended up losing his L plates. He later recalled, 'I agree cars are not the best places for making love but that's where it happened. Despite the uncomfortable, cramped circumstances, I christened my car and we did each other a bit of good.'

By now Bruce was no longer the Mighty Atom, having outgrown his first stage name. It was never feasible to perform under his real name – Bruce Forsyth-Johnson – which was far too much of a mouthful. Bruce's first choice for a stage name was Jack Johnson but that was already taken by a professional fighter who went on to become world champion. So he settled for Bruce Forsyth.

Gradually, Bruce's act started to gel and the quality of the venues he performed in improved too. His ambition then was to appear in the plush theatres owned by Moss Empires. 'They were a different thing altogether,' he explained. 'The dressing rooms were better, so were the bands, and seats were nice and plush rather than all worn and dirty. And there were boxes!' It was certainly a marked improvement on the Theatre Royal in Bilston.

Even with his career starting to take off, there would still be weeks when Bruce struggled to find work – a fate shared by almost everyone starting out in show business. Bruce was lucky that his parents lived in London and that he could live rent-free while he hunted for his next booking.

His next lucky break came when he saw that the legendary Windmill Theatre in Soho – which became notorious in the early 1930s when it became Britain's first nude revue – had advertised for 'juveniles' who could sing and dance. At 19,

Bruce was hardly a juvenile but he was still fairly boyish and he hoped that he might fit the bill.

The Windmill ran a programme of continuous variety from 2.30pm until 11pm. Inspired by the famous Moulin Rouge in Paris, the highlight was nude living statues or, to use the French, *tableaux vivants*, who were billed simply as the 'Windmill Girls'.

It was extraordinary in those conservative times that the Windmill had managed to get a licence for its racy shows. While the girls could appear naked, the one catch was that they had to remain completely still. The ruling stated: 'If you move, it's rude.' This, somehow, was considered to be high art and therefore in accordance with the Lord Chamberlain's strict laws on public decency.

The Windmill's shows became a huge commercial success and the Windmill Girls took their show on tour to other London and provincial theatres and music halls. The Piccadilly and Pavilion theatres quickly copied the idea and ran non-stop shows too.

Just a few streets away from the Windmill, there were plenty of far more risqué shows going on every night in the seedier end of Soho but these, of course, were unlicensed and completely illegal.

Bruce auditioned for the Windmill's owner, impresario Vivian Van Damm, and was immediately taken on as a member of its resident song-and-dance company for the princely sum of £25 a week – a huge jump on his previous earnings.

Bruce was thrilled but the job offer came with a warning – he was not allowed to even look at the naked girls on stage, let alone fraternise with them. Mr Van Damm, it was stressed, 'would not stand for any nonsense – and will step on it immediately'. Once again, the young Bruce would be surrounded by beautiful and sexually voracious women but sex, for him at least, was out of bounds! Ever the professional, Bruce took to these 'hands off' strictures without any problem. Work had always been the be-all and end-all for him – and if that meant not letting sex get in the way, so be it.

But just three weeks into his time at the Windmill, disaster struck – he was called up for National Service. With Bruce now on the brink of real stardom, his call-up could not have come at a worse time. The one consolation was that he had impressed Van Damm so much during those three weeks that he was promised his old job back as soon he came out of the forces. Even so, he still faced two and a half pointless years away in the Royal Air Force doing meaningless jobs when the country wasn't at war anyway.

He was first posted to Warrington in Cheshire where new recruits were knocked into shape and taught the joys of square bashing – the endless marching drills performed to instil discipline. Bruce also had to learn a skill in the RAF and so chose to become a teleprinter operator – figuring that if ever did fail to make it in show business, he would have a trade to fall back on. He also hoped that it would keep his fingers nimble for the piano. He was later transferred to Carlisle in Cumbria – about as far away from the West End as you can get in England. In this remote outpost 300 miles from the theatreland, he tried to his best to keep his hand in as the pianist in an RAF band that performed at dances.

Still, Bruce was never one to mope and he soon picked up a lovely new girlfriend. Clearly he couldn't take her back to the barracks, so the Austin Ten's back seat once again saw some action as a love machine. As Bruce joked, 'By then, I had become used to cars doubling up as love nests!'

Bruce finally left the RAF in the autumn of 1949. He went straight back to the Windmill to make sure they would keep their promise to take him back on again. Fearful that they would have forgotten all about him and that he would have to start from scratch again, Bruce knew it could go either way. He was told, 'Of course we'll have you back. Welcome home.'

He soon became one of the lead performers at the Windmill, responsible for arranging the song-and-dance duets. One of the young tap dancers he choreographed was Lionel Blair, who has enjoyed a career almost as long as Bruce's and later found fame as a team captain on the TV show *Give Us a Clue*.

It was a gruelling workload – six shows a day, six days a week. Bruce wasn't the only star to spend his early years at the Windmill. As well as Lionel, countless other big names were discovered there, including Peter Sellers, Harry Secombe, Michael Bentine, Kenneth More, Tony Hancock, Nicholas Parsons and Brucie's future comedy writing pal Barry Cryer. Bruce and Cryer became friends at this time and would work together several times over the next few decades. Cryer was one of the first gag-writers on *The Generation Game*.

Bruce later conceded that the sheer relentlessness of the schedule meant there was no better training ground for a young performer like him. He reckoned that he learned something new with each performance – when you are performing 36 times a week, it is one heck of a learning curve. It was a tough audience too because most of them – much the worse for wear at the best of times – were only there to see the naked girls.

This was the early 1950s – the heyday of the Hollywood musical. *Singin' in the Rain, Carousel, Oklahoma!* – Bruce lived for these cinema classics. By now Bruce's hero Fred Astaire had been superseded by a whole new generation of stars, including Gene Kelly and Judy Garland. Bruce, of course, longed for this kind of stardom.

Bruce was only in his early twenties but he had already been treading the boards for almost a decade. It was a job he loved but what was it going to lead to? Hollywood and mega-stardom, or a life of unfulfilled drudgery in provincial theatres across Britain? If Bruce was worried that he was never going to make it, he wasn't letting on. Everyone from the Windmill remembers his cheery optimism. Bruce was right to look on the bright side. These were happy days: he finally had a bit of money in his pocket and the dreary postwar hangover marked by deprivation and rationing was finally wearing off.

Bruce's parents had done everything they could to set their son on the road to stardom. But sadly neither of them would live long enough to enjoy his success. And the last years of their lives were scarred by a tragedy that haunted Bruce for the rest of his life, as we shall discover next.

CHAPTER 3

THE TRAGEDY THAT SCARRED HIS LIFE

They were like chalk and cheese. One a twinkle-toed showbiz dandy who refused to do any manual work for fear that he would damage his beautiful hands, the other never happier than when he was in overalls and smeared in grease beneath the bonnet of a car. Five years separated Bruce and his big brother John and they always occupied very different worlds but, despite the differences, they were very close. Bruce adored John, describing him later as a 'really loveable lad'. John's death, aged just 20, in what was an easily avoidable accident in an air-training exercise during the Second World War, changed Bruce for ever. It was tragedy from which his beloved parents never really recovered at all.

John had been itching to join up from the moment Britain had gone to war when he was 16. He was too young then and had to wait another two years before he achieved a boyhood ambition and enlisted with the Royal Air Force. He saw it not just as his patriotic duty but also as an exciting adventure. Bruce could not have been more proud of his big brother when he arrived home days later in his immaculate new blue uniform.

John spent the next two years away from the family, largely flying out of bases in Scotland. He was thrilled to be playing a crucial role in the war effort and loved every minute of his time in the RAF. He would write regularly to his family, and Bruce would eagerly read his dramatic dispatches.

Everything changed one spring day in 1943 – just two years before the end of the war. Bruce, still only 15, had returned home after several days away performing as the Mighty Atom. He would always spend any time off back at the family home in Edmonton, enjoying some home cooking and a bit of TLC from his mum. But from the moment Bruce opened the front door he could tell that something wasn't right. The Forsyth-Johnson house – attached to the family business and almost always a hive of activity – was unexpectedly empty and eerily quiet. Bruce looked everywhere for his mum and dad but they had vanished. Just hours earlier, there had been that unannounced knock on the door. A senior officer was standing solemnly in front of them with some terrible news. Like any parent with a loved one away fighting, they'd imagined the scenario. They had prayed it would not happen to them. Now they were grappling with the horrible reality: John's Wellington bomber had crashed on a training exercise in Scotland and, along with 11 others, he had been killed. Miraculously, seven of the men flying that night had been plucked from the icy water and survived. But not their John.

Eventually, his parents returned home and Bruce heard in more detail what had happened to his beloved brother, a flight sergeant serving with the RAF's Volunteer Reserve. The tragedy had happened while John was on a training exercise in Turnberry – home to the famous British Open golf course and very close to Ayr on the west coast of Scotland. It was one of the worst domestic flying disasters to hit the RAF during the Second World War. What was even more heartbreaking for the whole family was that John's body had still not been found. He was simply posted as 'missing while on low-altitude practice'. Was there just a slim possibility that John was still alive? So many service personnel were mistakenly assumed to be dead after being reported missing during the War, only to turn up later alive and well after miraculous escapes. Certainly that was the hope that Bruce's mum Florence in particular clung to over many years, even after the war ended. Perhaps he'd been rescued by a passing trawler and taken to some far-away place, such as South America or South Africa, and would return home one day. You could hardly blame Florence for not giving up hope but her wild theory seemed completely fanciful to Bruce and his dad, who knew that John would have been straight on the first ship home soon after his rescue. No, John was dead, right enough – but how had he died?

That mystery was only cleared up a few years ago when a Margaret Morrell, who had been researching many of the fatal crashes that had happened in that part of Scotland during the war, wrote to Bruce. It had been assumed until then that John had died on Friday, 21 May 1943, when seven aircraft were lost on the same night while on training exercises to lay sea mines and torpedoes. But the real story was very different.

Morrell sent Bruce official documentation showing that, in fact, only three Wellington bombers were lost that night during the training exercise. The first plane had misjudged its height and crashed into the sea while undertaking low-level attacks on a target ship. The inexperienced pilot had become confused because of the glassy appearance of the sea on what was a very dark night and had committed a serious error of judgement. Immediately, the crews of the two other Wellingtons out that night went in search of survivors. And as they desperately scoured for bodies the same horrible error occurred. Again the pilots were befuddled by the appearance of the sea and this time the two Wellingtons crashed into each other.

The news shocked Bruce to the core. It seemed such a needless loss of life. He was desperately proud of the fact that his brother had died serving his country. But he knew, too, that John would far rather die from enemy fire than in what later turned out to be a needless accident.

A report by Squadron Leader Tony Spooner DSO DFC – unearthed by Margaret Morrell – gave the reasons for the triple tragedy. It happened because the crews did not have low-level radio altimeters, which measure the height you are flying at. Instead they had more rudimentary pressure-sensitive altimeters that didn't have the detail needed to fly in such hazardous conditions. On that night in Turnberry, the low flying had to be judged solely by the pilot's eye. This is relatively straightforward when the sea is choppy because of the highly visible white waves but the sea became a death trap when it was calm and it appeared to the pilot as one huge black expanse. It ended up looking the same from 500 feet as it did from a few feet off the ground. Squadron Leader Spooner explained that, when the first Wellington ended up 'in the drink', the other crews put on their landing lights, flew low and scoured for survivors. The pilots in the two other aircraft tragically made the same mistake as the first one.

There were real tales of bravery that night despite the losses. The skipper of the first aircraft to crash spent six hours in the freezing sea before being fished out the next morning near the Mull of Kintyre. After being flown back to Turnberry, he quickly realised that they could muster a fresh crew from the eight survivors. 'Would it be all right, sir, if we formed up as a crew and finished the training course?' he asked Spooner, whose report concluded, 'He had already obtained the consent of the survivors from the other lost crews. What could we do in the face of such determination but say yes?'

Bruce was spooked by something that had happened to him on the very same day his brother died. He had been performing with the American Red Cross at a base in Bedfordshire and he had been given the afternoon off. It was a beautiful sunny day and a group of the lads had gone down to the river to play ball. During the game, the ball hit Bruce on the finger, bending it right back and really hurting him. He felt quite sick afterwards and was forced to lie down for a bit to recover in one of the bunks. It was then that he had this very strange dream, which involved him flying low in an aeroplane over the sea. In Bruce's fantasy, he suddenly felt the need to jump out of the plane. It was at this point that he woke up as he tried to jump out of the bunk in which he was sleeping. At the time, Bruce just dismissed it as a strange dream we all occasionally have, which has no bearing on real events. A few days later, when told of his brother's accident, he could see it as nothing other than an eerie premonition.

Despite being a talented mechanic, John, like Bruce, was also an accomplished pianist. After his brother's death, Bruce found it increasingly difficult to play the piano because it always brought back such painful memories of his brother.

In the months before he died, John had completed further training, before going to Pensacola in Florida to get his wings. He loved it in the States. After passing his training course, he was allowed to pilot a Catalina flying boat right across the Atlantic because they were so badly needed for the hostilities in Europe. It was just his bad luck to be posted to Turnberry as his reward – a station notorious at the time for its high accident record.

All of those lost 11 men are remembered to this day with honour at the Air Force Memorial at Runnymede in Surrey. Bruce shared the sentiments of the words carved on the stone plinth: 'Their name liveth for evermore'.

Bruce's mother Florence never got over the tragedy. She herself was to live for only another 14 years – dying, aged 63, on 19 September 1957. She had suffered a stroke three weeks earlier at home from which she never recovered. It was just a year before Bruce finally became famous starring in *Sunday Night at the London Palladium*. He knows he never would have had that success without her. Her favourite song in Bruce's act was 'When You Wish Upon A Star' from the Disney film *Pinocchio*. The song says, 'when you wish upon a star, your dreams come true' and that is exactly what Florence did for Bruce. When she was still alive, she would watch the *Palladium* TV show with Bruce on Sunday nights and tell him how she hoped one day he would star in it. If only she'd known how quickly her son would realise that dream.

Bruce's dad John was very lonely after his wife's death. They had been completely devoted to each other since meeting through The Salvation Army. The son he had expected to run his business with after the war had been killed, Bruce was away all the time on stage and his daughter Maisie was busy with her three children. Three years after being widowed, John, to the delight of his two surviving children, married his wife's sister Dolly, who had lost her husband when she was in her forties. Bruce wasn't surprised by their decision to marry because Florence and Dolly were so alike and Dolly had often been in their lives, even coming on holiday with them. Bruce's dad was a bit of a loner who was very naïve about the world around him. Bruce recalled once taking him to a Spurs game on a Saturday afternoon and having to explain the rules of football.

John lived long enough to see his surviving son become one of the biggest stars in Britain. He died on 30 December 1961, aged 69, after suffering a heart attack. Bruce had been working in Manchester at the time. His sister Maisie rang him with the news. She told Bruce, 'Don't cancel the show. Dad wouldn't want you to do that.' Bruce pondered his sister's advice and concluded that she was right. Bruce duly performed that night – still a little tearful because he had missed, through no fault of his own, his dear dad's final moments in hospital.

One of Bruce's biggest regrets was that his parents were never able to fully enjoy his fame – or his wealth. 'If it wasn't for them, I wouldn't have made it – it's as simple as that,' he said. 'I feel so sad when I think they did not live to enjoy the fruits of my labour. I could have bought them a house, a car, a boat – anything they wanted. They so deserved it. My parents were not wealthy by any standards but they were rich in love.

'They never got over John's death in the war. What parents would when their son was only twenty-one? John and I were very close. He was very musical but he was classically minded, whereas I was the jazz man.'

He was just thankful that his dad was alive when he enjoyed his first brush with fame on *Sunday Night at the London Palladium*. 'Dad was so happy for me but he was elderly,' Bruce said. 'I'm sure Mum was pulling the strings for me from up there. But Dad died three years later – it was heartbreaking because, although he did get to see me on TV, he never got to see how I turned out when things really took off.'

Just a year before the death of his brother, the family suffered another tragedy. Bruce's sister Maisie was in hospital having given birth to her third child when her husband Tom was killed while working at the family garage. A young assistant was siphoning petrol from a car into a can when there was a short circuit followed by an explosion of flames. The assistant panicked and threw the can straight at Tom who was taken to hospital with terrible burns and died a few days later. Maisie was left to bring up three children on her own, aged just 24. It was such a traumatic event – one that Bruce said later had 'scarred the end of my childhood'.

His brother John's death haunted Bruce for the rest of his days. Days after one of the proudest moments of his life – when he was told that he was to be knighted by the Queen – Bruce's thoughts immediately turned to his brother as he described his pride at being honoured in an interview with Sue Carroll at the *Daily Mirror*. He said, 'My brother was only 20 when he died. I've lived 63 years more than he ever had a chance to. It doesn't seem right. Why didn't he have a longer life? Or at least a share of my years? We could have split that time up between us. Perhaps he might have become a Sir before me, who knows?'

So the early years of Bruce's show-business career had been marked by terrible tragedy. These were grim and depressing years, with rationing continuing long after the war ended. But Britain would come alive again as the 1950s dawned. Bruce, too, was about to embark on a whole new era on his life. He was to break Mr Van Damm's cardinal rule at the Windmill and fall in love with one of the beautiful dancers. But this was one love affair that would end up having a very unhappy ending.

CHAPTER 4

PENNY FOR YOUR TROUBLES

It was the most unlikely beginning for a romance. Bruce had quickly become one of the star performers at the Windmill – impressing everyone with his energy, enthusiasm and general *joie de vivre*. While no obvious heart-throb, he had charisma in spades and this made him quite a catch to the young beauties parading naked on stage every night. The increasingly confident Bruce had realised that the strict 'No Hands' rule that banned male performers from even staring at their female co-stars had, shall we say, a certain degree of flexibility. It meant that, if you were very careful, you could date one of the showgirls. The basic rule was that, if the owner, the formidable Mr Van Damm, thought it was a suitable coupling, he would turned a blind eye.

There was one girl who caught everyone's eye: a delectable young blonde called Penny Calvert. One of Bruce's pals from

Edmonton, Jimmy Perry, came to the theatre every night just to catch a glimpse of her. Eventually, Bruce, happy to do an old pal a favour even though he fancied Penny himself, set the pair up on a date. Jimmy was thrilled but not so thrilled when Penny spent the whole night talking about the real apple of her eye – his best mate Bruce who, despite his flourishing self-belief, was convinced the petite Penny was out of his league. If only Bruce had left Penny to his old pal Jimmy. It would have spared him almost 20 years of heartache.

This was also the time when Bruce reached a crucial juncture in his career. He had been treading the boards now for more than 10 years. He had learned his craft and yet there were still long agonising periods when he could not find work, some of which dragged on for weeks and weeks. Even someone as dedicated as Bruce began to wonder whether it really was worth all the hassle, particularly after one disastrous booking when he bombed on stage seven nights' running. He eventually set himself a deadline: another five years and, if nothing had changed, he would quit show business for good.

* * *

Life had always been a bit of a struggle for poor Irish-born Penny. Still only 18, she was the main breadwinner in her family – her Windmill wages had to provide for her mother and three younger brothers. Her father had long since gone. It left little time for fun once she had finished her shift.

Penny had her eye on Bruce right from the start. She could tell that he was different from the other male performers who made up the show's resident company. It wasn't his looks – with a chin jutting out like the Rock of Gibraltar even Bruce's mother would accept that he was no oil painting. No, Penny saw something else in Bruce – put simply, it was star potential. She could see, long before anyone else, that he would soon outgrow the Windmill and go on to great things. The problem she had was how to bag her man. Though strikingly beautiful, so were dozens of other girls at the theatre. Bruce, who had long since lost the awkwardness with women that characterised his teenage years, was spoilt for choice. As he joked later on, 'It was rather confusing for a chap!' It wasn't so confusing for Penny, who knew that Bruce was the one from even before their first date. 'I saw this name, Bruce Forsyth, and suddenly there were green flashing lights in front of my eyes and I knew that this was the man I was going to marry,' she explained.

Bruce and Penny quickly fell in love after finally going on that first date. Penny recalled later how blissfully happy she was during those days. 'Bruce would drive me home to Brixton and we'd spend hours in his car every night. I actually lost my virginity to Bruce on Streatham Common,' she told the *Daily Mirror*.

Bruce's parents, in particular, really took to his new girl. The young lovers would often pop up to Edmonton for their Sunday lunch where Penny would spend hours chatting to Bruce's mum Florence. There she could see how a normal loving family operated. It was a world away from the tough upbringing she had endured. Simple things we all take for granted – birthday cards, presents around the tree at Christmas – had always been denied to Penny. It was obvious that Bruce was smitten with Penny too. There had been plenty of girls before but everyone around Bruce knew that Penny was different and that they were likely to tie the knot some time in the future.

Penny wasn't the only one to see that Bruce was outgrowing the Windmill. He was itching for a move himself. Bruce may have been the envy of all his mates in north London – in those dark days of the early 1950s, it was every young man's dream to be paid to dance on stage with dozens of naked women. Most would have killed for the privilege. But Bruce was fiercely ambitious, always eyeing the next opportunity. Yes, the money and the glamour had been exciting at first but he knew he wanted more from life than to be part of a simple showcase for a nude revue. He didn't just want his own name in lights – he *needed* it to be. And the way to achieve that was by striking out from the Windmill with a new act. The obvious option was to team up with his girlfriend and form a double act. As well as being beautiful, Penny was a highly talented singer and dancer. She had never been one of the nude models at the Windmill. They stood as still as statues while Penny and Bruce danced and sang around them. So they both quit their jobs at the Windmill and threw themselves into the new act.

Sadly, things didn't take off in the way they had hoped. 'We felt we were so well matched that we should strike out on our own,' Bruce later explained. 'But the truth was we didn't set the world alight.' Bruce and Penny were a song-and-dance double act and that was not the way show business worked in those days. You were either a singer or a dancer – not both. Agents found them increasingly difficult to place. It meant that they had to take cabaret bookings on slippery dance floors that had been designed for ballroom dancing, then all the rage. That was no use to a pair of tap dancers like Bruce and Penny who found it almost impossible to perform effectively, slithering around while trying to keep their balance. It was hardly the kind of magic formula that was going to result in return bookings. 'It was really terrible,' Bruce complained.

The only solution was to seek work abroad, which they did successfully by entertaining American troops still billeted in Austria, Italy and Germany after the war. It was exciting to be travelling the world with a beautiful young dance partner with whom you were madly in love. So when an agent offered them the chance to tour India and Pakistan for four months, they jumped at the chance. The only way to get there was by taking an ocean liner to Bombay (now Mumbai) – a gruelling journey lasting three weeks. In those days, the only way an unmarried couple could share a cabin on a journey of this kind was by marrying. And that was the dilemma facing Bruce: stay single and endure the trip from hell cooped up with a stranger in a dark cabin or tie the knot and snuggle up to the girl of your dreams.

So Bruce and Penny ended up getting married in a big hurry – which led to inevitable but unfounded speculation by their friends and families that Penny was pregnant. It was 1953 and the ceremony took place at the Methodist Hall in Edmonton. 'Bruce made a couple of gaffes during the ceremony,' Penny later recalled. 'And I had long nails at the time, the wedding ring got caught, and he was pushing and pushing, trying to get it on. Perhaps that was an omen.'

Bruce was 25 and his new bride was 23. It was an exciting

new chapter in their lives: young and in love and off on an unforgettable adventure to Asia. The first part of their honeymoon was spent cruising through the Middle East en route to Bombay, visiting places such as the Suez Canal and Port Said in Egypt.

India came as a big shock to Bruce and Penny. They had never experienced poverty like this before. Bruce was never been able to return, so traumatised was he by the sight of the beggar children minus limbs, some deliberately maimed by their parents to arouse more compassion and earn more money from rich foreign tourists. Bruce was so taken aback by this tide of human misery that he could barely stomach leaving their hotel in Bombay. It was far worse in Calcutta – the poorest of the big cities in India. In the station alone there were 400 refugees living in unbelievable squalor. Bruce grabbed the hand of his new bride and said simply, 'Breathe in, hold your breath and run!' Some honeymoon!

Surrounded by all this filth, it was inevitable that one of them would get ill. One night Penny was struck down with flu-like symptoms and was unable to perform. Of course, the show had to go on – that was the first rule of show business. It meant Bruce performing solo for the first time in 12 years. It was a formidable challenge for the young showman. Sure, he had years of experience to fall back on – but always as part of a double act or a revue, never on his own. Bruce had all the necessary skills: he could sing, dance, crack jokes, banter with the audience. But did he have the guts – and, crucially, the charisma – to cut it as a solo artist? Based on that first performance in Calcutta, the most charitable answer would have to be 'maybe'. He certainly didn't die a death but it would be wrong to say that he blew the audience away. But perhaps most importantly, he had survived. Bruce told Penny, 'Well, at least I have proved to myself that I can perform alone.' But where, in the long term, would this leave Penny? She was a talent in her own right and was desperate to carry on performing but solo female song-and-dance artists were rare in those days. A career on her own really wasn't an option for her. Bruce's decision left Penny with very little to do but look after her new husband. It created a crucial imbalance in the marriage that was to cause them no end of problems over the years. Penny would not be the first woman to discover that work came before everything else for Bruce.

Penny recovered from her illness after four nights and their double act – for the time being, at least – carried on. They travelled on to Pakistan to finish off a tour that had been an unforgettable experience for both newlyweds. The food had been largely inedible and they survived on boiled eggs for the rest of their six weeks away. Bruce, skinny at the best of times, was, in his own words, 'skeletal' when he arrived back in Blighty, having lost almost two stone.

Any hopes that things would pick up in Britain following their dismal start before leaving for India were quickly dashed. They couldn't get arrested before they went away and nothing had changed during their little Oriental adventure. It left Bruce with only one option: he had to ditch Penny from the act and go solo immediately. Penny later said Bruce was oblivious to how this would harm her career. She said he simply told her, 'Right, now you can get down to having babies.'

Penny would join Bruce on the road but, instead of

performing, she was now simply there to ensure that things ran smoothly for her husband and that his costumes were clean and ironed. They were so hard up that they could not afford to stay in hotels while travelling from show to show, so they bought a caravan that they towed around the country in an old Wolseley. Bruce would sometimes go for weeks without work and the couple would stay at his parents, simply parking the caravan down a nearby alley. In one bleak period, he didn't work for two long months. He admitted later that his parents were the only ones that saved them from 'serious hunger'. He told the *TV Times*, 'It was a terrible feeling: you're raring to go, firing on all eight cylinders and nobody wants you. Those were terrible times. The frustration – that was the worst thing of all.

'I once gave myself five years. I seemed to be going nowhere. I used to come off stage and one of my mates would be in the wings and he'd ask, "Any good?" meaning the audience, and I'd shake my head and say, "No." You do despair; you do get down in spirit. I said to myself, "If things don't change in five years, I'm packing it in." But you soon snap out of it. Or rather, I did, I'm happy to say.'

So it was a really topsy-turvy time for Bruce – one minute up, the next down in the dumps. There were few such highs and lows for a frustrated Penny. She may have been still in the first flushes of love but her job, in effect, was to clean the caravan. It didn't do a lot for an ambitious young woman's self-esteem, especially as she'd been so successful on stage when she first met Bruce.

At first, this didn't cause too much upheaval in the marriage because Penny did eventually become pregnant. Their first daughter, Debbie, was born on 24 June 1955, when Bruce was 27. In those days, fathers didn't attend the delivery, and Bruce was left to pace up and down nervously outside before being told they had a healthy baby girl. Bruce loved being a dad. Debbie, he recalled, was a 'darling little girl' with gorgeous blonde curls. Three years later she was joined by another girl – their second daughter, Julie, born on 4 June 1958. With two toddlers to care for, often on her own at home, Penny certainly had her hands full. Bruce did his best but work dragged him away from the family home more and more. He admitted that the 'prolonged absences' eventually did put a 'great strain' on their marriage.

Bruce's career hit rock bottom during a booking at a theatre in Brixton, south London, which he described as the 'unhappiest week of my entire life'. It was an old cinema with the atmosphere of a morgue. By now, Bruce had introduced comedy into his act and often did impressions of the leading stars of the day, such as Tommy Cooper. What made matters worse was that he had been unemployed for weeks before, so his confidence was already fragile. He was the second-spot comic in charge of getting the audience warmed up. That week nothing went right for poor Bruce – he couldn't have warmed up an Eskimo. Penny, worried sick about her husband, came with him every night to bolster his ego but to no avail – whatever gag he tried went down like a lead balloon. It got so bad that he would shy away from the other performers at the theatre – he was too timid to even go to the bar for a drink. This wasn't like Bruce at all, who, no matter how down he was feeling, would always try to put on a cheery public face. But show business can, at times, be a very cruel master.

Bruce felt he had created extra pressure for himself by moving into comedy. 'Nothing quite matches the pressure on a solo comic,' he later said. 'Call it guts, courage or a super-big ego, you need a special quality to get out there on your own. A singer can always finish his song and, even if he is rotten, the audience will wait till the end before they give a derisory patter of applause. But the comedian gets his reaction – a laugh, a chuckle or a stony, lonely silence – after every line. That's why I have always said comedy is the hardest profession of all. No one suffers quite like a bad comic.'

From Brixton, Bruce went to City Varieties Music Hall in Leeds for another booking. Now this really was make or break. Forget the five years he'd given himself – there was a limit to how much pressure any man could take and poor Bruce was at breaking point. Just to add to the pressure, he didn't have the time or the inspiration to change any of the material that had bombed so badly at Brixton. He was going to have to crack the same gags that had bombed every night for a week all over again. Only this time, of course, they worked. He went from having the 'worst week ever' to feeling fantastic. So what was the explanation for the change? Simple: confidence. The most important weapon in a comic's arsenal. It is difficult to explain where Bruce found this self-belief after such a bruising week at Brixton. Perhaps the simplest explanation is that it came from his almost maniacal determination to succeed. Bruce, like all great performers, was able to blot out failure – wipe it from his mind – so that every time he appeared on stage it seemed as though he owned it.

'I knew that after that week at the City Varieties I could make my way as a comic,' he said later. So he had gone from

48

zero to hero in the space of a fortnight. From there, there was the odd setback but Bruce rarely failed again. Things just got better and better. It was a crucial turning point in his career. Perhaps *the* crucial turning point. Somehow, Bruce had discovered a winning formula. In truth, his act had not changed much at all. What had changed was the man on stage – finally, he believed in himself. He knew he could do it. Not just when the going was good and the audience were on his side but every time he stepped on stage. He had the secret weapon which distinguishes the stars from the also-rans – that crucial *je ne sais quoi* that only big names have, which allows them to entertain even the toughest audiences. It showed every time he went on stage. After Leeds, he enjoyed another storming week on stage in London. A young producer from the BBC saw him and immediately booked him for a big new television variety show, *Music Hall*.

By 1955 Bruce was now just one small step away from the big time. He knew his act worked and he had added that vital element of comedy. All he needed now was a lucky break – the final spark that would see him go from being a consummate pro respected in the profession to being a household name. It finally all came together for Bruce during four highly successful summer seasons on the south coast – three of them in Babbacombe, near Torquay in Devon. The 600-seat theatre, perched right on the cliffs, was packed every night with holidaymakers desperate for the kind of easy-going family entertainment that was Bruce's meat and drink.

This was a key turning point in Bruce's career. Up until then, he had always been a performer, predominantly with his own one-man show. Now he was a compere – pulling together lots of different strands of entertainment into one coherent whole. It sounds relatively straightforward but, in fact, it was devilishly difficult – a consummate compere needs to spin several plates at the same time and constantly think on his feet.

Bruce, of course, was a natural. He didn't realise it at the time but this new skill was to be both his saviour and his curse. His saviour because who is to say if Bruce would have ever become such a huge star without these compering skills, which transferred perfectly to the game shows that were springing up on TV? His curse because, for years, compering was virtually all anyone in show business wanted him to do when Bruce's heart still lay in song and dance.

The seaside show he was compering was a real challenge – he had to hold the whole thing together over six acts. He was on stage every night for more than three hours, which meant, inevitably, that there was a fair bit of padding. To fill the time, Bruce would play games with the audience – his first real chance to try out his audience-participation skills, which, as we all know were second to none. Bruce devised all sorts of silly games, such as one where you had to eat a doughnut without licking your lips. The punters lapped it up. What had seemed like a bit of giggle to kill some time would end up becoming the cornerstone of his career. *The Generation Game* – the show which more than any other made him a megastar – was pretty much one long very silly game from start to finish. 'I got out there, relaxed, had fun with people and found that I loved not knowing what was going to happen next,' Bruce explained. He was such a hit that he even won his first award, A Bucket and Spade Oscar, for the best summer-season performer.

By now, Bruce had been in the business for 16 long years. He was so close to major stardom he could almost taste it. If anyone was ready to make the step up it was Bruce. Just a month after his final summer season in 1958, he was booked for a new ITV variety show called *New Look* starring Roy Castle, Lionel Blair and Des O'Connor. That helped Bruce to land a slot on *Sunday Night at the London Palladium*, then the biggest show on TV. From seriously considering packing it all in just a few years earlier, Bruce would soon be earning an extraordinary £1,000 a night.

CHAPTER 5

I'M IN
CHARGE

L ife as a true show-business star began for Bruce at 30. He
had been treading the boards since the age of 14 but now
he was on the brink of real stardom. Just a few weeks earlier
he had been performing in front of as few as 40 people in his
final summer season at the Hippodrome in Eastbourne. He
had been plucked from the bucket and spade circuit to host
the biggest show on TV, *Sunday Night at the London
Palladium*. Finally, he would be working with the biggest stars
in the world. Peter Sellers was one of the acts on his first show.
If he played his cards right, he could soon be earning more in
one night than he did in a whole year on stage. Could this
likeable jack of all showbiz trades hack it in the Big Time?
Bruce would find out over the next six years – and not all the
changes in his life would be for the better.

If Bruce could have invented a show to give him his break,

it would have been *Sunday Night at the London Palladium* or, as everyone called it, *SNAP*. The format was absolutely perfect, combining popular audience participation games such as 'Beat the Clock' with a guest list that featured the crème de la crème of show business, including many big names from Hollywood. It required song-and-dance skills but also – and much more importantly – a razor-sharp wit and a calm head in a crisis.

Bruce had first appeared on the show in 1957 when it was still being hosted by the comedian Tommy Trinder. Trinder had indicated that he was moving on and the Palladium's boss Val Parnell made no secret of the fact that he was looking for a talented newcomer for the role. Billy Marsh, a leading London agent, had been tipped off that Bruce was going down a storm in summer seasons on the south coast and would be perfect for the role. Marsh introduced Bruce to Parnell and they got on like a house on fire. Bruce was hired for a six-week contract on just £85 a week. He would have to prove himself before the big money followed. What attracted Parnell to Bruce was his ability to interact with an audience. All those years playing daft games on stage by the sea had finally come in handy. Bruce was the one person Parnell knew who could handle the popular middle segment of the show called 'Beat the Clock'. This was a very fast-moving feature where couples played games against the clock to win a cash prize. Each week the jackpot went up by £100 and, if it was not won when it reached £1,000, all the cash went to charity. The whole thing was completely unscripted and really played to Bruce's strengths.

Bruce's first catchphrase came about when he was trying to

show a couple how to throw plates on to a table-tennis board balanced on a trestle during 'Beat the Clock'. They were making a complete pig's ear of it and Bruce stopped the clock before showing them again how best to chuck the plates in the hope that they might improve. Bruce restarted the clock but then turned around to discover the couple had already restarted the game without his permission. This wasn't on. Bruce turned to them and shouted, 'It's my game – I'm in charge.' It doesn't sound like the most earth-shattering exchange but somehow it struck a chord with the public. Bruce knew he was on to something in the following days when taxi drivers – great judges of the popular mood – kept saying to him 'I'm in charge' as he journeyed around London. Never one to look a gift horse in the mouth, Bruce reintroduced the phrase the following week and then every week on *SNAP*. It was such a great catchphrase that theatres started advertising his stage show with posters saying, 'Bruce Forsyth is in charge.'

With Bruce's trial period coming to an end, Val Parnell thought re-signing his new hiring would be a simple matter. He knew he would have to up the money but that wasn't a problem. Bruce had been aware that £85 a week was taking the mickey when he first signed but he was hardly going to argue over a contract just when he was about to make it as a star. What was worrying Bruce wasn't the money, it was overexposure. Television was still a relatively new medium and Bruce was concerned that the show would kill his theatre career. He had already used up all the best sketches he had developed during the summer seasons. Perhaps scarred by all those nights of failure when trying to make it big, part of him wanted to get out while the going was still good. Of course, this was madness. He had struggled for 16 years to hit the big time and now he wanted to walk away just as it was getting started. Was he being serious?

Parnell told Bruce in no uncertain terms that he had lost the plot. He was still a newcomer. He wasn't overexposed, he was *underexposed*. Parnell quickly talked Bruce round and, so confident was he of his new star, he hired him for a further 33 shows – every week for more than half the year. And as for the problem over the shortage of material, there was a simple solution: they would get in some talented new writers to fill the gaps. Bruce realised just how wrong he'd been when, a few weeks later, he was second on the bill at a theatre in the Midlands. It soon became clear though that the only person the audience wanted to see that night was the new star of *SNAP*, not the headliner. Far from damaging his theatre career, the TV show was enhancing it and introducing him to a whole new audience. It was an early reminder to Bruce of the power of television.

As well as *SNAP*, Bruce starred in the Palladium's Christmas panto. By then, his money had gone up to £190 a week – big money in those days when you could buy a three-bed semi for £2,000. Finally, Bruce could afford to be a bit flash, splashing out on a plush estate car that had room for all his show-business outfits and props. For the first time in his life, he had enough money to dine out at smart restaurants. The irony was that just when he could afford to pay, no one wanted his money and he would invariably eat for free because the restaurants wanted the kudos of having Brucie at their table. Bruce was able to move his family out of their little three-bedroom terrace in St Albans

– first to Mill Hill and then to a gorgeous former coach house in exclusive Totteridge, north London, which had three acres of grounds. His little girls – growing up fast – thought they had died and gone to heaven.

Bruce was forced to miss the whole third series of *Sunday Night at the Palladium* in 1960 when he was struck down with a duodenal ulcer. Parnell hastily brought in Don Arrol, a Scottish comedian, as the new compere. But it was always only going to be a stop-gap measure before the real star returned. Arrol said at the time, 'Every time I did it, it was like working with a ghost behind me. Let's face it – it's Bruce's show.' As soon as he had fully recovered, Bruce was back.

By now, it was the early 1960s and London was swinging. Bruce was hosting the night the Beatles appeared on *SNAP*. This was after their first few number ones when Beatlemania was at its craziest. Val Parnell was terrified that their performance would be ruined by screaming girls in the theatre audience and that all the much more important audience – the 20 million sat at home in front of their TVs – would hear would be this hysteria and not the Fab Four's music. Parnell tried to ban girls coming into the auditorium but, of course, it didn't work.

The night itself was a huge success, thanks to Bruce's quick thinking. He developed a clever routine whereby four silhouettes of boys appeared at the back of the stage right at the start of the show. Of course, the audience assumed those darks shapes were The Beatles – and the wailing started. But when the lights came on only Brucie was there – in an early version of the famous 'Strong Man' pose that became part of his routine on *The Generation Game*. He smiled and told the audience, 'Don't worry, they'll be on at the end.' All the head-line acts on *SNAP* came in the third and final part.

Bruce wasn't the only one having a joke that night. John Lennon ended up playing a practical joke on Bruce later on when the band played live. Viewers at home were left confused when Lennon handed Bruce a note on stage. Bruce blushed and laughed with obvious embarrassment. But he didn't explain what the note said. The truth only came out several years later when Bruce's then estranged wife Penny explained what had happened. 'We had been to Paris the previous week with Matt Monro and his wife,' she said. 'Somebody took us to see a sex show and, while two girls were writhing on stage, Bruce was asked if he would like to participate. Of course, he declined. John Lennon had evidently heard the story and the note he handed to Bruce said simply, "Would you like to participate?"'

As for Parnell's fears that the fans would ruin the show, well, there was an incessant screaming throughout the hour, even when the Fab Four weren't on screen. And the stewards were kept busy pulling girls from the audience who had fainted with excitement. But, of course, the whole thing – possibly thanks to Bruce lightening the mood at the beginning – worked brilliantly and it was the most popular show in that whole series of *SNAP*. When you've got the hottest band in the world on your show, it is difficult to put a foot wrong.

By the end of his third series, Bruce could justifiably lay claim to being the biggest star in Britain. His pay had gone up from the original £85 a week but he still felt that he was being seriously short-changed by Val Parnell. And when he heard that Tommy Steele, the entertainer, had bagged £1,000 for a single television show, Bruce was determined to match that money. He had already been promised £750 but Bruce figured, not unreasonably given the success of the show, that he was worth the same as Steele, and he would dig in his heels until he got what he wanted. There then followed weeks of tense negotiations that could have seen Bruce exit *Sunday Night at the London Palladium* altogether. Of course, what drove Bruce on was simmering anger at the derisory money he had felt obliged to accept at the start of the show. A final offer was made: £850 a week. But it was stressed that this really was a final offer. Bruce would have to like it or lump it. He had been driven into a corner and felt he had no option – if they wouldn't increase the offer, he was off.

At the time, Bruce was appearing in theatre in Torquay. Just before he was due to go on stage, there was a call for him from London. It was Parnell. Until then, the negotiations had been conducted by Leslie Grade – part of the famous Grade family and one of the bosses at Associated Television, which made the show. Now the guv'nor was involved. Parnell cut straight to the chase.

'Well, what do you want?' he asked abruptly.

'A thousands pounds a week,' a by now terrified Bruce replied.

Quick as a flash, Parnell concluded the negotiations by saying, 'You've got it! Deal with me in future. What is all this nonsense?'

Two minutes on the phone and Bruce had become our best-paid entertainer. He was on top of the world. And he had learned a valuable lesson in show business: always know your worth.

News of Bruce's bumper pay packet made big headlines in

the newspapers. Hailing Bruce as the 'highest paid compere in British television', the *Daily Mirror*'s story was headlined, I'M IN CHARGE AT £1,000 A GO.

One of Bruce's big regrets was that they never managed to get Frank Sinatra on *SNAP*. He was one of the few big American names they missed. When the stars from Hollywood came over to promote their films and albums, the show was the first on their checklist. It meant that Bruce was able to work with several of his heroes, including his all-time favourite, Sammy Davis Jr, who appeared on several of Bruce's shows over the years. Sammy generously credited his old pal with making him a star outside America.

But Bruce is probably best remembered on *SNAP* for a show that almost didn't happen at all. The actors' union Equity had called a strike for a week, banning virtually every star from appearing on the show. Everyone except Bruce and the comedian Norman Wisdom, who both had an exemption. Somehow, improvising away, they managed to see out the entire show together in a truly unforgettable routine that quickly went down in show-business legend.

Bruce was by now recognised wherever he went. In truth, after years of obscurity, he enjoyed it. He was never one of those stars to refuse an autograph or be rude to fans that approached him, even when he was out with his family.

It would have been so easy at this time for Bruce to lose the plot. Yes, he spent years climbing the show-business ladder but when fame had come it had been sudden. Coming from solid Salvation Army stock, that was never going to happen. Bruce always had rigid self-discipline: he was constantly analysing his own performance to ensure that he never let his standards drop. Temptations like booze were never a big problem for him. That is not to say that he didn't drink, even occasionally when he was on stage. He soon cut that out. 'I used to keep a glass filled up with wine in the wings,' he explained in one interview. 'But one night when I was doing a lot of dashing on and off stage, I totted it up and discovered I had drunk about three-quarters of a bottle. So I gave it up. I figure that, if you're the only sober person in the theatre, you've got a head start. I had seen it all before becoming famous. I'd see the gambling, the drinking, the wasted lives. If I hadn't, how could I have coped? It would have been like winning the pools. I didn't want to squander my good fortune. I'd waited long enough for it.'

As well as eschewing the booze, Bruce developed little routines that he would repeat every time he went on stage. He wouldn't eat for four hours before a performance because he was convinced a full stomach slowed him down and made him lose his edge. Clearly this meant he had to turn down lots of attractive offers for pre-theatre dinners. That was of no consequence to Bruce – the job was everything.

There were other rituals: he would always gargle with Cockburn's port because he was convinced it was good for his throat. He gave up smoking. And he began taking vitamin pills years before they became fashionable. This health-orientated fanatical attention to detail is second nature to the successful stars of today but was far from the norm when it was pioneered by Bruce in the 1950s and 1960s.

By the end of 1962, Bruce really was ready to quit *SNAP*. He knew at last he had made it and he wasn't scared of trying his luck on new projects. This would be a recurring theme throughout Bruce's career, particularly during the golden years of the 1970s. He was always looking for the next big thing and was wary of becoming stale in the same weekly format. He had taken on board another of the golden rules of entertainment: always leave the audience wanting more. He was also worried about his health. He had always been a workaholic – terrified of returning to those days when he was forced to go cap in hand to his father for cash. But now he had the money and fame, he could afford to slow things down a little – and he also had the confidence to finally not say yes to every booking. He said at the time that he would never work seven days a week again. 'My health is more valuable to me than money. I've decided to live a little longer,' he said. He loved his time away from the show. He went on tour with a stage version of *SNAP* and also appeared in a three-hour panto of *Dick Whittington* in Manchester.

The next year he was back on *SNAP* and he stayed on for a further two years before once again being drawn away by the lure of more attractive theatre work, including his own one-man show, *Little Me*. It had been great while it lasted but Bruce was not sad to see the back of *SNAP*. The job was a monster, with the show running from September to May each series, taking up 40 weeks of the year. It was impossible to accept any other significant work while he was doing it, but it also didn't keep him busy for the whole week. He was thankful for the huge leg-up it had given to his career – it had made him a household name and the BBC would never have hired Bruce for *The Generation Game* if he had not first been on *SNAP* – but he was also eager to prove that he was more than a one-trick pony. He still felt he had the talent to emulate his big hero Fred Astaire and make it in Hollywood.

He was never going to do that starring in a British Sunday night TV show.

Bruce still maintains that *Little Me* was the best thing he ever did in his career. 'I don't think anything else could come along that would prove so satisfying,' he said proudly. In it, Bruce played 7 characters and had a staggering 29 costume changes – which worked out at one every 3 or 4 minutes. He played a huge variety of roles, from a 16-year-old boy in short trousers to the wizened miser Old Man Pinchley, who was in a wheelchair. Bruce successfully launched the show in Bristol before switching back to the West End, where it was hailed as 'the smash hit of the season'. Bruce proved not just to his fans but the wider theatre world that he was a lot more than just a talented TV presenter. It was choreographed by Bob Fosse, who went on to win the Best Director Oscar in 1972 for the musical *Cabaret*, starring Liza Minnelli.

One positive spin-off almost came from *Little Me* in 1967 when Bruce got a call from Lionel Bart, who had written the music and lyrics for the stage and screen versions of the musical *Oliver!* He had loved Bruce's portrayal of the old curmudgeon Pinchley in *Little Me* and he thought he would be perfect for the role of Fagin in *Oliver!* Ron Moody, who played the part on stage so brilliantly, was stalling over committing to the movie and Bart was looking for an alternative. This, to Bruce, was a dream role. When he came off the phone, he was walking on air. Sadly for Bruce, Moody resolved his difficulties with the producers and ended up taking the role. *Oliver!* of course, went on to win six Oscars and has been acclaimed ever since as one of the greatest British films of all time. Moody was nominated for the Best Actor Oscar and, although he lost out on that, he did win a prestigious Golden Globe award for the same role. All that could have been Bruce's if things had happened just a little differently. Bruce said years later, 'I was winded – so disappointed. That part could have been the "in" to a film career that I'd always hoped for but never quite believed would happen.'

Bruce was succeeded on *Sunday Night at the London Palladium* in 1965 by his old pal, the Scouse comedian Jimmy Tarbuck. Inevitably, with a new host, there were changes to the show and Bruce's old favourite, 'Beat the Clock', was phased out. The show was not really the same and the ratings never again reached the peaks of Bruce's 20 million.

Bruce's career then went through a bit of a lull. He was always busy but he failed to capitalise on his earlier success. He was never one to stand still though, using these years to work on his live act and make it longer and more polished. 'They were lean times but very important for me,' he admitted to the *Observer*. 'Before then, although I could do all the things I do – play the piano, sing, dance, impressions – the problem I had was that I didn't have a long act. Sammy Davis Jr had been over from the States and he went on and did an hour and a half. What I was learning was how to extend it and pace it. It meant that I could do my one-man show that has been such a success at the Palladium and other places – go on with a nice big orchestra and do two or two-and-a-half hours on my own.'

So Bruce's career may have been stalling but it was at least evolving. And it was all change at home too as Bruce and Penny split up in spectacular fashion and his squeaky-clean family-man image was ruined by one very public affair.

CHAPTER 6

LAUGHING MISS WORLD INTO BED

It would make a cracking trivia-quiz question: which much loved star has had sex with not one but *two* Miss Worlds? The obvious answer would be George Best but, in fact, he bedded three! No, the star with those two unlikely notches on his bedpost is none other than Brucie. We all know about one of the Miss Worlds: his lovely third wife Wilnelia, who won the crown for her native Puerto Rico way back in 1975. But what about Brucie's first Miss World? She was a pretty 19-year-old hairdresser from Bournemouth. And their affair was to have massive ramifications for both of them. For Bruce, it could have killed his career just as it was taking off. For Ann Sidney, the fall-out was even more devastating – it almost ended up killing her.

It all started in June 1964. Bruce's marriage to his first wife Penny Calvert was already in big trouble. They had previously separated and then got back together. Bruce knew deep down that it was over for good but he had not told Penny, who was living in the family mansion back in Totteridge, north London, with their three young children. Bruce, in his mind at least, was already a single man when he started a summer season at Bournemouth's Hippodrome theatre and rented a luxury apartment for the summer.

Bruce was out one night early on in the run when he caught sight of one of the most beautiful women he had ever seen. The girl in question was Ann Sidney. She was 16 years younger than Bruce, who was 35 by then. Ann simply took his breath away – she was that gorgeous. Bruce wasn't the only man who shared this view. Ann was a much-admired beauty who had recently won Bournemouth's Miss Front Page beauty contest.

Bruce made no secret of the fact that he was smitten. All evening he winked or waved at Ann from across the room at the ball, which had been held to mark the end of the beauty contest. Every time he got the chance, he would slip over to talk to her. And later, when a crowd went on to a local restaurant to talk and sing until 4am, they sat together and Bruce asked for her phone number.

Ann was impressed and flattered that a big star should pay such lavish attention to her. She was initially wary but Bruce had real charisma and he made her laugh. Bruce really should have known better. Yes, he was desperately unhappy at home with Penny. But he had a young family and he was almost old enough to be Ann's father. If he had had any sense, Bruce would have walked away. But Bruce was still high on the first real taste of fame. Let's not forget, he had only hit the Big Time six years earlier. And if a future Miss World was taking an interest – even one as young as 19 – he wasn't going to turn her down.

We'll see later on how beauty pageants came to play such a crucial role in Bruce's love life. All the significant women in his life first crossed Bruce's path because of these glamour parades. They seem very old-fashioned these days but it would be wrong to underestimate their influence back in the 1960s. Almost every little girl dreamed of being Miss World one day. There didn't seem anything remotely naff about parading in a swimsuit and being asked your favourite hobby and vital statistics. Bruce loved them. Not just because he enjoyed looking at beautiful women but because they were great places to pull. As one of the biggest stars of the day, he was often asked to be on the judging panel, which, of course, made it very easy to introduce himself to all the best-looking girls.

Back to Ann, who had always wanted to be a model. This had seemed unlikely in her early teenage years when she had long skinny legs and no chest to speak of. But she blossomed and, by the age of 15, was ready for the catwalk and a move to London. Her parents thought she was too young to make such a move. Instead, they persuaded Ann to stay in Bournemouth and learn a trade: hairdressing. It was to help publicise the salon that she entered the Bournemouth Regatta Queen competition. The rules stated that you had to be 16. Ann, still only 15, lied about her age. To her surprise, little Ann, in her girl-next-door gingham dress, was chosen as the winner. More contests followed, until she won the Miss Front Page pageant shortly before meeting Bruce.

The night after their first meeting at the ball, Ann agreed to meet Bruce for dinner. There was one question on her mind:

was this exciting new man in her life married? If he was, there was no question of her taking things further.

Bruce told Ann that was he was separated from Penny, which he admitted did sound like an old line. There was an element of truth in the claim because he had made up his mind that the marriage was over when he arrived in Bournemouth. But Penny still didn't know this and certainly believed the marriage was still on. Ann was happy enough with his answer. She couldn't help but be impressed with her older suitor. He was funny, charming and treated her like she was the most important woman in the world. Of course a 19-year-old girl was going to be impressed.

It should be stressed, however, that things progressed very slowly. Ann wasn't hugely experienced and made it abundantly clear to Bruce that, if anything was going to happen between them, he would have to wait before they slept with each other. For a start, she had an incredibly protective father who might view Bruce's claims that he was 'separated' from his wife with a little more wariness.

Bruce was happy to wait. They went out together whenever they could during that summer season in Bournemouth. Bruce would regularly send Ann little gifts – jewellery and flowers – and he also had an endearing habit of writing little notes telling her how special she was to him. Ann knew that she was falling in love with Bruce. And she knew, too, that this was all wrong. He was too old for her. And if she was ever going to make a big success of entering beauty pageants, she had to be single. She would be instantly disqualified if the judges discovered that she had a famous married boyfriend, albeit one who claimed he was separated.

Ann thought it best to make a clean break from Bruce. She quit her job at the hair salon and moved to Blackpool, where she stayed with some family friends. Her plan was to enter beauty contests in the north and make enough money to pay for drama or modelling-school fees as she furthered her career away from Bruce.

Once in Blackpool, she began to enter and win more beauty contests. But she could not escape the attention of Bruce. Wherever she was, he would send her a 'good luck' telegram. Aware that their romance would cause a big scandal, he signed them under false names. Two that he used were Fred Nurg and Charlie Forthright.

Ann had the kind of shimmering beauty that meant she was destined for greater things than beauty contests in the north. So it was no surprise when she won the Miss United Kingdom title in Blackpool shortly after her move. That win suddenly thrust her into the limelight and won her a place as the British entrant in the Miss World contest a few weeks later. Suddenly, Ann Sidney had become big news.

When Ann flew back from Blackpool to Bournemouth after her Miss UK triumph, there was a welcome party to greet her. Her mother, father, grandmother, even the singer Matt Monro... they were all there to say well done. And lurking in the background was the one person Ann longed to see but at the same time hoped wouldn't be there. And Bruce was so proud that he stepped forward from the crowd, gave her a peck on the cheek and whispered, 'Well done, darling.'

Dozens of pictures were taken that day but the one that was splashed all over the papers the next morning was of Bruce and Ann. Alongside it was a story suggesting that they were having an affair. At that stage, they had done little more than hold hands, though they were clearly in love despite the brief separation while Ann was in Blackpool. So the affair story was not strictly true but clearly something was going on.

Ann, aware that the press coverage could kill her chances of even entering Miss World, was distraught. Her father was angry too. And Bruce was panic-stricken. He was a loser on two fronts: he faced being dumped by his dream girl and he had also been branded an adulterer in the press just at the time his career was taking off on *Sunday Night at the London Palladium*. It could be killed stone dead by a big scandal surrounding an affair. If that wasn't enough, a furious Penny had finally found out about Ann and there was no way she was going to believe the claims that this young beauty had only held hands with her husband.

But first Bruce had to deal with Ann. He rushed to the Sidney family home at 1am to plead his innocence. 'It's all my fault for being at the airport and getting Ann involved in this coverage,' he told her father. He also explained that, yes, his marriage had been in difficulties but he and Penny were separated.

Ann's father sat down with his daughter and asked, 'Have you slept with Bruce Forsyth?'

'No, no, no!' she insisted.

Bruce's charm offensive worked and he was given the seal of approval by Ann's father. He told his daughter, 'He's a real gentleman.' The big romance was back on.

Penny, meanwhile, had read the reports and rushed down to Bournemouth to confront Bruce, telling reporters that their marriage was over. She insisted that she was not aware of any separation. Bruce met her at a nearby hotel and agreed to move out of the family home. Whether they were separated or not before he met Ann, they certainly were now. Lawyers were brought in and the separation was established on a more formal basis.

Despite the scandal, Ann went on to compete in the Miss World finals at London's Lyceum Ballroom in November 1964, just four months after she met Bruce. Along with the other contestants, she had to stay at the city's Waldorf Hotel for the week before the big day. She was heavily chaperoned and all telephone calls were monitored, which meant that Bruce could not get in touch with her.

All girls were told that, if they were involved in any scandal or disobeyed the strict rules of the organisers, Mecca, they would automatically be out of the final. But in spite of the security, Bruce found ways of telling Ann that he loved her. He got his elderly valet to dress up as a waiter and slip into her hotel room each evening with a bottle of champagne. With the bottle was a note saying where Bruce would be that night. And after midnight, Ann would sneak out of the back of the hotel to meet him.

On the big night, Ann was a bit nervous beforehand and cracked open a bottle of champagne with her roommate, Miss New Zealand, to bolster their self-confidence. But she needn't have worried: she was the unanimous choice of the judges and easily won the competition. It meant, though, that when they put a rhinestone crown on her highly lacquered head and the Miss World sash over the most prominent parts of her 36-24-36 curves, she was already a bit tipsy... and dying for the loo!

Even at her moment of triumph, her thoughts also turned to

Bruce and her fears that the romance would never survive the scrutiny of her being the most famous beauty queen in the world. She told herself, 'I have lost Bruce now.' She knew that as Miss World she would be even more in the limelight and there would be no chance of having a 'normal' romance.

Twice during the Miss World ball after the contest, Ann made her excuses to slip away to telephone Bruce. He was at home in the bachelor pad he had bought after his split with Penny, which overlooked Lord's cricket ground in north London. He knew there was no chance of seeing Ann that night. She wouldn't be that reckless.

Oh yes, she would! At 1am, Bruce was sipping the final few sips of a bottle of champagne he had opened to toast her triumph when there was a knock at the door of his flat. There was Ann in her wonderful Miss World ballgown but not her crown – she had left that at the hotel so as not to raise suspicion. She stayed with Bruce for a few hours before sneaking back to her hotel room undetected. With all those security guards and chaperones, they were both amazed she had got away with it.

If anything, their romance would be even more difficult to conduct now but they were determined not to give each other up. Ann had signed a contract with the International Wool Secretariat to act as a worldwide ambassadress. A clause in the huge £30,000 contract said that any misbehaviour on her part would see her instantly sacked.

Ann moved into a flat in Putney, south London, with a girlfriend. They still had to be highly secretive but Bruce and Ann were at least free now to become lovers for the first time. Convinced that his marriage really was over and she could do herself no harm, Ann let herself fall hopelessly in love with Bruce.

By then he was appearing in his first West End musical, *Little Me*. To keep the romance secret, he would don a series of disguises when he went to visit Ann in Putney. One night he would appear as the TV detective Columbo in a dirty old mac. Another time he would arrive wearing a funny little moustache. Ann found it hilarious.

But sometimes, even with the disguises, they were found out. One morning, they were walking arm in arm from the flat after Bruce had stayed the night. He was in disguise and confident no one could recognise him. They froze when someone in the flats opposite yelled, 'Come of it, Brucie! You can't fool us. We'd know that walk anywhere.'

Ann scurried away and Bruce, thinking on his feet, cracked a few gags with the man and explained that he was rehearsing for a film part. Ann loved the fact that he was so quick thinking. Her life seemed so exciting now she was with Bruce. It was impossible, Ann thought, not to have a good time with him.

The good times were not to last though. Despite their secrecy, the story of how Bruce was seeing the current Miss World refused to die. It created far too much pressure on the couple. The illicit romance that had seemed like a lot of fun in the first six months began to take its toll on both of them.

In December 1965, Bruce had to go to South Africa to appear in a variety show and Ann went with him. She told Bruce she had begun to hate their secret life in Britain together. She wanted the relationship to be established on a more formal basis and for Bruce to publicly say that they were together. Bruce and Ann's recollections of what happened after that are slightly different. She claimed that she asked Bruce if he had any intention of marrying her after his divorce from Penny came through. To her bitter disappointment, she said he told her he wanted to go along with things as they were without any wedding. Bruce, for his part, did not recall this conversation and just remembered that things were tense and that they were not getting along. What was true was that things were very difficult with Penny and any divorce was a long way off. Even if he had wanted to marry Ann, there was little chance of it happening.

Ann was feeling particularly fragile. Her year in the limelight as Miss World had just come to an end and she was facing a big crossroads in her life. She felt restless and missed all the attention she had received while she still held the title. She was in a bit of mess throughout the trip and craved more commitment from Bruce. One night on the trip, while alone in the hotel room she was sharing with Bruce, she drank too much alcohol and swallowed a lot of sleeping pills in an attempt to take her own life. How serious Ann really was in her attempt only she knows. Thankfully, she was unsuccessful and she suffered no long-term damage. She later bitterly regretted what she had done and said she was very ashamed.

Ann flew back to Britain on her own while Bruce carried on working in South Africa. He sent her loving cards, letters and cables before they were reunited a few weeks later. But things were not right between them and there was no going back. Bruce realised that he needed to get out of the relationship but, after what had happened in South Africa, he knew he had to be careful. After telling Ann the news, he also phoned her father. Bruce told him that Ann was very mixed up and would benefit from spending time in the family home in Bournemouth.

Ann and Bruce never saw each other again. Ann moved to Los Angeles, where she worked as an actress, singer and dancer. She later told the story of her affair with Bruce. She rang Bruce shortly after he had met his third wife Wilnelia in early 1983. Hurt about untrue claims Ann had made about him in the press, Bruce told Ann he had nothing to say to her.

It's worth asking at this point what had turned Bruce from being a contented family man with Penny into a bit of a boy about town. We know that relations with Penny deteriorated over the years but was there another reason? Bruce thought there was. It was all to do with his star sign and his late sexual development. Bruce was a Pisces, which astrologers reckon is the sexiest of all the star signs. As a young man in his late teens and twenties trying to make it in show business, Bruce dreamed of sleeping with the most glamorous stars of the day: Ava Gardner, Cyd Charisse and Loretta Young. Of course, they were all completely unobtainable to a fairly unsuccessful, second-on-the-bill British showman. Suddenly, with his success on *Sunday Night at the Palladium*, big stars – and plenty of other women besides – were attracted to the rich and successful Bruce Forsyth. After years of miserable underachievement, Bruce was like a kid in a candy shop as far as women were concerned. Also he had been so focused on his career as a young man that he had almost forgotten about his libido. The irresistible offers that came flooding his way after he became famous soon jogged his memory!

He admitted in his book *Bruce: The Autobiography*, 'I don't think I reached sexual maturity until my thirties. Ambition can take the place of everything – even sex. "I want to be successful" is what drove me in my youth and throughout my twenties. I was always so busy rehearsing and practising new things that it left little time for anything else. Sex took second place.

'Only when I hit the Big Time, got the job at the Palladium, became the "name", did I gain confidence, not only in myself as a performer but as a sexual being. Then, after being on that show for six weeks and seeing my name outside the Palladium, my libido grew and I became sexually of age!'

Bruce lost count of the number of women who tried to get him into bed. 'There have been times since, of course, when I regretted passing up some potentially splendid moments with some of the lovely girls I met – especially when I knew I could have pushed matters further,' he said. 'When I was with Ann Sidney I was doing loads of shows and, not surprisingly, there were endless opportunities. But I let them pass me by!

'Temptation, to use a golfing term, is par for the course in show business. If you are successful – and this is especially true if you are in the spotlight on the stage – women easily became enamoured, just as men do with female stars. There are, shall we say, opportunities that you wouldn't get in ordinary occupations – I guess it's one of the perks, and sometimes complications, of the job!'

One opportunity Bruce didn't turn down was with a beautiful young singer dubbed the British Marilyn Monroe. This was when he was going through another sticky patch with Penny and was a year or so before he fell in love with

Ann Sidney. Kathy Kirby may not be a big name now but in the early 1960s she was one of the biggest stars in Britain. Bright, blonde and bubbly and with an unforgettable soprano voice, she had stormed the charts with two big hits, 'Dance On' and 'Secret Love', which sold more than a million copies worldwide. She could fill any theatre in the country and was earning a fortune at the peak of her success. She was an incredibly charismatic performer in her heyday and it was no surprise when Bruce immediately fell for her one night at the Savoy Hotel after they appeared in cabaret together.

As ever with Bruce, there were complications. Although estranged, he had Penny and his young children lurking in the background, and Kathy was in a long-term relationship with her manager and Svengali, bandleader Bert Ambrose, who had discovered her when she was just 16 and made her into a star. Ambrose – or Ammie as she called him – was also married and 40 years older than Kathy. She had been deeply in love with Ammie but over time she came to realise that he was stifling both her career and her emotional development, and she longed to escape his iron grip. Ammie was also insanely jealous – and he was not at all happy when Bruce appeared on the scene. Despite all these issues, Bruce and Kathy enjoyed a passionate six-month affair – meeting for secret trysts at her flat in Grosvenor Square, Mayfair.

Kathy, who also went on to have an affair with the singer Tom Jones, described in an interview with the *Sunday Express* how Bruce pursued her relentlessly after that night at the Savoy.

Ammie missed the performance and after the show she went with Bruce to the restaurant for a meal. 'We danced – and what a superb dancer the man is!' she said. 'Then we just sat and talked, first about his life; how his marriage had broken up and how worries lay behind his cheerful television face. Then we talked about me.

'After a while he said, "You don't have much fun, do you?"

'I just smiled.

'Bruce said, "How about lunch tomorrow?"

'"I can't, Bruce," I said. "He wouldn't like it."

'Bruce more or less echoed what my sister and my closest friends had been telling me for a long time: "You're a big girl now. You've your own life to live."

'"You're probably right," I sighed. "But please, Bruce, let's leave it at that."'

But Bruce didn't leave it at that. The next day he phoned Kathy but Ammie answered and told him she wasn't there. She recalled that he kept phoning but always got Ammie, who always told him she was out or too busy.

Kathy knew nothing of all those calls until, by chance, she answered the phone herself one day. 'Bruce asked me to lunch and I accepted. Then Ammie came in and asked who'd called. For a moment, I felt as if I were back at school, caught by Reverend Mother talking to a strange boy. But I said firmly, "It was Bruce. He's invited me to lunch." Ammie grunted and said, "Why doesn't that guy stop bothering you?" I said, "He's not bothering me. I'm lunching with him this afternoon."'

Kathy and Bruce met again and again, she said, adding, 'Gradually our relationship grew warmer and I knew that here was a man who really understood me. Here was someone I could trust with my life.

'Had he asked me to marry him, I'd have accepted, for looking back I think I was truly in love as a young girl should be for the first time. And I know he felt deeply about me.'

But Ammie wasn't happy about this. 'We would go to a restaurant and everything would be fine and then suddenly he would scream out, "Bruce Forsyth, that goddamned son of a bitch!" and a lot worse,' Kathy recalled.

The situation became so intolerable that she began meeting Bruce secretly. 'Soon I found Ammie was checking on all my movements. And nothing could stop him sulking – not even exciting news from New York.

'One of my records was high in the American Top Twenty and Ed Sullivan invited me to appear on his famous coast-to-coast chat show. We accepted, of course. But on the plane Ammie just sat staring out of the window, refusing to answer when I spoke.

'And it was worse when we reached our hotel on what should have been one of the happiest occasions of my life. When I walked in, the living room was a mass of flowers. They were from Bruce. And there, too, were half a dozen telegrams from him sending his love, wishing me luck.

'My happiness was overshadowed by the fear of what Ammie would say. Then the phone rang. It was Bruce. While I talked to him, Ammie stayed in the room, which made our conversation awkward.

'Afterwards, I could not stand his silence. "Please talk to me," I pleaded. "Please let's be friends."

'Struggling to control himself, he said, "Promise me you'll never see Bruce Forsyth again."'

It was a heart-rending decision for her to make, she said.

'My love for Bruce was deep but if I rejected Ammie, I might destroy him. For without me he would have no reason for living. I heard myself say, "All right, Ammie, I promise."'

She wrote to Bruce, explaining what had happened. After that they never met unless they happened to be appearing in the same show. 'And for my sake he didn't go out of his way to meet me even then,' Kathy said.

Kathy later blamed the affair with Bruce for wrecking her show-business career. Ambrose remained her manager after the split with Bruce but things were never the same. He was wary of pushing her too hard because he was worried that he would lose her again to another man. As a result, she missed out on a big Hollywood role.

'I discovered that a Hollywood movie producer was offering me a three-picture deal. They thought I could become the British Doris Day or Monroe. Like Doris Day, I was not a trained actress but they said I could sing and I had presence,' she recalled.

'I was keen to break into Hollywood but Bert decided not to go through with it. I was also doing the *Kathy Kirby Show* for the BBC and had offers from other television companies but all that began to dry up too. Bert was turning down work for me because he thought I would leave him after having the affair with Bruce Forsyth but he should have known I never would.

'I think I could have played romantic leads or light comedy roles in movies but my silly affair with Bruce had inadvertently brought it all to an end.' Not wanting to become frustrated or bitter, in the end she just put it down to experience.

'Bert kept my head busy with singing jobs and appearances,'

she continued. 'I know I was big in my day and there are times when I think I could have had a bigger career but I loved Bert and I hated the fact that the affair was playing on his mind so much.'

As well as trying to deal with Ambrose's jealousy, she was also discovering that he was a compulsive gambler who was losing most of her earnings in London casinos and clubs. It was only after he died in 1971 that Kathy discovered he had lost £5 million of her money.

After finishing runner-up in the 1965 Eurovision Song Contest, Kathy's career petered out towards the end of the decade. After a series of flings, she married for the first time in the mid-1970s, to policeman-turned-writer Fred Pye. However, that relationship lasted only a few years, perhaps doomed when she lost a child. From living a life of luxury, she found herself penniless and she had mental problems. Like Ann Sidney, she took a drug overdose. However, she pulled herself back from the brink and enjoyed a revival on a nostalgia tour, performing for the last time in public in 1983 at the Horseshoe Bar in Blackpool for a television show.

For the last 25 years of her life she lived largely as a recluse in a flat in Kensington, west London, surviving on her memories, welfare benefits and the occasional gift from an astonishingly loyal fan base. She died of a heart attack, aged 72, in May 2011 shortly after being transferred to Brinsworth House – a retirement home for entertainers in Twickenham, Middlesex. It's the same home where Bruce's first wife Penny also lived as an elderly woman.

Shortly before she died, Kathy reflected on her affair with Bruce and whether she should have married him when she had the chance and left Ambrose. She said, 'I often wonder, at this stage, if I would have been in the same mess today if I had married Bruce Forsyth. I could have done. He was the one real love that I have ever known.

'It was the saddest moment of my life as I turned my back on Bruce. He has always proved to be a gentleman and the kind of husband that a woman can rely upon. I myself was never lucky enough to meet a man like him again.'

Bruce briefly referred to the affair in his autobiography. He said that it was secret by mutual consent. He described his lover as 'a soft person who had a Marilyn Monroe quality about her'. He talked about how Kathy's fortune was gambled away by Ambrose, before adding, 'Female stars have always been vulnerable – have always found it very difficult to find a man who will not only be a good manager but also a good partner or husband. This has happened to so many over the years – Doris Day and Judy Garland are just a couple of examples. I am so sad that Kathy fell on such hard times. But that's the other side of the business we are in.'

Having put two tricky relationships with young starlets behind him, Bruce soon had even bigger problems to deal with when it came to women. Disastrously, he decided once again to return to his wife Penny – a decision that landed him in even more trouble.

CHAPTER 7

THE HOKEY-
COKEY YEARS

Bruce's split and eventual divorce from Penny Calvert dragged out for almost 10 cruel years. He first walked out of the family home way back in the early 1960s. By then, their marriage had become a bit like the hokey cokey – he was in and out and in and out (and by his own admission, there was a fair bit of shaking it all about as well, as he had several affairs). Where did it all go wrong? And why did Bruce make such a bitter enemy of his ex-wife for most of his adult life, before they enjoyed a tender reconciliation when they were both in old age?

Let's start at the beginning. Young glamorous couple in show business fall in love and decide to go on the road as a sexy girl–boy, song-and-dance double act, travelling all over the world and performing in exotic locations. It sounds perfect, doesn't it? But there was a problem: no one wanted a duo of this kind and they struggled for bookings from day one. It soon became clear there was only option: Bruce would go solo while Penny would join him on the road and take care of his every need. This was fine for a while, though frustrating for Penny who still longed to be on stage herself. But she enjoyed being away with her charismatic new husband, so they rubbed along fine despite the tensions. Children followed – gorgeous, golden-haired little girls. Inevitably this kept Penny at home and meant that she could no longer join Bruce while he was away.

So there were all kinds of elements that could have lead to a break-up. But what really killed the Bruce and Penny marriage wasn't the long separations; it wasn't the exhaustion caused by young children; it wasn't the imbalance created in their careers as Bruce carried on treading the boards while Penny stayed at home. No, the real killer – the third woman in this marriage – was what Bruce had craved all his life: stardom. When it finally came, he found it took over his whole life, to the detriment of everything else including his marriage and children.

By 1958, Bruce was starring in *Sunday Night at the London Palladium*. At the time, he was living with his family in a small house in St Albans – a 90-minute trip from central London. As well as the Sunday night TV show, which required several rehearsals and endless preparation, he was appearing in pantomime twice a day, which ran from before Christmas right through to April. Clearly it was impossible to nip back to the family home for bathtime or to read a bedtime story. Home became simply a bed for the night – a glorified hotel room. Bruce would be there simply to sleep and not to spend quality time either with his children or, perhaps more crucially, with the increasingly neglected and frustrated Penny. Bruce knew that he was losing touch with what should have been the most important things in his life. But he had spent 16 years longing for this moment. In later years, Bruce was prepared to compromise. He happily achieved a work life balance and made sure he set aside time to keep his home life happy. But not then – his career was everything.

Throw into this toxic mix one final factor that has killed millions of marriages, that of temptation. Not just temptation but something far, far more dangerous: opportunity. Bruce, by now, was a star – and that meant there were women everywhere who wanted him and would do everything to get him.

Bruce tried hard to be faithful. Unlike his parents, he was not religious but he nevertheless took his marriage vows very seriously: he knew very well that adultery was a sin. But he was floundering in this new world. He summed up the difficulties he was facing in his 2001 autobiography.

'I found the Big Time hard, but exciting – and suddenly becoming so well known was wonderful,' he wrote. 'Pretty girls were now giving me an extra long look and temptation was being thrown my way 24 hours a day. As a married, young, heterosexual male in his prime, it was not an easy situation to find myself in. I'd always been a flirt, but when I think back on some of the opportunities I passed up – especially when it was going on all around me – I don't think I was too awful. Promiscuity was, after all, common in our business – as indeed it is now everywhere.'

Sex was becoming much more open and acceptable in the

late 1950s and early 1960s, he went on to explain. 'And, because I had achieved something – was now a "somebody" – a lot of my shyness was beginning to disperse. Hitting the Big Time was a boost to my all-round confidence – business and sexual. It made me aware of what was going on and I began to take advantage of this.'

He admitted he had been unfaithful to Penny but that she also shared some of the blame. 'Looking back, I have more of an idea why all this happened. I've certainly shouldered my fair share of the blame but I know that Penny would be the first to admit her faults, not forgetting her fiery temper!'

Before things went horribly wrong, there was happy news for Bruce and Penny. On 19 November 1962, Penny gave birth to their third daughter, Laura. They now had three highly demanding young girls – the eldest, Debbie, was by then aged seven and their second child, Julie, was four. For Penny, so often left home alone, this was exhausting. It wasn't fashionable then to have armies of nannies to take care of all the drudgery. Penny herself would change virtually every nappy. And unlike so many other women, she didn't have a strong family of her own to provide support. Her mother was miles away in Brixton. Tragically, there was little support from Bruce's side either. Neither of his parents was in the best of health in their later years. Bruce's mother died just two years after the birth of Debbie. His father only lived to see the birth of Bruce's first two children, dying from a heart attack in 1961. Penny was very much on her own.

By 1963, the marriage was approaching breaking point. 'We were not getting on at all well,' Bruce admitted. 'I do think that, as much as Penny always wanted things to be good for me, there was – and I certainly don't blame her for this – an ongoing sense that she was missing out on her own career.' If they'd had their time together again, Bruce and Penny both accepted it would have been better to wait five years before starting a family. That would have given Penny a decent chance of making it in her own right. Hindsight is a great thing but it was too late for regrets now.

Very occasionally, Penny would appear on stage with Bruce. She starred alongside his Dick Whittington at the Hippodrome in Bristol, playing the Queen of Catland. And they both appeared in *Showtime* at the Wellington Pier Pavilion in Great Yarmouth. Even after they started a family, she would perform with him in summer-season shows, with a babysitter waiting in the wings. But it would be wrong to say these were regular bookings. The day-to-day reality for Penny was nappy changing and long stretches on her own at home.

Of course, there was bitterness on Penny's part. Yes, she was thrilled for her husband – and grateful for the financial security blanket his fame provided. For years, they had scraped by, at times having to scrounge money off Bruce's parents just to put food in their bellies. The irony was, of course, that when they were at their happiest, they had nothing. Now Bruce was earning £1,000 a week and Penny could not have been more miserable. What added to her sense of dislocation was that her career had been snuffed out without ever having a chance to flourish. Maybe, just maybe, she could have been a star if she had only been given a chance. 'By then I had become a top-of-the-bill name and Penny hadn't – probably because she never had the chance,' Bruce explained. 'Looking back, although we had some fun and nice years working together, it would have been marvellous for her to have made her own way, to get in a few shows that would have fulfilled her ambitions, rather than waiting for the summer season so that she could continue working with me.'

Bruce eventually decided that there was no way back for him and Penny early in the summer of 1964. He went to Bournemouth to appear in another summer season and rented an apartment on his own. It was here that he fell in love with Ann Sidney. While Bruce knew in his heart the marriage was doomed, he had yet to tell Penny. She clearly knew that they faced real difficulties but she felt very much that their marriage could be saved. When the newspapers first reported that Bruce and Ann were together, this was a bombshell to Penny, who had no idea about the affair. Understandably, she was bitterly hurt and she lashed out very publicly. She announced that the marriage was 'over' and that she was heading immediately to Bournemouth for a 'showdown'.

Bruce had been incredibly selfish. He was big enough to acknowledge this years later but at the time he could not see the wood from the trees. The fact was he had been taking Penny for granted for years. Now he was quickly moving on with his life. Meanwhile, his still-young bride – who had always hankered for the limelight and felt, rightly or wrongly, that her big chance of fame had been stolen from her by her husband – had been dumped in the most humiliating fashion. Penny had every right to be angry.

The fall-out from this very public spat could have been disastrous for Bruce. It's worth remembering that he had only been a big star for a few years. Yes, he was a household name but he was new to stardom – he hadn't built up years of goodwill with the public to see him through the bad times. His fledgling career could have been killed stone dead by weeks of bad publicity.

These were very conservative times. Divorce was frowned upon. The tabloids had none of the ferocity they do these days but, even so, he got a bit of a kicking. He had always been seen before then as the 'happy family man'. Now that carefully cultivated public image – there were glowing press photographs of a beaming Bruce and Penny posing outside their first home in St Albans with little Debbie during happier times – had been shattered. In the eyes of some media commentators, the Brucie 'brand', as it would be known these days, had been 'irrevocably tarnished'. Penny was happy to talk to passing reporters out to make a bit of mischief and the whole thing was played out on the pages of our bestselling newspapers.

Of course, Bruce wasn't the first star to outgrow his first marriage and start a new relationship with a pretty girl. It was happening all the time. But other stars – perhaps with a bit more experience of the limelight than a newcomer like Bruce – were a little more discreet. It was possible to have affairs and not be splashed all over the papers if you were careful.

Penny finally arrived in Bournemouth for the 'showdown' promised in the papers. The glum couple went to a hotel for lunch. Bruce knew immediately that there was no going back – not least because he was by then madly in love with Ann Sidney. 'Our marriage had really turned sour and the conversation didn't get far,' he recalled. 'Penny was up and gone from the table in a flash. It was one of those moments that married people are so familiar with. I decided that, for both our sakes, things could not go on as they were; that Penny and I should formally separate and I should move out of our lovely house in Totteridge.'

So Bruce quit the family home, taking just his desk, golf clubs and trophies, a drinks trolley and his beloved Steinway piano. He moved into a new apartment overlooking Lord's cricket ground in London. It was so close to the ground that he could watch the cricket from the window. At the time, Bruce was happily settled with Ann. Despite constantly being targeted by other women, he remained faithful to his new love. But, as we know already, this romance was doomed too.

Over the next few years, Bruce and Penny remained close, despite their very public fall-out when the relationship with Ann had first been revealed. Bruce found it difficult to completely give Penny up. She was a beautiful woman and he was still attracted to her. And, of course, they were linked for ever by their three lovely girls, who, whatever his differences with Penny, Bruce still doted on. He would see little Debbie, Julie and their youngest daughter Laura most weekends, and often went back to the family home in Totteridge, a short drive from his new flat. Often on these occasions, Bruce would stay late to catch up with Penny and they would happily reminisce about the good times and end up in bed together. They both knew it was probably a bad idea to get back together but couldn't stay away from each other for long.

Over the next few years, there were several reconciliations between Bruce and Penny. Bruce put the figure at two. But Penny insisted there were far more – as many as seven.

At first it would work well but then all the old problems would return: Bruce's long absences, the temptations of new women, Penny stuck at home. The rows would start again and Bruce, with a new flat readily available to him at Lord's, would move out again. These were the hokey-cokey years, when neither Bruce nor Penny was sure if the marriage would survive.

Their separations became so frequent that there were farcical scenes at the house in Totteridge. Moving a Steinway piano is no easy feat. They are so valuable that Bruce would insist specialists came from the Steinway to shift it every time he and Penny had a row and he was packing his bags. 'The last time they called to collect it I had stuffed all his press cuttings inside,' revealed Penny. 'One of the movers looked at the piano and then at me and said, "Mrs Forsyth, if your husband leaves again, he can fetch his own piano. This is the last time."'

There were other little squabbles. They owned a cut-glass decanter, which kept going backwards and forwards after each separation. Penny got so fed-up with Bruce asking for it back that she stuck on the stopper with glue.

Penny spoke in detail in several interviews to different newspapers about why she felt the marriage failed after the final break-up. She believed that it was killed by his success on *Sunday Night at the London Palladium*. Until then, in her eyes, Bruce had been reasonably grounded and family orientated. In her view, the first whiff of real fame changed her husband for ever. She was warned that fame would kill the marriage by Bernard (later Lord) Delfont, a TV bigwig who had played a crucial role in getting Bruce the *SNAP* job.

'I remember Delfont asking me if I was sure I wanted Bruce to be a star,' Penny told one interviewer. 'I replied, "Yes, of course – that is what we both want. It's what we have always dreamed of." Now I realise what Delfont must have been thinking. He probably suspected stardom would cost us our marriage. It's not the success itself but the fame that goes with it that whips a person up and takes them so far away there's no coming back.

'Suddenly there were lots of people in the wings, waiting to tell him when he came off stage that he'd been fantastic. Why did he need me offering suggestions when there were all those people waiting to slap him on the back and say everything was just great.'

She spoke about the first moment she realised she was losing him.

'One night in the Palladium dressing room, I said, "You're doing so-and-so all wrong, Bruce." It was a natural thing to say. After all it had been my job to do so for years. He always called me his "eyes". But that night he looked at me and said, "What do you know?" It was the beginning of the end. Right up until then it had been, "Was it alright, Penny?" and "How did I do?" Now I was a stepping stone he no longer needed.

'There were rows and then there was not time for rows. Bruce had a show to do, Bruce mustn't be upset. What did he want to know if the baby wasn't taking its milk properly, or had measles, when everybody was telling him important things like he was a star?'

Bruce had several affairs during this time that went unreported. But Bruce was very publicly outed as an adulterer when he fell in love with Ann Sidney. There was another long affair with the pretty showgirl Kathy Kirby that only fully came to light almost 20 years later when she sold her story to a Sunday newspaper. Penny was aware of plenty of other women too.

Strictly speaking, Bruce wasn't always being unfaithful to Penny at this time. There were long periods when they were formally separated, so he could claim justifiably that he was a single man. Bruce had left the family home and for several years was living a bachelor existence – first in the flat at Lord's, then at a slightly bigger place in Kensington.

Penny said she always knew when Bruce was having an affair because he would not have sex with her. 'He didn't like to be untrue to them,' she said, fully aware of the bitter irony. 'Every one was like Anthea Redfern – young, pretty, leggy girls who thought he was smashing and never knew what the hell they were talking about. They just loved his fame.'

Bruce once presented Penny with a new pet dog. Her woman's natural sixth sense told her he must have been covering up in some way for another affair. 'He came home and presented me with a poodle,' Penny remembered. 'I said, "But Bruce, you didn't want me to have another dog." He told me he'd been somewhere, seen this dog and thought I would love to have it.' She recalled the conversation.

'I asked him, "Which girl did you go with? Was she buying a poodle too?"

"How dare you think like that," Bruce stormed.

Not that long after that, I met this girl singer backstage and she said, "How's your little doggy? Bruce and I bought them together."

Then she showed me her dog and told me it was the sister of the poodle Bruce had given me.'

Penny would occasionally make concerted attempts to pep up

93

the marriage during the brief interludes when they were back together and there wasn't another woman on the scene. She recalled one night when she splashed out on expensive lingerie, a matching negligee and sexy slippers. She cooked a fabulous dinner and had the candles lit just as Bruce arrived home from another night working at the Palladium. She recalled, 'I swung the front door open to greet him and he walked straight past me, saying, "God, what a rotten audience tonight!"

'And with that he went up the stairs to bed. I just sat there and tore the negligee to pieces. The next morning I was going to be so angry with him. But he said, "I've got no time to talk, darling. I've got to be at the television studios." I said, "Just a minute, did you notice me when you came in last night?"

'"Oh yes, you looked ready for bed and so was I," he replied.'

Penny became short-tempered around their friends, who were unaware of the fireworks going off behind closed doors. 'Your whole life is lies to your friends and they say, "Penny's a bit stand-offish, isn't she?" But they don't know why,' she said. 'You become the villain. In the end, after seven years of it, I just said to everybody, "Look, he's a right bastard. He sleeps around and that is what has made me so strange to you."'

It's clear from his own admissions and Penny's, albeit rather jaundiced, account of their marriage that Bruce was no angel. This carried on right through to 1971 when he fell in love with his *Generation Game* hostess Anthea Redfern. Anthea recalled that he had been juggling four women at the same time before she came along and made sure he only had eyes for her. By this stage, Bruce and Penny had been living apart for years.

We perhaps know rather more of Penny's views on why the

marriage failed than Bruce's because she was never shy of speaking to the press. Various barbs were aimed at Bruce in countless newspaper articles over the years. It all culminated in a major series in the *Daily Mirror*, which was published the same week that Bruce and Anthea were telling the rival *Sun* newspaper why their marriage had failed. Not the best of timing. Bruce was so incensed by the *Mirror* series – which he felt was highly sensationalised and full of inaccuracies – that he issued a very public challenge to the journalist who had written the pieces to have it out with him publicly. This was an extraordinary way for a major star such as Bruce to behave. But that's Brucie all over – he always wore his heart on his sleeve. When he felt he had been wrong, he was not shy in shouting the fact from the rooftops. He would do this several further times in his career, particularly if he felt he'd got a raw deal at work.

What slim chance they had of saving the marriage was killed by his romance with Anthea. Because Bruce had said little about the turbulence in his love life, the public perception at the time was that he and Penny were still together. In fact, the last of their reconciliations had failed a few years earlier and Bruce had been happily living as a bachelor for some time. So when Bruce and Anthea's relationship became public, it was reported that his '20-year marriage was over' – which simply wasn't true.

Penny wasn't going to allow the facts from getting in the way of having another blast at Bruce. 'Frankly, I can't wait to get rid of him,' she stormed. 'I treat him like a naughty son. He's just a silly boy, that's all. I am writing a book all about our marriage. It's called *Darling, Your Dinner's In the*

Dustbin. Writing it has helped me a lot to keep my balance and dignity. Marriage is the most difficult job anyone has to work at.'

To Penny, the marriage had failed for one simple reason: Bruce's womanising. 'Bruce really was a Don Juan and this often broke my heart,' she said. 'He could not resist a pretty face. It was not that he was particularly promiscuous. He just couldn't stop himself falling in love. I view his relationship with Anthea as a mother would: getting a troublesome son off her hands.'

She said that after they split for good she was cut out of the lives of all their famous friends. 'All these stars were our friends – people such as Tommy Steele, Tommy Cooper, Morecambe and Wise, and Sean Connery,' she said. 'We had been entertained by them all. But when a show-business marriage ends, everything stops for the other half. Des O'Connor and his wife lived down the road and I put notes under their door inviting them to drop in. But they didn't. I can understand it. People don't want the responsibility of dealing with the "failed" half of the relationship.'

Penny said that she was glad to be rid of Bruce. 'It made me cross when people looked at me and whispered, "She still loves Bruce." I didn't. He was soon dead to me. He died when he had the affair with Ann Sidney. And he died when I saw his affidavit to the registrar over the divorce settlement.'

Penny admitted that she had stuck with Bruce for so long because of the money. 'I was frightened I would come off badly financially,' she said at the time. 'Under the divorce law we have to give our mutual consent and I shall not give my consent until a satisfactory financial agreement has been worked out. The solicitors are fed up with us. We've been the most nearly divorced couple in the world for ages!'

She didn't feel jealous of his new relationship.

'No, I used to be jealous but not any more. He has a tremendous amount of sex appeal – I'm not surprised that young women fall for him. He has been falling in and out of love with girls for the last six years. In the past six years he has left me and come back seven times.

'Bruce and I have been together for 20 years. I still love him but I'm not in love with him, if you see the difference.'

Bruce's divorce from Penny did not come through until 1973 – more than 10 years after their first separation. For Bruce, it was very expensive. The divorce negotiations were marked by more rows and recriminations. Those rows became so heated that Bruce stormed out of one hearing at the High Court. Their lawyers had big arguments about money while they tried to thrash out a deal. Penny believed, wrongly, that Bruce was not fully declaring all his earnings and that she would be left short-changed in the final settlement. After months of protracted negotiations, a deal was agreed and Bruce was free to marry Anthea. He paid Penny a lump sum of £65,000 – half the value of their Totteridge home. He also paid £2,500 a year each for their daughters as well as their school fees. And he set up a trust fund for the girls that would give them a regular income after they left home. This wouldn't be the only time Bruce was hit with a huge divorce bill. His manager Ian Wilson used to joke that, if Bruce had just stayed married to the one woman, he would have been a billionaire!

Bruce escaped the stresses of going through the divorce by throwing himself into work. He told the *Sun* just as the settlement was coming through, 'It's been going on for nine years. It's been a great mental block for me. But whenever anything upsets me I can switch it off, go out and do some work. If I couldn't, I wouldn't be here now. I don't know where I'd be.'

Penny felt no bitterness towards Anthea. 'She was pretty and she was kind to him. She would go, "OK, Bruce, anything you say, Bruce." I could watch him on television and enjoy his performance. For all his failings, he was terribly talented – more than anybody has ever seen.'

Bruce finally detailed the inside story of their explosive marriage in a big interview with the *Sun* in 1979, by which time their daughters had grown up and Debbie had married. 'Our life together in those latter years was one of constant squabbling and rows,' he revealed. 'And many is the occasion she finished throwing things at me. Once she hurled a whole china tea service out of the kitchen window on to the lawn. Another time a heavy radio set went through the window. The way she squandered money just added to our marriage difficulties.

'My marriage to Penny, despite my two reconciliations, was the biggest mistake of my life. My daughters apart, I regret it completely. One of Penny's constant accusations against me was that I was a mean person. She claimed I penny-pinched over Debbie's wedding day. That I imposed a strict budget that orange juice had to be mixed with sparkling wine to disguise the fact there was no champagne. Penny, as usual, was in a fantasy world. We certainly had champagne at the wedding. I remember taking two dozen bottles myself. The wedding was a complete success.' Debbie backed up her father's recollection.

Bruce claimed that Penny had allowed their home in

Totteridge to fall into disrepair, to the extent that it was actually sold for less than they had bought it – diminishing her divorce settlement. 'Just before the house was put up for sale, she wrenched every fixed appliance out of the kitchen, ripped out fitted wardrobes, and wrecked the plumbing and tiling,' said Bruce angrily.

Bruce further claimed that many of their problems had stemmed from Penny's heavy drinking. While Penny had always acknowledged she enjoyed a drink, she felt Bruce had exaggerated her problems.

Long after the marriage had ended, Bruce took a more reflective tone, accepting more of the blame for its failure. Speaking in 1987, he conceded, 'Thirty years ago, I was getting my act together, rehearsing, performing, travelling. I was away almost constantly touring and that puts a great strain on a relationship. I'm sure I was very difficult to live with, simply because I wasn't there and everything was geared towards work rather than home.'

There were several reasons for the softening of Bruce's attitude. Obviously time is a great healer. And there is no doubt that the happiness Bruce enjoyed after meeting his third wife Wilnelia made him far more reflective and able to admit to mistakes in the past. Having three daughters together, of course, meant that he and Penny never lost touch. Whether they liked it or not they were reunited at regular intervals over the years – weddings and christenings, not just of grandchildren but great-grandchildren

In 2003, in a sign that all their bitter wrangles from the past had been well and truly forgotten, Bruce was spotted visiting Penny at Brinsworth House, a nursing home run by the

Entertainment Artistes' Benevolent Fund in Twickenham. Penny, who had suffered a stroke, was a full-time resident. 'It was a very tender meeting,' one friend said. 'Bruce was really affectionate towards Penny – they appeared to be like two very good, very old friends, which, I suppose, in many ways they were. Penny was genuinely thrilled to see him. Whatever anger she had felt before had long since gone.'

Penny had shown there were no longer any hard feelings by researching the Forsyth genealogy. She had discovered that Bruce's great-great-great-grandfather, William Forsyth, was George III's head gardener at Kensington Palace (the forsythia shrub was named after him).

So the marriage to Penny had been a disaster. Bruce's career had hardly been blossoming either as he and Penny finally went their separate ways. But his luck was to change at just the right time. He would land the biggest show of his career – and a beautiful new wife too.

CHAPTER 8

GIVE US
A TWIRL

It all started at a Lovely Legs competition at a nightclub in London. Bruce was already one of the best-known faces in Britain and he was about to embark on what was arguably the most successful period of his career. It was May 1971 and he was spending an enjoyable evening with a female pal acting as a judge in the competition. Suddenly, a very pretty girl appeared on stage as the compere. As the then-unknown Anthea Redfern swished past in a stunning lavender outfit with an eye-catching mini-skirt, Bruce's friend gushed, 'Oh, Bruce, what a beautiful girl!' She was just 23. Bruce was 43. And little did he know then that this would be the start of a tumultuous decade-long romance that would finally kill his already dying marriage to first wife Penny but also lead to fresh heartache.

Bruce could not take his eyes off Anthea. She had just

returned from a holiday in the South of France and was a sporting a gorgeous golden tan. She was one of the most beautiful women he had ever seen. If she had entered the contest herself, she would have been the runaway winner. Bruce would have made sure of that.

Later in the evening, Anthea popped over to chat to Bruce and his pal at their table. But while Bruce was attracted to the leggy beauty, romance was the last thing on either of their minds. 'It wasn't a case of love at first sight,' Bruce later recalled. And anyway, Anthea lost no time in telling her new pals about her boyfriend – Louis Brown, a rich nightclub boss who owned the club where the contest was being held. She even showed them pictures of the happy couple on the same holiday where she'd picked up that lovely tan.

Four months later, Bruce and Anthea met again. He was to star in a new BBC One Saturday-night game show, *The Generation Game*, and bosses were looking for a glamorous hostess to act as his sidekick. They had already drawn up a shortlist after auditioning 50 girls, picked largely because they had appeared on other TV shows. But it soon became apparent that what they really needed was a new face, someone fresh that viewers had never seen before. Then Bruce remembered Anthea. Or more accurately, he remembered those legs. Well, not just the legs but also the calm and professional way that she had compered the competition. He knew she would be perfect for the new role and got a friend to ask her to come along for the audition.

Anthea quickly realised that this was her big break. She left nothing to chance in making sure that the job was hers. She even persuaded her rich boyfriend Louis to lend her his chauffeur-driven maroon Rolls-Royce, which allowed her to make a spectacular entrance in the BBC's exclusive VIP car park.

It took the producers just 10 minutes to decide that they had found their dream hostess. Bruce didn't even need to put in a word on her behalf. She was hired for the princely sum of £100 a show – a fortune for a girl who'd previously only enjoyed modest success as a model.

Anthea was about to become one of the most famous women in Britain – a meteoric rise for a girl born in Newton Abbot in Devon whose only real ambition in life was to be a wife and mother. She was the classic ugly duckling, a slightly awkward schoolgirl who grew up into a beautiful swan. 'I was so skinny and incredibly unattractive as a child that people would say to my mother, "Isn't she plain? Isn't she thin? Whatever is she going to do in life?" I don't think they meant to be cruel but I was aware of it and I think that's why I wanted to be a model,' she recalled.

Anthea had enjoyed a troubled upbringing – to the disgust of her mother, her father had given up a successful career as a green grocer to dedicate his life to his first love: gambling. He at least had the sense to become a bookmaker and, despite being successful enough to send his three striking daughters to private schools, there were long losing streaks too. Anthea always knew when he had fallen on hard times because the family car would change from being a Jaguar to a more humble Volkswagen.

Anthea blossomed in her teens and, with those never-ending legs, her mother gave her the confidence to pursue a career in modelling. 'With your height you'll make a beautiful model,' she told her daughter. Anthea took a modelling course and, aged just 17, had left her life in Devon behind to stride down the catwalks of Paris modelling for Christian Dior. However, a career in high fashion never really took off and it was not long before she became one of the first models to appear on Page 3 of the *Sun*, albeit not topless. She also worked as a Playboy Bunny, working in the London club in Park Lane in 1969 using the name Sasha. A year after that she won the Miss London beauty pageant.

So Anthea was not exactly new to the world of celebrity but this was her first time on television. Bruce used all his show-business experience to help a very nervous Anthea on the road to stardom. Understandably, she was nervous during rehearsals and he would remind her to raise her voice and also help her with her lines. Other aspects of the job came naturally to her – her time on the catwalk gave her real poise and, of course, there were those looks.

Fans took immediately to Bruce's new television companion when *The Generation Game* first aired a month after her audition and delighted BBC bosses quickly realised they had a monster Saturday-night hit on their hands. Bruce and Anthea's double act became more assured and, within weeks, they were performing little routines together on the show.

Anthea's outfits soon became a big part of her appeal. In the first series, there was a strict budget on the show and all her dresses were brought from High Street shops. Later, bosses realised they were missing a trick and had Anthea's dresses specially made for her by the designer Linda Martin.

Every week her TV entrance would bring gasps from the audience. Letters would pour in from fans asking for more details about the outfits. One night, when Anthea was looking particularly stunning, Bruce blurted out, 'Oh, Anthea, that's lovely. Let the viewers see the back. Come on, give us a twirl!' Instantly, the phrase stuck. Like all of Bruce's famous catchphrases, it was ad-libbed rather than scripted.

With such an immediate rapport on screen, it wasn't long before Bruce and Anthea became closer off screen too. At first, Anthea had been wary of getting involved. As far as she was concerned, Bruce was still a married man. There was no way she was going to be a marriage wrecker. What she didn't know was that Bruce had been separated for years. This had been reported but Anthea had not picked up on the news. Eventually, she learned the truth. She was delighted that her glamorous co-star might be available after all.

Bruce discovered that Anthea loved doughnuts and would buy her six every week. They would sit together having cups of tea and eating the doughnuts. It tickled Bruce so much that he started calling Anthea 'Doughnut'. The pair would also take a break between rehearsals at a little café called Oddies. At first, conversation was strictly about work and how they could improve their act. But, gradually, things became far more intimate.

Anthea told Bruce how she was experiencing problems with her long-term boyfriend Louis. She had been grateful for his help in establishing her as a model. He was kind and generous and he loved her to death. But he was also quite jealous and controlling.

Anthea was given very little freedom. His maroon Roller – which had whisked her to that fateful audition – was always there at the studio to pick her after the shows. Often he would watch her in the studio audience during recordings of *The*

Generation Game, which always put Anthea on edge. And afterwards he would often be critical of how she'd performed, adding to the tension. Though reluctant to be disloyal to a man who had done so much for her, it was obvious to Bruce that Anthea was deeply unhappy.

Anthea began to really open up to Bruce as they huddled together in Oddies and soon a romance began to blossom. They began holding hands as they spoke and giggled as their knees touched under the table.

Anthea was wary of getting involved with Bruce. She was aware that Bruce had severed all ties with Penny but there were also other girls on the scene. 'When I met him, he was juggling four very beautiful girls so I certainly wasn't the cause of the break-up of his marriage,' she said. Whatever juggling Bruce was doing, it soon stopped. He realised that, if he was to have any chance with his young co-star, he had to show her that he was serious.

One day, Bruce couldn't hide his feelings any longer. By then, he had sensed that Anthea felt the same way. He was determined to tell her his true feelings and he burst into her dressing room. He was greeted by Anthea in rollers, wearing no make-up and caught completely off guard. But even stripped down to the basics, Anthea looked stunningly beautiful to her besotted co-star. He swept her up in his arms and they kissed for the first time. Whatever doubts Anthea had about embarking on a romance with a man who was effectively her boss were swept away in the same moment.

It still left the problem of Penny, who was to remain a thorn in Bruce's side for many years to come. They had separated several years earlier after various failed attempts at reconciliation. Bruce had long since moved out of the family home in north London and was rebuilding his life in a flat in Kensington, which even he described as 'grotty'.

After that first kiss, Bruce invited Anthea to dinner. She turned up and made straight for the fridge. She expected to see barren shelves and possibly a few bottles of champagne – a life indicative of a lonely bachelor. In fact, it was fully stocked with the best cuts of meat and everything needed for a lavish banquet. Bruce was a proud man – perfectly capable of looking after himself, even if the décor of the flat lacked a woman's touch. And he had always loved his food. Anthea was impressed.

Bruce cooked Anthea a steak and they both drank from a chilled bottle of champagne. Later, they went to bed and made love for the first time. It was a momentous night for both of them. They both knew they had fallen deeply in love and wanted to be together. But there was still the problem of Louis. Bruce didn't mince his words, giving Anthea a stark choice: 'It has to be Louis or me!'

Bruce went off to a health farm for a few days to relax, keen to give Anthea some breathing space to make up her mind. He was confident that she would choose him but didn't want to appear too desperate. 'I am not going to contact you. You telephone me when you have made up your mind,' he told her. 'You know I want us to be together.'

Anthea soon made her choice – it was Bruce, of course. She rang him breathlessly and said, 'Yes, I want to be with you.' She quickly moved into the same Kensington flat and, with a few feminine touches, she soon got rid of the grot, turning it into a comfortable home for the new lovebirds. She also took over the cooking.

It was inevitable that news of this sensational show-business romance would leak out to the press. And sure enough, it happened when Bruce went to Canada with a touring version of his London Palladium show and asked Anthea to join him. As luck would have it, an eagle-eyed Fleet Street show-business reporter was travelling with the show. He quickly deduced that their on-stage chemistry had spilled over into real life. When the reporter gave them an ultimatum, 'Either I write a nasty story about you being here with the hostess of your TV show, or you tell me the truth,' Bruce was happy for the truth to come out. He replied proudly, 'To hell with it, I have nothing to hide. I love Anthea. And yes, if things work out right, I *will* marry her.' For Anthea, this stunning and very public declaration of love was perfect. But she had always been plagued by a lack of self-confidence.

She turned to Bruce and said excitedly, 'Do you really mean that?'

'Yes, I do mean it, darling,' he replied.

Anthea was never bothered about the age gap. 'People often asked about the twenty years that separated Bruce and me,' she explained. 'When they asked if that worried me, I would say, "Yes, [it] does." Not that I worry about losing my looks, because everyone grows to look older. But I never want to grow old mentally. If I did that, I'd feel much older than Bruce, because he will always stay young at heart.'

The happy couple enjoyed an idyllic few final days in Canada before returning to Britain to face the music. For Bruce this meant more recriminations from his estranged wife Penny. And for Anthea, this meant dealing with the fall-out when the press finally contacted Louis.

Bruce had sensed there were would be problems with Penny before embarking on the trip to Canada. He knew that, if news leaked out of his secret romance while he was away, all hell would break loose. So before setting out, he had told Penny that he and Anthea were in love. Her fears were quickly realised when news broke of the romance before their return home. Almost immediately, inaccurate press reports soon appeared saying that Bruce had walked out on Penny and their three children to take Anthea to Canada. Penny said bitterly, 'I thought he'd take a bird with him. I'm not surprised. Bruce is always falling in love. I wouldn't be surprised if he didn't fall in love with the Queen next.' While it was true that Bruce *had* conducted affairs during their marriage, this time he had behaved entirely honourably. He and Penny had been living apart for a while.

Certainly Anthea felt no guilt over Penny's anger. 'Penny wasn't always complimentary about us,' she said later. 'And I understand the meaning of the saying "Hell hath no fury like a woman scorned". Some women can't handle it and I don't blame them. But if a man is happy in his marriage, even if he does have the odd indiscretion, he will do everything in his power to cover it up. But if he's not happy in a relationship, it becomes something more than just an odd indiscretion.'

Louis – 25 years older than Anthea – put a brave face on being dumped so horribly. He had met Anthea in circumstances very similar to Bruce – spotting her in a beauty contest when she was just 19 and struggling to get over the break-up of a disastrous first marriage to former Torquay United footballer Robin Stubbs. They had wed in 1966 when she was only 17 – and it only lasted 10 months. It was wrongly reported that the marriage had never been consummated. Robin hit back angrily, saying, 'Of course the marriage was consummated. We definitely made love on our honeymoon but I really didn't fancy her.'

Anthea put their marriage failure down to the simple fact that she had tied the knot too young. 'When he asked me to marry him, I was so flattered and overwhelmed that I just didn't think about being too young to take on that responsibility,' she explained. 'I was only seventeen, far too young, and I got married partly as a gesture of independence. Neither of us realised that you have to work at a marriage – not just sit back and hope it works out, which is what we did.'

Anthea was just getting over the split when she met millionaire Louis after winning the 1970 Miss London contest he helped to organise. She moved in with him after a few weeks. He became her manager and promoter and spent thousands making Anthea 'beautiful' by paying £1,200 – an absolute fortune in those days – to have her teeth fixed. He even named a £50,000 club after Anthea. And he bought her a £1,500 ring and took her on expensive holidays.

Bruce even befriended Louis and they, along with Anthea, would often go out as a threesome, with Louis completely unaware that the big star was wooing his girl. He only found out about their secret romance as he was driving through London in March, 1972, when he saw a newspaper billboard saying, MY NEW LOVE – BY BRUCE FORSYTH. Louis was stunned. 'I still can't believe it has happened,' he said at the time.

He hit out at Bruce in an interview with the *Sunday Mirror*. 'I had lived with Anthea for more than a year and I always had at the back of my mind the thought that one day she might leave me for somebody else. But never in a million years did I think that somebody would be my mate, Bruce Forsyth,' he stormed.

'I trusted Bruce implicitly. I looked on him as a personal friend, someone I could confide in and tell my problems to. I even told him private details of my life with Anthea – about our rows and tiffs. About her wanting us to get married and my saying I thought we should wait a little longer to be sure. Now I can see that all I was doing was providing him with ammunition – ammunition that made it easier for him to take Anthea away from me. Bruce has wonderful chatter – he is the man with the golden tongue. I can't believe Anthea is in love with him.'

Despite the break-up, he was still fond of Anthea. 'I would still rush round after her. Anthea is the sort of woman who can make you feel you are the only man in the entire world. Deep down inside Anthea, with those lovely legs and such smashing looks, is a little suburban wife just looking to get out.' As Bruce would later discover, Louis was unerringly accurate in his description of his former lover.

Bruce and Anthea thought they had weathered the storm – but there were problems to come. This time, they came from their bosses at the BBC.

The Generation Game was one of the most popular shows on British television, regularly attracting more than 20 million viewers every Saturday night. Viewers loved Bruce and Anthea's sizzling on-screen chemistry. Audience numbers hadn't dipped at all when viewers discovered that the two stars were together in real life. However, there were conservative elements within the Beeb who were not at all happy. While Bruce had been separated from Penny for years, they felt it looked bad for the married presenter of a family show to be in a very public romance with his much younger co-star. Unbelievably, they wanted to destroy the winning formula by dropping Anthea from the show.

Anthea explained, 'One day the producers came to the flat. They said, "We want to talk to just you, Bruce." But he insisted, "Anything you want to say to me you can say in front of Anthea." I didn't want to force them into a corner, so I agreed to go out and do a bit of shopping while they talked. While I was away, they explained that, because he was married and we had fallen in love, they couldn't use me because of the bad press it would generate.'

Loyal Bruce was having none of it. His reply was simple: if she goes, I go. And such was Bruce's popularity at the time that it was inconceivable they could go on without him. 'I told Bruce that he shouldn't threaten to quit the show because of me,' Anthea said. 'This was a huge, huge show for him and I didn't want to jeopardise it. But he just said to me, "It's not fair. I've been separated all these years and I will go out with whoever I want."'

Bruce got his way and Anthea stayed. But a compromise was reached whereby they reduced her input by bring in four extra hostesses for the new shows. Producers hired the most glamorous girls they could find to work with Anthea. And to really rub salt into the wounds, they gave Anthea the frumpiest outfit they could find for the first show in the new format – a grey dress with an unsightly frill just beneath her chin. Anthea hated her look; she said she looked like a choirboy. This contrasted sharply with the glamorous halterneck gowns worn by the other girls. To make matters worse, the girl with the twirl was shunted into the background and given a lesser role than the new hostesses. The viewers couldn't understand why the changes had been made. They wrote in their hundreds to ask to see more of Anthea, not less. After this very public show of support, there were no problems at all – and all talk of Anthea being booted off the show quickly ended. The fact that Bruce had been prepared to put his career on the line to save his new love only brought them closer together.

The bosses at the Beeb were right in one respect: there was a formidable press backlash, albeit one which probably boosted rather than harmed the show's ratings. Anthea was portrayed quite unfairly as a scarlet woman who had wrecked a 20-year marriage and ripped three girls from their father. Understandably, she was distraught – not least because the stories were simply wrong. 'I was made to look like a horrible painted blonde who stole husbands – and that really hurt,' she later said bitterly. 'What everyone forgot to mention was that Bruce had left Penny years earlier, so I didn't split them up. I don't think his wife had been sitting all alone at home crying all those years, just as Bruce had many lovely girlfriends before he met me.'

Anthea and Bruce moved into his Kensington home together. Anthea was convent-educated and had very traditional views on marriage. She would only live with a man if she felt sure that there was the prospect of wedlock. Bruce wanted to marry her too but there was one big problem: he was still married to Penny. And getting out of that marriage was proving far from easy.

The divorce dragged on and on and cost Bruce a fortune. It took a further two years to finalise. With almost 80 per cent of Bruce's earnings going in tax anyway under the punitive rates levied by governments in the 1970s, he was having to work seven days a week to cover the bills, taking on vast amounts of cabaret work. With the divorce finally through towards the end of 1973, Bruce was finally free to marry Anthea and he lost no time in proposing. She excitedly said yes.

For a great showman like Bruce, the plans for his second wedding were a little surprising. He wanted no crowds, no press photographers and no big fuss. For those reasons he picked one of the most unlikely days in the world in world to tie the knot: Christmas Eve. It was two and a half years since he and Anthea had first fallen in love.

Bruce planned it all meticulously. They would marry quietly and then he would tell his three children by Penny his happy news the day after Boxing Day when a family day out was planned. That way, despite missing out on the wedding, the girls would hear the news first from their dear old dad. Bruce knew that, if Penny found out in advance, she was bound to tell the children – and it would ruin their Christmas Day.

The banns were called at Windsor Register Office. The registrar entered into the spirit of the thing by promising to pin them in a corridor where 'they wouldn't be noticed'.

Anthea wore a long velvet wedding dress in Bruce's favourite Roman purple, the rich colour bringing out the blue in her huge eyes. Her fair hair fell about her shoulders and rippled down her back, and on her head was a white coronet of baby rosebuds and sweet lily of the valley. Just a dozen guests were invited, meeting for a quick drink in a pub before the ceremony. There was a quiet reception at a nearby hotel and then all the guests went home, sworn to secrecy, having attended what was probably the most low-key showbiz wedding in history. In the days before camera phones and the Internet, there was no reason to believe the details would leak.

But Bruce hadn't reckoned on a photographer – a friend of the family, who they had invited along to take a few snaps for the family album – selling a picture of the wedding to the *Daily Express*.

Bruce had been due to meet his three girls – Debbie, Julie and Laura – on the same day the *Express* was planning to publish the picture. Bruce had been due to have lunch with his girls and then they would all go to see the hit movie of the time, *The Sting*, starring Robert Redford and Paul Newman. Soon other papers were also on to the story and had phoned Penny with news of the wedding. She told their daughters, and Debbie rang Bruce to ask if it was true. Bruce lied. 'I remember so clearly my words on the telephone: "No darling, no darling. It could be a rumour. They are always saying we have got married. Would I lie to you? Of course I wouldn't."'

Bruce was simply buying himself some time. When he was talking to Debbie, he didn't know that the pictures had been sold and would be published the very next day – that was when he hoped to soften the blow by telling his daughters face-to-face. Of course, by then it was too late. And the girls were in tears after getting confirmation of their beloved dad's second marriage by reading about it in the papers.

The trip to the cinema was quickly cancelled as Bruce

attempted to right the wrong. In the end, the girls quickly forgave him. They knew, in his heart of hearts, their dad had behaved honourably in wanting to tell them this momentous news himself. Debbie said later, 'All he wanted was to spare our feelings.'

The newlyweds didn't let the trauma spoil their honeymoon, which they spent in sunny Barbados. Anthea recalled how Bruce had always boasted that he was a fantastic surfer. On their first day away, he took to the crashing waves in a tiny inflatable Li-lo they had been given on the plane on the way over. For a second, Anthea was panic-stricken, thinking, 'Oh my god, what has happened to him?' Then she heard a voice further up the beach saying, 'Darling, darling.' He was lying flat out in the sand, hair everywhere, sand in his nose and his ears, washed-up and completely bedraggled. He clearly wasn't the expert surfer he had claimed to be.

Bruce and Anthea settled down to married life, quickly moving out of Bruce's bachelor pad to a new home in Ascot while they waited for his divorce with Penny to be finalised. They were blissfully happy with only one little complication: their little Yorkshire terrier Bothwell! Bruce went off on a club tour of Britain, taking Anthea and Bothy with him. But the mutt didn't adapt to life on the road and was soon off his food. Animal lover Anthea became upset and the stress and aggravation soon got to Bruce too.

Bruce sent Anthea and Bothwell to her mother's. 'It's Bothwell or Brucie! Him or Me!' he joked to Anthea. Thankfully, Bothwell settled down and became a wonderful addition to the family, accompanying Bruce on his regular rounds of golf, always sitting quietly on the side of the green as his master putted, and never once picking up a ball. But in the house, his first love was Anthea – he would always walk away from Bruce with a disdainful look when she was in the room.

They moved to a wonderful new home on a fortified private estate overlooking Wentworth golf course in Surrey. It cost £75,000 at the time and they spent a further £150,000 on extensive renovations. With help from her new hubby, Anthea lost no time in creating the perfect home, with six spacious bedrooms including a master bedroom with separate his-and-hers dressing rooms. Off the sitting room there was a bar, wood-panelled library and indoor swimming pool. Bruce lived there for the rest of his life and it is worth at least £6 million. It has been completely remodelled by his third wife Wilnelia but it remains a palace. You reach it through a grand tree-lined avenue and it is set behind big electric gates adorned with a gold leaf 'F'. Yes, Bruce could be flash when he wanted to be. The faux-Georgian pile has grandiose pillars on each side of the shiny front doors, expansive landscaped grounds and a sunken tennis court.

Even with this gorgeous house to show off, Bruce and Anthea didn't entertain much. They were happier in each other's company. When they did, it was mostly by hosting a dinner party with celebrity neighbours such as Jimmy Tarbuck, Kenny Lynch and Val Doonican.

So everything seemed perfect for Bruce and Anthea. Bruce already had three lovely grown-up children from his first marriage. But there was one thing Anthea craved more than any other – a family of her own. Bruce was happy to go along with this. 'It would have been perfectly understandable for me to have insisted that there be no children in our marriage. To have told Anthea, "No, Darling, I would rather not have a family." But as a Pisces, I always see the other person's point of view. I knew Anthea desperately wanted a child. If a woman demands a child, why deprive her of her right?' he said.

It was that quest for a child — and the lonely life of motherhood Anthea was about to endure — that would ultimately kill their marriage. But before we deal with that, we should look at what made *The Generation Game* such a phenomenal success.

CHAPTER 9

DIDN'T HE DO WELL?

Bruce's career hit a rocky patch towards the end of the 1960s. He had always been busy but he hadn't properly been able to capitalise on his success with *Sunday Night at the London Palladium*. What he needed was another big hit. It was to arrive from an unlikely place... across the sea in the Netherlands. *The Generation Game* would prove to be the biggest success of Bruce's long career – propelling him into the mega-league of fame and spawning many of his most memorable catchphrases, including the most famous one of them all: 'Nice to see you, to see you nice.' It was also to have huge repercussions on his private life.

Things didn't get any better as the new decade dawned. Bruce said he was hit by 'a bit of a low'. He had split from his first wife Penny – though there was the odd fiery reconciliation, almost always short lived – and he was living the life of a bachelor in a flat that had seen better days in Kensington, west London. His career – which had meant everything to Bruce – just wasn't firing. From being the hottest star on TV in the early part of the decade, he was scratching along making only the odd appearance on ITV. He kept busy by taking cabaret bookings across the country – basically a slightly shortened version of his one-man show featuring singing, dancing and Bruce on the piano. Mostly this was well received but he recalled with a shudder one disastrous night in Manchester where he had virtually been booed off. 'I just wish I was dead!' Bruce said afterwards. A bit over the top, yes, but a clear sign that a man never normally short of confidence badly needed a break.

It came in the spring of 1971 when his agent Billy Marsh arranged for Bruce to see Bill Cotton, head of light entertainment at the BBC and one of the most powerful men in television. Bruce pitched an idea at the meeting – a talk show but with an entertainment element where the guests would also sing or do comedy. That was never going to be a runner because Cotton was just about to start Michael Parkinson's eponymous talk show the same year. It would become a huge hit and run throughout the 1970s.

Cotton had another plan. 'There's a videotape I'd like you to see,' he told Bruce. The tape showed a Dutch television show called *Een Van de Acht*, or *One Out of Eight*. The game had eight competitors – 'Let's meet the eight who are going to generate' – split into four teams of two. Each team came from the same family but were a generation apart – most often a father and daughter or a mother and son. In the first two rounds, two couples would compete against each other and the couple with the lowest score would be eliminated. The games involved professional people performing a skill – pottery, painting or dancing – that the contestants then had to imitate. Of course, they always got things wrong and with hilarious results. It was all overseen by a charismatic host who knew how to run a game and keep it light and funny. As Cotton well knew from watching 'Beat the Clock' in the 1960s, there was no one better at that than Bruce. The two highest-scoring couples made it through to the final, which would often be a big set-piece number such as a drama or a farce where they would dress up in costumes. The couple with the highest mark then competed in a quiz to determine the outright winner who made it through to the famous conveyor-belt round. The winner watched prizes pass on a conveyor belt and then won as many as could be recalled during a set time.

The Dutch show had been a huge hit but ran for a tortuous two hours. There was no way audiences in Britain would stick through it for that long. Cotton wanted to do the whole thing in 45 minutes and throw in a guest singing appearance from a star at the end. An experienced TV pro like Bruce knew immediately this would be impossible but he said it could work if it was stretched to 55 minutes. So that's what they agreed. All they needed now was a name. Cotton had that too: *The Generation Game*. Perfect.

Bruce was teamed with a brilliant young producer called Jim Moir, who later went on to become a highly successful controller of Radio 2. They made a pilot show but everyone on the show agreed that it was a bit lacklustre – it was too slow and lacked the slickness you get when a show beds in and everyone knows what they are doing. Still, the pilot had captured the flavour of the Dutch show and wasn't all bad.

Bruce went away to do a summer season and wrote an opening song for the show with the famous line, 'Life is the name of the game – and I wanna play a game with you.' In the early autumn, the team reassembled to film the first proper show but it was a disaster – even worse than the pilot. This prompted a crisis meeting at the Beeb involving all the major players, including the head of BBC One, Paul Fox. Time was fast running out and, with just two days to go, they decided to kick off the series with the pilot, which was put through a hasty re-edit. *The Generation Game* was launched on 2 October 1971 with everyone at the BBC clueless as to whether viewers would take to it. Seven million people watched the first show – a perfectly respectable audience. And then, as it bedded in – with the clunking errors from the pilot not repeated and the whole operation faster and well oiled – the audience grew and grew. Within two months, 14 million were watching and Bruce had another monster hit on his hands.

The show worked because Bruce handled both the contestants and the audience so brilliantly. He knew he was balancing on a tightrope every week. The contestants, let's not forget, basically had to make fools of themselves in the tasks, which were impossible to master in such a short space of time. It therefore required a real deftness of touch from the host to ensure that this was all played for laughs and that no one was humiliated. In the wrong hands, it could have ended up a disaster. How did Brucie always manage to get the balance just right? It was a question that often bothered his friends. The comedian Alfred Marks once told Bruce, 'I could never get away with treating people the way you treat them. I'd finish up with a black eye. But they just take it from you – let you get away with it.' As Bruce explained, 'That's because I play it for laughs and always show that I'm the one who is really suffering – they are ruining my show.' It is this subtle understanding of the nature of human interaction – and of comedy too – that has been the cornerstone of so much of Bruce's success.

Bruce was such a natural that he wouldn't even meet the contestants on *The Generation Game* until the show was recorded. It was felt that way the whole thing would seem lighter and more spontaneous. The contestants had all been very carefully selected by the production crew and lots of research had been done into their past. Primed with this information, Bruce would then effortlessly crack affectionate jokes about their lives as he introduced them to the audience.

The show improved every week but the producers soon ran out of games. In the end, the whole crew was charged with the task of thinking up new ones. They became so successful at this that they ended up sending games to the Dutch show from which they had bought the originals.

A trademark of the show was that a cuddly toy was always among the prizes on the conveyor belt. This led to an affectionate joke: 'Dinner service… fondue set… cuddly toy! Cuddly toy!' often quoted whenever *The Generation Game* is mentioned. This final round often came in for criticism because the audience – and Brucie himself if the contestant was struggling – was always shouting out the names of the prizes, allowing most contestants to win easily.

In that brilliant first series, most of Bruce's famous

catchphrases were born. Bruce was asked by Jim Moir to come up with a line after a contestant had finished the conveyor belt round. 'What about, "Didn't he do well?"' he suggested. It worked perfectly and still gets used today.

Of course, nothing topped his most famous 'Nice to see you' catchphrase. This actually pre-dated *The Generation Game* and came from a TV ad Bruce had made for the *TV Times* in the 1960s. Bruce didn't actually say the phrase at all. In the ad, he is approached by a stranger in a pub who says to him, 'It is you, isn' it? Nice to see you, to see you nice.' After that, people started shouting it to Bruce in the street. But with him largely off our TV screens at the end of the 1960s, it would be incorrect to say it had caught on widely. Once he used it in *The Generation Game* – inviting the audience to say the final 'Nice' – it caught on immediately. It remains his most popular catchphrase to this day. Other simpler catchphrases also stuck, such as, 'Good game, good game.'

Some memorable features of the show came out of nothing. Moir wanted the whole thing to start with Bruce in silhouette at the back of the stage. Bruce felt it would be boring if he just stood there 'like an idiot', so instead he created his famous 'strong man' pose. It was a bit like the famous Rodin statue *The Thinker* – except that Bruce was standing up. This also became a weekly staple of the show.

Moir explained at the time that the show worked so well because of Bruce's charisma. 'Bruce is a genius because of his spontaneous humour and, of course, his professionalism,' he said. 'Our programme is done without a script. But things rarely go wrong – we're there to see they don't. However, if something does come unstuck, Bruce is literally in charge. And all goes well in the end. I remember in the Christmas programme, a woman competitor playing Cinderella came on jerking about like a puppet on a string. That could have spoiled everything. But Bruce just jumped about in time with her. Then he leaped on a table and danced on it. He turned the whole incident into something hilarious.'

Part of the show's appeal was, of course, Bruce's lovely assistant Anthea Redfern – 'the hostess with the mostest'. We saw how she was chosen for the show and subsequently fell in love with its star in the previous chapter.

Bosses on *The Generation Game* feared there would be a backlash from viewers when news of Bruce and Anthea's affair became public, even though he had long been separated from Penny Calvert. There were plenty of negative headlines. But they did nothing to dent the show's popularity and, by 1976, when it notched up its 100th edition, its audience had soared to 20 million. The *Sun* dubbed Bruce 'The Most Important Man in British Television' and he easily topped their readers' poll to find the year's Top Television Personality, beating *Starsky & Hutch* stars Paul Michael Glaser and David Soul, who came second and third. Bruce was so thrilled that he had postponed a holiday in Portugal to pick up the award. Bruce said at the time, 'This last year, things have been fantastic, incredible, two hundred per cent. Sometimes, you say to yourself, "How can things be this good?" You don't trust it. I don't think about whether it could go higher still. I daren't even think about that.'

It is worth remembering that there were only three channels on British TV at the time. Bruce was the undisputed king of all three. In Britain, at least, he was a superstar – far bigger than any television star today. Marcus Plantin, who went on to run ITV and hire Bruce to host *Play Your Cards Right*, was at the time a lowly assistant working on *The Generation Game*. His job was to wrap up the prizes for the conveyor belt. Looking back on those days, he said, 'He [Bruce] used to park his Rolls-Royce (it had the registration plate BFE standing for 'Bruce Forsyth Entertainer') outside the studio. And always on double yellow lines. He knew he could pay the fines.'

The Generation Game was recorded in a 13-week run between September and Christmas. It left Bruce with plenty of time to carry on doing club dates, which he needed to pay for the divorce from Penny. Also, no one, in those days at least, got rich working for the BBC, which paid a lot less than its commercial rivals.

With the show such a soaraway success, Bruce started to become restless. He loved *The Generation Game* but was he really going to spend the rest of his career as a game-show host? He was a showman who always felt happiest when he was singing and dancing. Let us never forget, his ambition had always been to be the British Fred Astaire. He was never going to achieve that larking about playing silly games on TV.

This meant he could often be prickly in his dealings with his bosses at the Beeb. One of his big bugbears was how early – at 5.45pm – the show was screened. This was far too early for Bruce, who wanted to be on at primetime – 7 or 8pm – where he was sure of getting an even bigger audience. The BBC at that time boasted a stellar Saturday-night schedule. It kicked off with *Doctor Who* just after the football results. Then there was *The Generation Game* – followed by *The Duchess of Duke Street* (a classy and hugely popular period drama), *Morecambe*

& Wise (probably the only two stars at the time who could claim with some justification to be bigger than Bruce), *Parkinson* and *Match of the Day*. Bill Cotton explained to Bruce just why he was on so early. 'You're The Hook, Bruce – the most important element of the lot. You bring in all the viewers and they stick with us throughout the night. Never underestimate the power of The Hook.' These were the days before TV remote controls so, once viewers had decided on a channel for the night, they tended to stick with it because a change would mean getting up off the sofa to switch over. Once it was all explained, Bruce got Cotton's point immediately and he never complained about the show's timing again.

Bruce summed up the show's appeal in one snappy sentence: 'Everyone likes to see ordinary people having a go.' Of course, he was right. The wider TV industry woke up to the phenomenon of 'the people show' (an early forerunner of the reality shows which dominate TV today) and a string of copycat shows was spawned. The result was that Bruce's beloved variety – much more expensive to stage than a simple game show where the contestants were paid nothing except expenses – largely disappeared from our screens. Bruce had ended up killing the form of entertainment he loved best.

Bruce worked on other TV series during these years. In 1976, he was lucky enough to be one of the few British stars asked to appear on Jim Henson's brilliant creation *The Muppet Show*, which was filmed in the US. Bruce wasn't well known in the States at the time but the production team had seen him on TV in Britain and felt he would interact well with the puppets. Bruce later described it as 'one of the most rewarding and enjoyable things I ever did'.

Bruce said the joy of working on the show was the fact that the Muppets were so like real people that you stopped thinking of them as puppets. He kicked off by enjoying some banter with the show's host Kermit the Frog before doing a jokey routine with Fozzie Bear. The highlight was the finale – an intimate duet of the Nat King Cole classic 'Let There Be Love' at the piano with Miss Piggy perched beside him.

After an unforgettable day's filming, Bruce went to the workshop where all the Muppets were by now hanging on their pegs. He found it strange seeing all those lovely faces hanging from hooks when, moments earlier, they had been so full of life. He said that, when he left the room, he actually felt sorry for them!

By 1977, Bruce had had enough of *The Generation Game*. There were only so many games he could play with contestants and, while the show was as popular as ever – for the first time, it was consistently topping 20 million every week – its star feared the whole thing would go stale. It was time to get out while the audience still wanted more. 'This is so much better than hanging around for a gradual fade and then going down with a sinking ship,' Bruce explained. Bruce told his bosses at the BBC that he was off and went back on the road, starring in a musical, *The Travelling Musical Show*.

While his new theatre show was a critical hit, it never really connected with audiences and it was cancelled just four months into its West End run. Inevitably, some critics sniped that Bruce had got too big for his boots and should have never left the BBC. *The Generation Game* ratings juggernaut, meanwhile, carried trundling on with a new host in Larry

Grayson and a new hostess in Isla St Clair. It actually achieved its record audience – an astonishing 25 million – in 1979, with Grayson hosting, although it did benefit from a strike that blacked out the ITV network.

In 1981, the rights to *The Generation Game* were sold to the American TV network ABC and Bruce was asked to host a pilot for the show that had been renamed *A Piece Of Cake*. The Americans disastrously wanted to cram the whole thing into just 30 minutes – sandwiched between lengthy commercial breaks. It didn't play to Bruce's strengths – the zany interaction with contestants and audience – and so it was no surprise when the decision was made not to commission a full series.

Bruce, who was now 62, returned to *The Generation Game* with the BBC in September 1990. The press greeted the news ecstatically with the headlines REGENERATION GAME FOR BRUCE and A GENERATION ON, AND STILL IN THE GAME. It was the first time he had worked for the BBC since leaving the show 13 years earlier. By then, relations with his new bosses at ITV's London Weekend Television had become strained and the offer from the Beeb could not have been better timed. Bruce said, 'It's nice to be back at the BBC. I spent ten years at LWT. You know what it stands for? Limp Wristed Television. Mind you, they bent over backwards for me.' In these politically correct times, Bruce would be crucified for such an obvious homophobic gag but, at the time, critics were more concerned with his brazen attack on his old bosses.

Bruce had agonised over whether it was the right move for him. Did he really want to do another game show? He finally made up his mind after watching some tapes from its mid-

1970s heyday. If he could create just half that magic, he would have another hit on his hands. Another key factor in him choosing to return was that his old producer Jim Moir was back pulling the strings.

The new show was much faster paced than the old version and Bruce was much ruder to the audience. It had a new hostess too – singer and actress Rosemarie Ford was plucked from her role as the lead dancer in Andrew Lloyd Webber's musical, *Cats*. Inevitably, there was a new catchphrase too. When Bruce checked how the contestants were doing by looking at the famous scoreboard, he would say, 'What's on the board, Miss Ford?' And Bruce managed to bring in another glamorous female star – his third wife Wilnelia, or Winnie. She was introduced to help on some of the games involving Latin American dancing, which she excelled at. In fact, Wilnelia was so good that many people on the show assumed she was a professional dancer.

The show – scheduled at first on Friday nights – was another big hit. Its ratings started at 9 million and soared up to 12 million. It was 8 million down on the peaks of the 1970s but all TV audiences had fallen sharply since then because there were more channels to watch. BBC bosses were so impressed that they promoted it in the schedules to Saturday nights where it ran for another five years.

Bruce decided to walk away from the show again in 1995 because he was fed up working at the Beeb. He felt that he was being taken for granted and was seen as a bit old and unfashionable. He hated the fact that younger, hotter names had overtaken him in the pecking order. As ever, Bruce didn't keep this to himself. He lashed out in a very public way. This was to a be recurring theme throughout Bruce's later career – he would switch network, there would be a honeymoon period where he swooned over his new bosses and slagged off his old ones, before relations would deteriorate and there would be another switch, followed by further recriminations.

'I am very happy to have left the BBC,' he stormed shortly after his departure. 'They don't really cater for family audiences any more. It is very obvious they have their particular favourites and perhaps I'm not one of them. I have nothing in common with them and I'm glad they have nothing in common with me. Although I have run out of ambitions these days, one of them was definitely to get out of the BBC.' As we all know, he would return to the BBC in spectacular fashion years later with *Strictly Coming Dancing*.

Bruce's anger also came from what he acknowledged was a dark side to his personality. 'I am, by nature, not always happy,' he explained. 'I suffer intense bouts of depression. I am incredibly restless. The catchphrase, "I'm in charge", though it arose purely by accident, actually reflects another side of my personality – the irritable, domineering side that viewers don't often see. The thing that irritates me above all is incompetence. And it is the thing I tried to guard against most of all. If I can be nothing else, I can, at least, be efficient.'

It was this anger, which Bruce often had difficulty suppressing, that lead to repeated bust-ups later on in his career. The remarkable thing was how he was so easily able to switch between ITV and the BBC when he had been so critical of both. It would impossible to achieve this in most other businesses but show business is unique. There's a high turnover of bosses so, by the time Bruce was ready for his next move, the boss he had previously lambasted had often moved on. And TV executives are not, on the whole, the types to bear grudges when they sense a star can deliver them ratings.

Part of Bruce's estrangement from the BBC was simply old age and fatigue. He had been around the block many times and was not as respectful of authority as younger up-and-coming stars. Bruce felt that, at his age, he had earned the right to tell it like it is. Doing *The Generation Game* a second time had turned out to be one of the most gruelling jobs of his long career. It had left him completely washed up. He found that every time he was due to start a new series he would be struck down with the flu – an illness which terrified Bruce because it always went to his chest and could easily have lead to pneumonia. He began to feel that he was risking his health every year in persevering with the show. 'Why am I killing myself doing this?' he kept asking himself. Bruce was also co-producing the show and that meant lots more work because he was a perfectionist who wanted every single part to be right. He was so tired after each recording that he was dead on his feet and unable to go out for the rest of the weekend. This was no way to live his life – particularly when he had a beautiful young wife, Wilnelia, and a demanding toddler son, JJ, by this time, who were both craving his attention. In all, Bruce had done 12 years of *The Generation Game* – 7 series in the 1970s and another 5 in the revival. This was more than enough for anyone.

When Bruce told his bosses at the Beeb that he was going, they were worried that he would announce the show was being axed for ever at the end of the last show. Of course, a professional like Bruce would never have done that. And *The*

Generation Game did carry on for another eight years with the comedian Jim Davidson hosting.

Bruce, meanwhile, had somehow patched things up with his old bosses at LWT, who had chosen to forget his 'limp wristed' jibes. Soon he would be hosting two big shows on ITV.

But first, we must look at the end of his marriage to Anthea.

CHAPTER 10

THE COUPLE EVERYONE HATED

On the surface, they seemed like the happiest couple in Britain. They were starring together in the biggest TV hit of the time, *The Generation Game,* and viewers loved their sizzling on-screen chemistry. But by 1975 – two years after their Christmas Eve wedding – things were beginning to go badly wrong for Bruce and Anthea. All sorts of problems were bubbling beneath the surface. They went through a nightmare trying to conceive their first child. Then Bruce made the disastrous decision to quit *The Generation Game* at the peak of his fame to launch a big new show on ITV, *Bruce Forsyth's Big Night Out*, which flopped horribly. Anthea also appeared on *Big Night*, just as she had done on *The Generation Game.* Viewers turned on not only Bruce but on the Forsyths as a couple. As Anthea said sadly, 'We seemed to have gone from Golden Couple to the couple everybody hated.'

The omens weren't good when Bruce and Anthea married. Beautiful young television hostess weds workaholic middle-aged entertainer with a grown-up family. Both with broken marriages behind them, it wasn't hard to see that the chances were it might go wrong. And that's exactly what happened.

Anthea had always been rather misconceived by fans. They saw her as a leggy blonde who revelled in the glamorous world of show business – exotic parties, Michelin-starred restaurants, globe trotting with superstars. In reality, Anthea didn't fit this image at all. All she really craved was a settled home life with a couple of children. And, in truth, she didn't want her husband away all the time – she wanted him by her side.

The first signs of trouble came as Anthea began to tire of her role as the supportive wife while Bruce tirelessly pursued his career. This didn't just involve weekly appearances on *The Generation Game* – it was a 52-weeks-a-year grind, with theatre tours, personal appearances and an adoring public making never-ending demands on their favourite star.

Before they were married, Anthea was always uncomplainingly by his side, travelling with him and watching patiently while he performed for up to three hours on stage. There was nothing really for her to do but sit around and wait. This might be fine when you are in the first flushes of love but it starts to wear thin when you've been together a few years and are trying for a baby. 'A leopard cannot change its spots overnight,' Bruce later said. 'At times I desperately needed her by my side, just as she yearned for someone to be with her when I was away. I can understand how she felt. Hanging around while your partner does a night's work is not my idea of fun either.'

Anthea began to turn down Bruce's offers to go away with him and some of the romance began to ebb away from the marriage. There were no big rows. Anthea had always been very insistent that they should never go to bed on a row. If an issue needed resolving, they would talk it through. But you simply cannot talk through a lack of spark between two adults; it is either there or it is not. And the flame that had burned so brightly for their first four years together was starting to go out.

The couple had always prided themselves on giving 100 per cent commitment to the marriage. But they both began giving less and less and found themselves drifting apart.

Neither was interested in anyone else – there were no affairs, not even any misunderstandings over harmless flirtations. If there was a third party in the marriage it was the one thing that Bruce was addicted to and would never go away: show business. He had known nothing but the smell of greasepaint since he was 14. It wasn't Bruce that Anthea came to resent but show business, or 'It' as she preferred to call his profession. Celebrity was a mistress endlessly beguiling to Bruce. Anthea was simply unable to compete.

The other mistress in the marriage was, of course, golf. Bruce loved the game so much that he bought a house overlooking the first tee-off of the West Course on his favourite golf course, Wentworth. Bruce could walk out of his garden gate straight on to the fairway – something he had always dreamed of. But while that obviously cut down on travelling time to the course, he would still be out for 4 hours playing 18 holes with pals. Then there would be another 2 hours catching up at the 19th hole, which Anthea felt excluded from because it was all middle-aged men. Even if the course was just at the end of the garden, a round of golf would take Bruce away from home for the best part of a day. Bruce insisted he only played twice a week. Anthea recalled that he was more dedicated, playing up to four times a week. Either way, it brought added tension in a marriage that was already fast heading for trouble. Anthea tried to take up the game but her legs were like 'great stilts' and she didn't have the right balance to develop a decent swing. She preferred faster sports like tennis and squash.

Anthea's reasons for going cold on the marriage were perhaps more complicated than Bruce's and they revolved around her initial inability to have a child. 'I think things started to go wrong between us when I lost my first baby. That was the first crunch in our marriage,' she said.

All miscarriages are heartbreaking but this one was particularly traumatic. Anthea did not lose the baby immediately; the agony dragged on for months, leaving deep mental scars that Bruce was slow to recognise. Anthea was bed-ridden a lot of time with agonising back pain.

She needed her husband by her side but he was, as ever, busy working in Manchester. Her condition deteriorated and she began to haemorrhage daily. She needed two nurses, one during the day and one during the night, to be on hand to help her twenty-four hours a day. Sadly, nothing could be done to save the baby. She was on stage at a charity event when she felt shooting pains. She thought immediately, 'This is it.'

At first, Anthea refused to accept that her baby was gone. She would not call a doctor. But then her condition deteriorated again and the doctor came and told her the baby was dead and had been for three weeks. In the end, surgeons had to carry out an emergency abortion. By this time, delirious with grief, Anthea was losing her mind. She was convinced that the medics were lying to her and that the baby was still alive. She rang Bruce, raging, 'They're all liars, darling. They're trying to make me believe my baby is dead and it isn't so.' The operation eventually went ahead but Anthea was never truly the same.

Clearly Anthea was unable to work throughout this time. At the same time, she understandably wanted to keep news of her trauma private. She ended up taking eight weeks off from *The Generation Game*. Producers simply said that she was suffering from a 'cold'. Some cold! As Bruce said, 'That was the nice "official" way of putting it.'

Bruce later described those dark days in 1975 as 'a terrible ordeal for Anthea'. Note the 'for Anthea' – it apparently wasn't an ordeal for him. It perhaps is one of the reasons he was nominated for Male Chauvinist of the Year at the same time. Bruce tried to understand his wife's feelings but it was a struggle. 'What happens when a woman loses a baby I just cannot begin to understand,' he later admitted. 'It is not just a physical experience, it's a mental one. God is a little cruel at times, not allowing us that little extra bit of understanding of each other's feelings and emotions. No matter how tender or understanding you are, it cannot compensate for what has gone wrong. I wonder if a woman does ever really get over losing a baby?'

It took years for Anthea to recover. She went through a long period of depression. To make matters worse, there were further miscarriages – thankfully not as physically agonising as the first.

Bruce expected Anthea to again join him on the road once she was better. But she now saw his entertainment-business life with a chilling new perspective. 'I went back to travelling with Bruce to all the grotty hotel rooms in awful places and I was very low,' she explained. Anthea later realised that perhaps she had been too demanding of her husband. 'I should have accepted and understood deep in myself how much his work meant to him and how much it would take him away from me. I didn't realise, I really didn't realise.'

Fearful that she would never be able to conceive naturally, Anthea persuaded Bruce that they must adopt a child. In those days the restrictions on couples adopting weren't nearly as prohibitive as they are now. Two divorcees with a 23-year age gap would never get a child today but the Forsyths breezed through the application process. And in the spring of 1977, they were presented with a beautiful adoptive daughter, Charlotte.

Anthea was stunned by the negative reaction in the press. 'Why do people attack Bruce and me for having an adopted daughter?' she lamented. 'I know they feel that a show-business marriage isn't a suitable background for a baby. This has hurt me deeply.'

The couple had been told about Charlotte on Christmas Eve, 1976, their third wedding anniversary. They both saw her for the first time on Boxing Day. 'I immediately loved her,' Anthea said. They weren't able to take her home straight away but Anthea still visited Charlotte daily, changing her nappy and behaving just as she would as a full-time mum. 'At the time I really felt that I wasn't going to be able to have a child, so I yearned for one,' she said, remembering it as the happiest time of her life.

Weeks after Bruce and Anthea had first seen Charlotte at Christmas, Anthea fell pregnant again. Bruce felt that his wife, fulfilled at last by motherhood, finally relaxed and this made it easier for nature to run its course. The happy couple announced the pregnancy on the same day that Charlotte came home with them. The *Sun* marked the double event with the headline: DIDN'T HE DO WELL, DO WELL, adapting one of Bruce's favourite catchphrases.

But nothing seemed to run smoothly for poor Anthea at this time. It was another very difficult pregnancy. Almost as soon as she became pregnant her body tried to miscarry the baby. It meant that making love to Bruce was out of the question for the duration of the pregnancy. Anthea eventually went into labour a month early. There was still a danger that she would miscarry even at this late stage but, thankfully, baby Louisa was fine. Bruce had rushed to the hospital and stayed with Anthea throughout the whole birth.

It meant that by November of that year the couple had two highly demanding babies on their hands. 'It all seemed so wonderful,' Anthea explained. 'Bruce was as thrilled as I. But it did change our way of life.' It was a case of too much, too soon for Bruce. 'It would certainly have been easier had there been a year or two in between,' he later said. 'Very few women, the mothers of multiple births apart, experience motherhood twice in such a short space of time. The children brought us so much joy. But they put more pressure on the marriage. It meant less opportunity for Anthea to travel with me.'

There was a huge row six weeks after the birth. This was rare for the couple. Normally any disagreement would amount to little more than a freezing silence of 15 minutes, then they would patch up their differences. Bruce had been left exhausted – his punishing workload and two babies in the house were just too much for him. He badly wanted a holiday – without those two screaming tots! He insisted he and Anthea go away together on their own to Barbados. Anthea could not bear to tear herself away from the children. Bruce eventually insisted, 'I'm either going with you, or without you.'

Anthea went on the trip but admitted that she was 'crazy with unhappiness because I was missing the babies'. She had left an 'absolute entourage' at home, plus her mother, to care for them but that didn't stop her worrying. 'I could feel the growing problem between us,' she said.

On their return, Anthea admitted that she became far too possessive and antisocial. It was nothing to do with Bruce supposedly being a Casanova – he had lost his roving eye long ago, when his first marriage died – but more to do with Anthea withdrawing into the home. 'I didn't want to do anything or go anywhere,' she explained. 'Basically I had a home and babies and I wanted to sit there happily with my man.'

Anthea had always had this antisocial trait and motherhood simply exacerbated it. 'At the start I was so totally wrapped up in him that I wanted him to myself the whole time,' she said. 'I didn't want to go out and meet his friends. Not because I didn't like them. I liked them but I didn't like them as much as Bruce. Complete madness, I know, but I didn't want to share him.'

Poor Bruce would end up saying, 'We must go to some things. We can't be hermits all the time.' Anthea would reply, 'Do we have to go? I don't want to.' Sometimes Bruce would go on his own and Anthea began to feel lonely.

The whole nature of their marriage was changing. Anthea began to realise not just how starkly they differed as people but how they both viewed their marriage differently. It was as though the love they had for each was different. For Anthea, this love was all encompassing, her whole life. For Bruce, his love for her was only part of his life.

With the couple rapidly going in opposite directions, quirky traits which Anthea had found rather endearing when they were first together now started to annoy her. Like Bruce's painstaking attention to detail. 'I was married to a perfectionist. Everything had to be perfect,' she said. When they first got together she was never allowed to wash his shirts in case she didn't do it right. He washed everything himself – by hand! His shirts had to be drip-dried on a special hanger with the top button and third button done up. When Bruce finally decided to show her how to do it, Anthea thought, 'My God, what am I getting involved in?'

Bruce was equally fastidious about his suits – the legacy of his years of struggle before hitting the Big Time when he could only afford one stage suit. 'I used to see some of the others nipping across the road to the pub, spilling beer all over their stage clothes and I used to think what a waste of a suit it was,' he explained. 'I made it a firm rule that I would never sit down once I had put my stage suit on before a show. I still keep to it. I never sit down in my show suit – it spoils the creases. My socks have to be hand washed too. I do that myself, more often than not. If you put socks into a machine and it's too hot all the elastic goes and you have to buy new ones.'

It's this fanatical attention to detail that kept Bruce at the top for so long. Great if you are a fan or his agent – not so much fun if you are the downtrodden wife constantly having to meet his exacting standards.

Bruce knew that he needed to loosen up a bit. And he made determined efforts to become a bit more laid back – which ran completely against his true nature. 'When people see me perform, they think I look like a person who can never relax,' he explained in an interview at the time. 'But if I sit down, I can turn off the Bruce Forsyth who is the vitamin pill on legs. I couldn't keep that up all the time. I can close my eyes and go off to another world.'

So maybe he was a little less uptight at home but he remained a fanatical workaholic, another legacy of his early years when he spent long weeks and sometimes months scratching around for work. 'I don't think about money that much,' he explained. 'I suppose it's easy to say that because I've got a few bob. But I haven't really taken a lot of time off. It's the old variety performer in me. I think, if you have more than two or three weeks off, you get that restless feeling that you are never going to work again.'

There is no doubt that Bruce could be a right handful at times – both at home and at work. It wasn't because he was nasty or unkind; it was because he was a perfectionist who hated getting anything wrong and was not afraid to speak his mind if the slightest thing went awry. Journalists were not allowed to see *The Generation Game* being recorded. A publicity agent for the show explained at the time, 'He can be

very, very difficult – one of those people who controls everything and everybody. On the programme day, no one is
allowed near him. If a journalist tries to speak to him, he will
blow his top and then everyone suffers from the fall-out.'

Bruce made no secret of the fact that he could be a tough
taskmaster. 'I hate incompetence,' he said. 'If I do one little
thing wrong in a show, I will be kicking myself afterwards
and will make sure I do it right next time. If I lose a laugh, I
will try to work out what went wrong and correct it.
Lackadaisical people make me angry. If I think someone is
not trying hard enough and is incompetent as well, I can't
bear it. I would rather not have that person around me. I
want him out of my sight.'

Of course, we are talking about Bruce the showman here,
not Bruce the man at home. He drew a clear distinction
between life on stage and time with his family. But even so, it
is clear that at times that fiery temper would explode at home
too – and Anthea would be walking on eggshells until he
calmed down.

Bruce was a man of clockwork routine. He would be up at
8am every day to do his morning exercises – a stint on the
rowing machine and then a short jog. Breakfast was always
the same – fruit and oatmeal. No white bread, no milk in his
tea. This all seems perfectly normal today but it was
considered downright bizarre in the mid-1970s. He had all
sorts of weird superstitions, such as never eating a green sweet
before a show. He loved Fruit Gums but, if he bought a
packet, he had to throw all the green sweets away.

The couple discovered that the things they had once enjoyed
doing together they no longer did. Bruce's idea of a perfect

evening was an early dinner and then a night at the theatre. He enjoyed a party and loved to take centre stage, cracking jokes and holding court with show-business friends such as Jimmy Tarbuck and Des O'Connor. Anthea felt uncomfortable in starry company. Gradually, friends picked up on this and they received fewer and fewer invitations to go out. When the invitations did come, Bruce would often go alone.

Bruce never really stopped loving Anthea, despite the difficulties in the marriage. And, if anything, his respect for her grew. He was always furious at the way she was mischaracterised in the press as a 'dumb blonde', a simple 'hostess with the mostest'.

In fact, she had a tremendous business brain. Bruce credited Anthea with saving his Broadway debut in New York in June 1978, after a big entertainment backer pulled out. Anthea tirelessly worked the phones to get the show back on the road. Eventually a new backer was found and the show went on.

If the strains of actually getting the production on stage were not enough, the 'Butchers of Broadway' – the fearsome New York critics – had their knives out for Britain's favourite entertainer. He had hoped to curry favour with the American audience by getting his old pal Sammy Davis Jr to introduce him. But even that added little bit of stardust was not enough to save Bruce's reputation. He was absolutely buried by some of the most influential critics. *The New York Times* said that Bruce had 'an enormous ego' and was 'casually vulgar, very brash and very broad'. The tabloid paper the *Daily News* was even more vicious, with the caustic headline: THE BRITON NOT FITTIN'. It added, 'Forsyth does everything except wear a lampshade. He'd be a riot at a neighbour's wedding but not on

A young Bruce Forsyth in the Fifties, by now he had already created his famous pose.

Above: The Royal Variety Performance at the London Palladium. Performing for the Queen, 1967.

Below: With his first wife, Penny Calvert, and children, from left, Deborah (aged 9), Laura (aged 1) and Julie (aged 6) celebrating Christmas in 1963.

Above: Alongside fellow British entertainment icon, Cilla Black, in 1969.

Below left: With Ronnie Corbett on *The Bruce Forsyth Show*.

Below right: Brucie with the finest hostesses in showbiz, 1972.

Above: *Sunday Night at the London Palladium* with the Tiller Girls.

Below: From 1973-1979, Bruce was married to Anthea Redfern, one of the hostesses on *The Generation Game*. During their marriage they had two children, Charlotte and Louisa.

Above: Performing alongside Julie Andrews (left) and Beryl Reid (right) in the film *Star!*

Below left: Bruce had a long stint hosting the popular quiz show *Play Your Cards Right*.

Below right: Showing no signs of retiring from showbiz, Brucie signed up to co-present *Strictly Come Dancing* with Tess Daly in 2004.

Above: Bruce and his third wife, Wilnelia Merced, were married for over thirty years and had one son together, Jonathan.

Below: The happy couple enjoying a day at the races.

Above left: Posing with a prestigious BAFTA in 2008.

Above right: At Buckingham Palace in 2011 with his children and wife, ready to receive his knighthood. From left, Charlotte, Bruce, Wilnelia, Jonathan and Laura.

Below: The highest, and most long-overdue, honour of them all: a knighthood from the Queen.

All images © Rex Features/Shutterstock

Broadway.' Another critic likened him to 'Uriah Heep on speed'. In fairness, at least half the reviewers were positive, with the *New York Post* concluding that Bruce 'amuses and charms'. But you would never know this from the coverage Bruce attracted in the British press. As far as his most acerbic critics were concerned, he had got too big for his boots in trying to make a success of his career away from his homeland. It's what Bruce called 'the British disease' – the constant need to bring down those who are trying to better themselves. He loved that the Americans viewed the world so differently. But sadly for him, his core audience was still back in Britain, along with a wife and two young children who were seeing so little of him.

More than 30 years after those write-ups, Bruce was still angry at the injustice of it all. In an interview in 2011, he told the *Mail on Sunday* that it had been a 'ridiculous response', before pointing out how many of the notices were the best he has ever had. 'The big mistake I made was only taking the theatre for a week and not giving it a chance to move on,' he explained.

Back in Blighty, Bruce's career continued to sail through choppy waters. Hideously overhyped, *Bruce Forsyth's Big Night*, which he made for London Weekend Television – his first big outing for ITV after quitting the Beeb – also came in for a barrage of criticism. It was suggested that Bruce didn't want Anthea on the show – that he resented the fact that people were coming to regard them as a double act. Certainly it was true that Bruce had a big ego. He would tell Anthea, 'I'm the star around here.' In fact, LWT insisted on Anthea being in the show right from the start and Bruce was happy to agree. Big headlines were made when it was said that the couple were eating separately at the studio canteen. The truth was rather more dull: on one occasion Anthea was seeing a friend and on another her dress designer.

Bruce could handle all the criticism. He had already been in show business for more than 30 years. It was water off a duck's back to him. As his friends said at the time, 'Brucie always bounces back.' Anthea, however, was far more brittle. For the first time, she was having to deal with vicious barracking, not just of the man she loved but of herself too. It was all too much for her and she retreated into her shell. 'The attacks went on and on and, of course, he brought his tension home and that made things worse,' she said.

By 1978, the couple knew their marriage was in crisis. Bruce accepted the lead role in *The Travelling Music Show*, a long, demanding theatre tour. It meant him working away from the family home for almost a year, appearing in a different theatre every night. Bruce explained, 'I would want to relax afterwards, take Anthea out for a meal, talk about the show, generally let off steam. Any performer will tell you that after two and a half hours on stage with an audience, your adrenalin is so high it takes you another two hours to bring yourself back down to earth. But only rarely did Anthea feel like joining me.'

Nine times out of ten he would drive home to Surrey after a performance but he did not often return until the early hours. Anthea, after a hard day looking after their children, would be asleep upstairs. And Bruce would creep up the stairs 'like a burglar', anxious not to wake her. It was no way for a couple to live and something had to give. To make matters worse, the show flopped and stopped running after four months.

The couple put on a brave face as they enjoyed their last Christmas together in 1978 – their fifth wedding anniversary. They bought each other lavish gifts – Anthea designed and had a special pendant made for Bruce. Anthea admitted that she was 'like an ostrich' – her head buried in the sand – hoping that the problems would just mysteriously disappear.

By this stage, rumours that the marriage was coming to an end dogged the couple. It was said that they drew up a list of 'rules' to help patch things up. One of them was to go out at least once a week. Anthea admitted she needed to change and become less antisocial. In March 1979, those rumours hit a peak and Anthea hit back with a firm denial, saying the reports of an imminent split were rubbish. 'Bruce and I are still in love,' she insisted. Two months later, she gave a further interview at home in Wentworth, saying, 'Bruce and I are like two teenagers in love. You can call me a lucky woman. From being a couple who can do no wrong, we can now do no right. This last year has been hell. I've lost weight and broke out in what the doctor's called a nervous rash as a result of the tension we've been through. Of course I would love to be with Bruce all the time. But it's not fair – or comfortable – to take kiddies of that age halfway round the world, in and out of planes and hotels.'

In the final year of their marriage, Bruce was travelling constantly – to America, New Zealand and the West Indies. He only saw Anthea for a few weeks in the entire year before the split. The final break came when he returned from New Zealand and had been asked to play in a charity golf match in Tobago in the Caribbean. He asked Anthea to come along with their two young daughters. Sadly, she didn't want to go.

And when he returned, they both knew the marriage was doomed. 'After a period away you know instinctively, just by looking into each other's eyes, whether you have really missed one another,' Bruce explained. 'I knew Anthea hadn't missed me as a husband. And I knew I hadn't missed her as a wife. Sadly, Anthea and I did not feel the vibrations any more. Our love had gone. It was very, very sad.'

It was actually Anthea rather than Bruce who finally called time on the marriage. She told her husband that there was no way back and that they needed to make an official announcement and put an end to the speculation. She was fed up with lying to the press. 'In the end, I think it was my decision. It was made because it had become clear to me that you only get one life. This is the main event,' she said. 'If you have found that there's an episode in your life that you're unhappy with, you must take a risk. Do something. Change it.'

The couple formally announced their separation in a terse two-line statement from their solicitors on 27 July 1979. It read, 'We have been instructed by our clients Mr and Mrs Bruce Forsyth to state that they have formally decided to separate upon the most amicable terms. No further statement will be made by either party, or on their behalf.' Just two days earlier, Anthea had again been denying anything was wrong.

Anthea stayed at Wentworth with the children while Bruce escaped the press furore by playing golf while staying at the Costa Brava villa of his pal, soccer pundit Jimmy Hill. Neither said anything. One person who was happy to talk about the news was, of course, Bruce's bitter ex-wife Penny. 'Nothing Bruce does ever surprises me,' she sniped. Asked if she would give the marriage another go, a fuming Penny stormed, 'Have him back? Jesus, Mary and Joseph, I would kill myself. Never again.'

Bruce and Anthea led largely separate lives but carried on living together at their home in Wentworth for almost a year after the split. It prompted inaccurate reports that they had patched things up and were not divorcing. In fact, Anthea had started a new romance with Lawrence Matz, a car dealer three years younger than herself. Matz told how he and Anthea had become close during the dying days of her marriage when she was stuck at home while Bruce worked in the States. 'Anthea was ripe for someone like me to come along,' he said. 'It was no secret that things were not too well between her and Bruce. She wanted some enjoyment. I did it by taking her to the races and out to dinner.'

Bruce and Anthea finally divorced in 1982, by which time Anthea had moved on from Matz and was now dating millionaire hotelier and property developer, Freddie Hoffman. The divorce was actually on the grounds of her adultery with Hoffman. But this was just agreed so that the whole thing could go through speedily and without fuss. Bruce, at the time, was already in a relationship with his soon-to-be third wife, the Puerto Rican beauty Wilnelia Merced.

Anthea explained, 'Bruce and I had always been perfectly honest with each other. I knew about Winnie but the rest of the world didn't. The press, however, knew about Freddie and, as one of us had to admit adultery, I thought it might as well be me. I hadn't committed adultery when I admitted it. That's the truth. But we needed to get divorced quickly and cleanly, and I wanted to protect the children, and Bruce and

Winnie.' Anthea got custody of the children but Bruce stayed in regular contact with the girls and they all lived near to each other.

'I didn't envisage that, when he and Winnie met, we [Bruce and I] would end up as such good friends,' Anthea said. 'There has never been a problem between us. Bruce has always been close to our daughters. He has been, and always will be, there for them. But he has also taught them that whatever they get in life, they have to deserve it. He has worked very hard, starting from nothing, so he has given them a good education. Both our girls went to university. If either of them fell flat on her face, Bruce would be the first one to help but now they pay all their own bills and don't expect a helping hand.'

Just two months after her divorce from Bruce, Anthea secretly married Hoffman at Maidenhead Register Office. Asked about the wedding, Bruce said simply, 'It doesn't matter to me.'

Anthea had a daughter, India, with Hoffman but again love was not to run smoothly for her and she divorced him after 16 years on the grounds of his unreasonable behaviour. 'He is a gentle, reserved man who was a wonderful stepfather,' she explained. 'Of course there was some animosity at the time but negative thoughts breed negative situations. You can't carry that hate within you.'

Anthea now spends a large amount of her time at her home in Marbella, Spain, with her new partner David Adams. They have never wed. She is very happy.

'I'd be a liar if I was to say I'd be happy living on my own,' she explained. 'I don't want to be this toughie who says, "I don't want a man in my life." David leaves me notes and sends me flowers for no particular reason. If he's in Marbella and

I'm in Britain, we phone each other ten times a day. But I don't want to marry again. I believe you should be married when you have children, which I was, but marriage is a passion killer. The fact David and I are not married is what keeps the excitement between us.'

Anthea has largely retired from show business. She was last seen on TV here on Channel 4's *Celebrity Come Dine with Me* in 2010. It was a crazy episode in which the comedian Michael Barrymore ran riot, licking dip off Anthea Turner's foot, stealing the other contestants' food and smashing their plates. Anthea Redfern did not come across as the same woman at all.

After the split with Anthea, Bruce once again threw himself into work. All alone in that huge house in Wentworth, he was not going to be single for long. And when he crossed paths with another Miss World winner, a new exciting chapter in his life was about to begin.

But first, let us deal with the one great love of Bruce's life from which he never wavered – golf.

CHAPTER 11

GOOD GAME, GOOD GAME

'An obsession, a religion, a way of life, a character-builder, a mental torture, a business lever, a business-breaker, a marriage-maker (if both play), a home-wrecker (if they don't), a relaxation (for only a few), a drug, a time-taker, a humbling experience, a humiliating experience, a walk into the sunset... or into oblivion!'

Has there ever been a better description of golf than the one above, as detailed by Bruce Forsyth in his autobiography, *Bruce*? It perfectly captures his lifelong love affair (one phrase he didn't use) with a game he adored so much he bought a house overlooking his favourite course, where he lived for 40 years. Everyone in the world who loves golf will understand the passion and also the exasperation that golf inspired in Bruce. When it goes well, it's the best game there is; when it's going badly, it is sheer hell.

Bruce reckoned that every golfer would recognise at least two of the descriptions he came up with – mostly the negative ones. They pretty much all applied to Bruce, with the possible exception of marriage-maker (none of his wives were particularly keen on the game, although his third wife Wilnelia tried hard to get interested and does have a handicap). It would certainly be fair to say that it was, in part, a home-wrecker for him. Anthea Redfern, Bruce's second wife, often moaned about his obsession with the game. She felt it dragged him away from the family home far too much when she longed for him to be around to help look after their young children.

It was with Anthea that Bruce bought a house overlooking the magnificent Wentworth golf course in Surrey. He simply needed to pop to the end of his garden and he was on the West Course, where all of the sport's greats have played. They moved there in 1975 and spent a fortune doing it up. When Bruce first saw the house, he thought it was 'an ugly monstrosity'. It looked like the back of a factory: red bricked, three huge garages and awful 1930s metal windows. But then he saw the view from the back of the house, straight on to those wonderful lush, green Wentworth fairways. Suddenly Bruce started talking about the positives to Anthea. 'We could change the horrible flat roof and we don't need all those garages – I think this house could work for us,' he told her, never forgetting the wonder of that view. It took 18 months to sort it out but finally Bruce had created his own little idyll. Anthea described the house as her husband's 'seventh heaven', adding with a trace of bitterness in her voice, 'He was living at long last on a golf course.' To Bruce, this wasn't any old golf course; this was Wentworth, one of the highest ranking in the world. He could still recall as a hard-up young showman in his twenties visiting the luxury-gated estate where his mansion now was and thinking, 'If only I could afford to live here one day.' Now that dream had become a reality.

When he fell in love with his third wife Wilnelia in 1980, Bruce feared he would have to move out of the house so that they could start afresh in a new home. But Wilnelia loved it too, so they stayed – and renovated it again, this time to Winnie's taste.

Bruce lived the perfect life for a golf fanatic. He spent late spring and summer at home in Wentworth – perfect weather for golf, which he played up to four times a week with a group of chums. Most of the winter months were spent with Winnie in Puerto Rico. Their luxury home was on another golf course in one of the most beautiful spots in the Caribbean. Situated on the northern shores of the island, it is secluded and has wonderful views of the championship fairways and greens. Bruce was there for four months every year and had a separate group of pals on the island who shared his love of the game. He reckoned you can play the 'best golf ever' in Puerto Rico.

Bruce was long closely associated with the game, which led to many positive spin-offs. For years, his was the first name on the guest list for the best pro-am celebrity golf competitions. It meant that Bruce played with just about all his golfing heroes. A few of them reckon that he might have had the talent to make it as a pro if he'd taken the game up earlier. Certainly it is incredibly rare to find a golfer who has had a single-figure handicap in his prime, as Bruce had, and who reached such a high standard without having had any prolonged professional tuition.

He first took up the game in the late 1940s. He was in a double act at the time with a drummer and dancer called Les Roy. For a while, they joined Jack Johnson's band – Bruce on piano and Les on drums. Jack, as well as being a very popular bandleader, was also a scratch golfer (a golfer whose handicap is zero) with a lovely natural swing. He loved recruiting fellow golfers to the band because it meant they could get a round in before their evening performances. Almost all of his musicians – with the exception of newcomers Bruce and Les – were accomplished players. The big truck that travelled around the country with all their instruments and props also had to find room for at least 24 golf bags. Bruce, at first, didn't feel the need to join them on the course. He had always thought of golf as an 'old man's game'.

One Christmas, Bruce was appearing with the band in Dundee for a fortnight. The landlord who had put up Bruce and Les at his digs hated them sitting about all day and told them, 'You are wasting the best years of your life – get outside and play a round of golf.' Bruce and Les didn't even get out of bed until 11.30am most mornings. Why on earth would they want to disrupt their morning routine with a freezing round of golf? Every day for the next two weeks the landlord was on at them. 'Get out there, boys,' he would drone on. Eventually, just to shut him up, they agreed to play a round with him the next day.

They were roused from their beds at 7am – it might just as well have been the middle of the night to Bruce and Les. And off they went to Carnoustie – one of the finest courses in Scotland and a regular venue for the British Open. The ground was so frosty that they had to play with red balls. The landlord set Bruce and Les a challenge: he would give them two shots at each hole and compete against whichever of them came up with the best score. The new pair didn't win a single hole. But it didn't matter. Bruce was hooked. He said later – without a hint of exaggeration – that the day out in Carnoustie 'changed his life'. He certainly no longer thought of golf as an old man's game. Lugging a big bag of clubs for four miles – roughly the length of most good golf courses – was exhausting.

Bruce admitted that golf quickly became 'one of my obsessions – my favourite pastime'. His mate Les was hooked too. They quickly joined up with all the other members of the band who played before the concerts. At first Bruce and Les had to tee off long before the others because they weren't as good and would take longer to complete a round. But as their games improved, some of the more patient band members let them tag along and gave them a few tips on how to improve their game. Bruce found that he learned best by analysing his own game and not repeating any obvious mistakes. He found formal lessons difficult to digest. It was an approach that worked for him – most of the time.

Bruce often played golf with celebrity pals. It was he who persuaded his old mate Jimmy Tarbuck to take up the game. The Scouse comedian succeeded Bruce as compere on *Sunday Night at the London Palladium*. They lived near each other in Surrey and were good mates for almost 50 years. Jimmy quickly developed into an excellent golfer and was soon beating Bruce. 'It's something I have never forgiven him for but we still manage a lot of laughs along the way,' Bruce joked.

The one thing we know about Bruce is that he was not one

to hide his feelings; if something was getting on his nerves, he was not afraid to let rip. So you can imagine what he was like playing a game as frustrating as golf. Even Bruce admitted that he could be a 'bit of a Victor Meldrew'. Like many golfers, he insists that he only moaned when he was genuinely unlucky, but his pals didn't see it that way.

Jimmy recalled playing with Bruce at Sotogrande in Spain. Having had a bellyful of Bruce's whingeing during the early games, Jimmy decided to lay down the law early. He told Bruce that under no circumstances was there to be the merest hint of a moan over the next 18 holes. When they got to the third hole, Bruce noticed a rake that had been stuck in the ground in an upright position when it should have been lying on the ground. Bruce told Jimmy that if he was to hit that rake – only an inch wide – he would be justified in having a moan. Bruce hit a perfect eight iron, which was heading straight for the hole when – you've guessed it – the ball smashed against the rake and landed in a nearby bunker. Bruce and Jimmy collapsed into laughter and yes, Victor Meldrew had a good moan.

Bruce reckoned he wasn't the only golfing masochist. He wrote in his autobiography, 'Can I suggest you stand on the 18th green of your home club and watch the faces of the golfers when it's all over? How many of them walk off the 18th green with a smile on their faces? But golf can be fun too. If you have the right four-ball and a sense of humour, the dialogue and ad-lib lines are often worthy of the finest comedy. I certainly find it great fun – sometimes!'

Bruce's favourite golf companion was his old comedian mate Kenny Lynch, who also lived near him in Surrey. 'I love him and hate him,' Bruce said, smiling. 'And he loves to hate me.' Bruce and Kenny loved golf so much they once played three rounds in a single day. Any golf fanatic will tell you that is bordering on the obsessive. This wasn't at any old course either: it was Gleneagles, another Open venue. They started after breakfast, had sandwiches for lunch, went out again, then stopped for a light snack early evening, finishing on the 18th hole of the Queen's Course. This was during the summer in Scotland when it often doesn't get dark until as late as 11pm. Even so, it was virtually pitch black by the time Bruce and Kenny got to the last hole.

Bruce was the only person to play in every series of the BBC Two's *Pro Celebrity Golf* series. One time he was paired with the comedian Peter Cook and the former world-champion racing driver James Hunt. Hunt had an Alsatian dog called Oscar who came with him to each hole, waiting patiently while his master went about his business, before they all took a break for lunch. Cook, known for his madcap humour, returned to the course with a pet of his own – a goldfish! Explaining that it was 'the only pet I've got', Cook proceeded to carry the goldfish in its bowl to all the remaining holes, carefully putting it down before each shot. 'He just loves to come along when I play,' Cook joked. Bruce described it as the most 'hilarious piece of comedy I had ever seen on a golf course'.

Bruce played celebrity golf with some of the biggest stars in the world, including Sir Sean Connery, Burt Lancaster and Bing Crosby. The American stars loved coming over to Scotland to play on the famous 'links' courses by the sea where the Open is often played. Bing was probably the only celebrity golfer more fanatical than Bruce (he actually died of a heart attack while on a golf course). Bing used to smoke a long pipe when he played. And the one time they competed together, Bing thrashed Bruce. Bruce mischievously wondered whether he was using that pipe to line up his shots.

Golf was the perfect escape for Bruce during times of stress. After his very public split from Anthea Redfern, for instance, he headed straight to Spain for a golfing holiday at the villa of his close pal, the football pundit Jimmy Hill. And whenever Bruce was single – not often – he would throw himself into the game.

In 1981, the first 'Bruce Forsyth Pro-Am Charity Classic' was held at Moor Park in Hertfordshire. The guest list was like a who's who of show business and sport, including Terry Wogan, Connery, Ian Botham, Nick Faldo and Greg Norman. Bruce was a very proud man that day and he raised a fortune for his favourite charities. He told the *TV Times* at the time, 'If I wasn't an entertainer, I'd have loved to be a professional golfer, provided I was good enough to be in the top 10 or 12 in the world. I wouldn't want to be anything in life unless it was at a world-class level.' He wasn't asking for much then!

Bruce played a lot of golf with Connery in the 1970s and 1980s. A hardy Scot, the former James Bond star insisted they carried on playing even when it was pelting with rain on one occasion. 'Sean, we're not making a war film!' Bruce told him. Another time, Bruce invited Sean to play with him at Moor Park and told a few of the members that the famous actor was joining him. Word quickly spread and by the time the ex-007 was due to arrive a sizeable crowd had built up. Imagine their disappointment when he turned up in the car park not in Bond's sexy Aston Martin DB5 but in his real car: a clapped out Mk 10 Jaguar. Sean told everyone, 'I've just been stopped by the police. The silly buggers didn't think my car was roadworthy. They made me late for the game.' Bruce looked at Sean's old banger and joked, 'Really, what on earth made them think that, Sean!'

Bruce celebrated his love of golf in a 1989 book, *Golf... is it Only a Game?* He affectionately recalled countless encounters on the course with celebrity pals and golf pros. He tried to convey a few useful tips – like the one the American golfer Jerry Pate gave him on how to blast through a bush, if it wasn't too thick.

He also featured a letter sent to him by two legends of the game, Lee Trevino and the late Seve Ballesteros. Bruce had been playing with them in a pro-am event. Trevino told him, 'You are hitting the ball as well as anyone.' Ballesteros readily agreed. 'Am I?' asked Bruce. 'Definitely,' said Trevino. 'Will you put that in writing?' said Bruce. And so they did. It was written on Gleneagles Hotel headed notepaper and said, 'We, the undersigned, being of sound mind and body, do hereby solemnly swear and declare that Mr Bruce Forsyth is, in our opinion, the most proficient celebrity at the game of golf that we have so far encountered during our stay at this pub.'

He was not sure what the bosses of one of the world's greatest golf courses felt about it being described as a 'pub'. Obviously it was a gag and the two golf legends' way of explaining that they were half-cut when they wrote the letter! Bruce, of course, treasured the letter. Even with its obvious irony about Bruce being the best. But Bruce really did think he was the best celebrity golfer, particularly given that Bing Crosby had died in 1977!

Seve, who sadly died from a brain tumour in May 2011, was always one of Bruce's favourite golfers and they often played together at charity events. Bruce's golf book featured a picture of Seve lying on the ground with a golf tee in his mouth and the caption: 'Always have confidence in your pro-am partner!'

'I wanted to put across what I love about the game and why I spend so much time doing it. It's difficult to think of a pro I have played with who hasn't been 100 per cent a gentleman. I find they all inspire me a bit. But they are different in pro-am games to what they are in tournaments. Seve laughs and jokes, he's the most wonderful guy. Of course, in an actual tournament he doesn't talk much. When he played Arnold Palmer they both had a completely different look in their eyes. They were men with a different attitude.'

Another former Ryder Cup player, Ian Woosnam, was a close pal of Bruce's. 'Everyone wonders how a guy as tiny as Ian hits the ball as far, if not further, than a lot of the long hitters,' said Bruce. 'One of the things said about him is he has strong forearms. That's why there is a picture in the book of me arm-wrestling with him. I reckon it can't be the forearms because I was dead level with him!'

Bruce said he loved golf because it was a game he could never master – meaning it was always a challenge. 'Nobody will ever find the secret. No matter how good you are, what your name is, nobody will ever go round a golf course in 62, 63, 62, 63. That is impossible. Even if golf is still being played in the 25th century, it will always be the elusive thing because of the mental side of the game.

'There's not another game that humbles you the way golf does. Look at what it does to Jack Nicklaus, a man who's achieved everything. It still stabs him in the back. All those achievements mean nothing when he's just hit a 78.

'I know how he feels. A bad round used to stay with me. I'm better now but I always say what an unlucky golfer I am. I have always liked the former American President Gerald Ford's way of describing golf's frustrations. He said, "I know I'm getting better at golf because I'm hitting fewer spectators."

People say that your bad luck on a golf course evens out at the end but Bruce reckoned that wasn't the case.

'I'm one of those people for whom it never evens out. If I have a day when I've had a few pieces of luck – do I suffer. For at least a month afterwards. I'll give you an example. I'm in Palm Springs and we're playing the water hole. It's a short hole, over the water, and you've got about a 140-yard carry before you get to the green. It's quite a tricky hole. All my three partners have played and I get all set up, address the ball, take the club back, I'm at the top of my swing... and a frogman comes out of the water. He shot out of the water like a bloody killer whale. Now my club has gone flying, my three friends are in hysterics and that's just typical of my luck. If I'm playing next to a garden, everybody else will take their shot and just as I go to play, someone will set off their mower. Or somebody will suddenly appear out of the trees. Or a dog will run up. It's staggering.'

Bruce worked a gag into his act about the four great characters in golf – the Show Off, the Slogger, the Short-Sighted Player and the Old Man of Golf. 'Golfers the world over have known and suffered these characters,' he explained.

'You find them on fairways and greens wherever you go. The Show Off is usually a good golfer who isn't happy until he knows everyone is watching him. He just loves to pose. The Slogger wants to beat the ball to death. He usually does but unfortunately has such a wild slice the ball ends up behind him. The Short-Sighted Golfer is the one who is never able to see where his ball ends up, even if it is just a few yards up the fairway. My favourite is the Old Man of Golf – the rickety old codger who takes an age to get round but always makes it in the end.' So was that Bruce? 'No, he is not modelled on me,' he said, laughing. 'I think I've got a while to go yet. But you see a lot of old fellas on courses everywhere. A lot of them are excellent golfers, just a bit on the slow side.'

The golf commentator, Peter Alliss, is one such old codger and also one of Bruce's closest pals and Bruce was touched when Peter and his wife Jackie asked him to be godfather to their eldest son, Simon. Often when he is commentating on events at Wentworth and a golfer slices his ball, Alliss will quip, 'That could have landed in Bruce's Forsyth's garden. Bruce is always out there with his field glasses and a bucket, hoping that will happen.'

After Anthea Redfern essentially accused Bruce of abandoning her for the golf course, Bruce was desperate for his third wife Wilnelia – or Winnie – to take up the game. She knew next to nothing about golf when they first met but was keen to learn and would often go to competitions to watch Bruce in action. One time, he was playing at an event in Spain when he lost his ball in the rough. Lots of people were looking for it, including Winnie who suddenly shouted, 'I've found it, I've found it.'

She ran to Bruce excitedly brandishing the ball over her head – and quickly earned him a two-shot penalty because the rules of golf make clear that you cannot move a ball while playing a hole, unless it is agreed in advance and the ball's position is marked.

Winnie said she had so many distractions in her life that she didn't have time to develop her game. 'I am so busy doing other things like painting and sculpture and tennis. I do not have the patience.' Bruce reckoned that Winnie has the most wonderful swing and a natural talent. Her game has improved over the years and she now plays off a handicap of 26 – perfectly respectable for a woman in her fifties.

Bruce could now enjoy the game with his son JJ, who has been golf-mad almost from birth. 'He has been swinging a little plastic club since he was thirteen months old,' explained his proud dad. 'He's got a great little swing.'

Bruce described himself as a 'pretty adequate 10 handicap player', although as he got older, like all players, he needed a few extras shots to get round.

He recalled how he had hit three holes in one. 'The first was the most tragic because I was on my own and whenever I tell anyone they laugh because they don't believe I did it. My second one was playing with Jack Jones and the wonderful Bob Newhart. And the last one was in a game on Christmas Eve. We were in Puerto Rico and I hit a lovely seven wood a hundred and eighty yards. It bounced on the green and rolled in.

'Am I a happy golfer? Jimmy Tarbuck says I grumble like an appendix. But we have fun. Once I was playing with Telly Savalas, who stuck his lollipop in his mouth before hitting a wicked slice. I said, "It's your fault, Telly – that's where the lollipop was pointing.'"

There's no doubt that all that time spent on the golf course – getting plenty of exercise – was one of the reasons for Bruce's remarkable longevity. The other reason was his strict fitness regime. He followed a regime called Fountain of Youth, originally created by Tibetan monks and recommended to him by Winnie's mother. It involves taking two royal jelly tablets before breakfast, and two garlic tablets and Efamol marine oil to cleanse the body of contaminants with every meal. 'I do the Tibetan workout every day,' he explained. 'It really wakes you up and makes you feel good.'

Bruce often used golf to escape the stresses of show business. He badly needed a stress reliever at the end of the 1970s when he took the controversial decision to quit *The Generation Game* at the peak of his fame, only to embark on the biggest flop of his career.

CHAPTER 12

BRUCE'S
BIG FLOP

It was time for a change. Bruce had been doing *The Generation Game* for seven arduous series by the end of 1977. It was still a great show and the ratings had not dipped at all. But to a perfectionist like Bruce, things weren't quite the same: the games were starting to get a little tired and were simply rehashed versions of ones they had used years before. He felt the whole thing was in danger of getting stale. He took the momentous decision to quit because he feared that, if he stayed, he would be 'going down with a sinking ship'. But Bruce could not have been more wrong. *The Generation Game* went on to even greater heights without him and he was to go from hero to a very spectacular zero with two very bruising flops that left him close to breaking point.

Bruce's first big role after *The Generation Game* was in *The Travelling Music Show*, a big on-stage musical. Bruce was basically playing his former self: a struggling, bottom-of-the-bill music hall artist desperate for a break. He was Fred Limelight, a performer attempting to put on a variety show and win the support of a successful theatre owner. There was no real plot to the show – the storyline, what there was of it, was there to showcase the wonderful songs written by the composers, Anthony Newley and Leslie Bricusse.

'Fred is a Bruce Forsyth who never made it, the man I had the fear of becoming,' Bruce explained. 'If the break had not happened as it did, it could have happened to me. Fred is a good performer; he is an attacker like I am. It's just that he is a little bit off sometimes. He can make contact with the audience but he does not get the breaks. And that is show business. You fall by the wayside unless the lucky break happens at the right time. Luckily, it happened to me.'

Bruce grew a moustache for the role that he kept on pretty much ever since. He loved being back on the stage full time and really threw himself into the production. 'For two months, I have done nothing but eat, drink and sleep this show,' he said shortly before it opened. 'It is like a never-ending jigsaw puzzle.'

The show opened at the beginning of 1978 in regional theatres and attracted what could only charitably be described as mixed reviews. Everyone loved the songs, everyone loved Bruce in the lead, but as for the rest of the show and the non-existent plot, well, the less said the better. One reviewer noted tartly, 'An invasion of starving termites could hardly have provided a more rickety, hollow structure,' before adding more positively, 'Bruce Forsyth doesn't so much carry the show on his back as toss and twirl it like a drum majorette. If he has ever charmed you on the box, beware: in the flesh his magnified skills may well defy all shortcomings and charm you into enjoying the whole evening.'

After a tour of the provinces, *The Travelling Music Show* made the switch to London – at Her Majesty's Theatre on Haymarket. For whatever reason, the show just didn't gel in the capital. After a lacklustre first night Bruce was left saying in all seriousness, 'That really was a terrible audience.' The reviews reflected this lack of enthusiasm and the show never really recovered from that faltering start. It closed after four months, by no means a disaster but hardly the triumphant switch back to the stage that the then all-conquering Bruce was looking for. The really disappointing consequence of the closure for Bruce was that the show would never transfer to Broadway in New York – any faint hopes he had of cracking America appeared to be fading fast.

The British press love to kick a man when he is down – particularly one as famous as Bruce. He was castigated for taking a 'terrible gamble' in giving up *The Generation Game* for a second-rate musical. Bruce wasn't bothered – he knew he had another ace up his sleeve.

ITV had been desperate to sign him throughout the 1970s as he wiped the floor on Saturday nights. With *The Travelling Music Show* petering out, ITV's boss Michael Grade sensed a chance and took Bruce out with his agent Billy Marsh for lunch. What Grade had in mind for the king of Saturday night was beyond even his wildest dreams. His flamboyant, cigar-chomping new boss had created pretty much the perfect vehicle for Bruce: a two-hour Saturday-night special featuring just about everything. It was like Bruce's entire career rolled into one and was called, appropriately, *Bruce Forsyth's Big Night*. Bruce had a variety of roles on the new show: host, games master, performer, interviewer, you name it. There would be audience-participation spots, comedy sketches, dancers, singers and a big star guest each week to finish it all off. Even Anthea Redfern – the hostess with the mostest and still Bruce's wife at the time – would be making a comeback. The budget was enormous: £2 million for the 14-part series, unheard of in those days. And at the centre of this huge ball of fun was the all-singing, all-dancing Bruce finally achieving a lifetime ambition he'd held since the 1960s to bring back variety to primetime television. Now this was why he had been so right to walk away from *The Generation Game*.

Bruce's *Big Night* was a bit like the *Titanic* – horribly overhyped and quickly heading for disaster. With the fanfare it was given by ITV – who sensed that they might finally be in a position to end the Beeb's Saturday-night ratings' dominance – viewers' expectations were raised to such dizzying heights that no host, even a charismatic old pro like Bruce, would ever have left them satisfied. It would have been far better to kick off slowly – as the BBC had done with *The Generation Game* – and let the show grow as the audience bedded in. But the difference was that Bruce was now a big star and the hype was unavoidable.

If the show failed, it wasn't through a lack of stardust. The big names were quickly signed up, a who's who of late-1970s talent: Elton John, Karen Carpenter, Dudley Moore, Dolly Parton and Bruce's hero Sammy Davis Jr all did headlining spots. Bruce also showcased some emerging talents who were on the very brink of superstardom. One such name was Bette

Midler, just about to go mega in the movie *The Rose*. Bruce hadn't heard of Bette when she was booked, so he decided to check out her act when she performed shortly beforehand at the London Palladium. She was sensational – like nothing Bruce had ever seen before. For a start, she was so confident and relaxed that she would perform lying down. No one had ever done that before. Bette told the audience sexily, 'This is my favourite position.' In fact, the whole thing oozed sex – to such an extent that up in the dress circle a group of men were holding a banner saying, 'Bette, show us your tits'. A star as outrageous as Bette was never going to ignore such a brazen invitation and, at the end of the act, she pulled down her tank top to reveal all. It was a stunning piece of bravado and left the whole theatre in uproar. 'In all my years in showbiz, I have never heard such a shocked laugh,' Bruce remarked afterwards. 'When they say, "The roof nearly caved in..." well, it nearly did.'

Bruce borrowed a trick from her stage show and interviewed her lying down on his new show. Of course, it worked brilliantly as the two stars flirted outrageously snuggled up together and cracked jokes.

'Parkinson could never do this,' Bruce told Bette, referring to his BBC talk-show host rival.

'Is that a disease?' the American, new to Britain, asked.

'Well... every Saturday night it is a sort of disease in this country!' came back the wisecracking Bruce.

Bette was wearing skin-tight black trousers that looked as though they had been sprayed on. As she left the stage, his hand slipped on to her bottom.

'Sorry,' he said, 'no hard feelings.'

'No hard feelings,' she retorted as quick as a flash to shocked laughter from the audience.

If Bette hadn't been a big star in Britain before this appearance, she was afterwards. *Bruce Forsyth's Big Night* ultimately failed but it wasn't the disaster it was portrayed as at the time, or in subsequent years. Its ratings were very respectable. More than 14 million saw Bruce and Bette almost get it on together. But the trouble was that the audience didn't grow – it went down. And as soon as that happened, the critics circled around Bruce – and Anthea too – and really put the boot in. With that kind of backlash, the only way was down – and try as he might, Bruce was unable to stop the whole ship from sinking.

His biggest problem wasn't the content of *Big Night*; it was what was happening over at the Beeb. Far from going down like a 'sinking ship' as Bruce had predicted, *The Generation Game* was bobbing along very nicely under new host Larry Grayson and his likeable hostess Isla St Clair. Ratings didn't dip at all after Bruce's departure and, in fact – thanks to an ITV strike – they actually went up. At 55 minutes, Bruce's old show seemed somehow more nimble and fun than this two-hour extravaganza he was manfully trying to hold together.

Mistakes were made. Cannon and Ball, then on the brink of real stardom just like Bette, were booked as the comedians but the sketches they made were never used. However, another comedian about to make it very big did survive the cutting-room floor. Russ Abbot had been appearing with showband the Black Abbots. *Bruce's Big Night* was his first big solo slot. It was a big success and Russ was so popular they brought him back later in the series.

Bruce also had to deal with tantrums from some of his star guests. Elton John walked out of the show during rehearsals because he was angry at the quality of the piano track for his performance. This was a disaster – it was the climax of the whole show. Bruce was charged with the task of smoothing Elton's notorious ego and persuading him back. He did this really cleverly by devising a routine whereby Elton would come on and explain to Bruce how he created one of his favourite songs. Then Elton would do a trick he had perfected at the time of making up a song from the words on the studio admission ticket. After 30 minutes with Bruce, Elton was raring to go.

Even with brilliantly improvised star turns like this, Bruce still couldn't turn the whole thing around. And after 14 shows, *Big Night* was canned. Bruce has always been one to see the positives in all his career setbacks. But even he admitted that this was one mistake he could not rectify. He admitted ruefully, 'In the end, I suppose I have to say that, although by the time it finished *Bruce Forsyth's Big Night* was doing reasonably well, it proved to be a better idea in conception than it was in execution.'

What made it worse for Bruce was that the show had been coming under fire throughout its entire three-month run. And all this was being played out while he and Anthea were battling without success to save their marriage. The newspapers were on to this too and repeatedly reported that they were on the brink of splitting up. It was a double whammy that left poor Bruce close to cracking up. 'When you are faced with this type of thing, you either fight or crumble,' he said. 'I decided to fight but the strain was enormous.

Whoever – or whatever – we did on the show, they continued to slate it. Michael Grade took the blame, along with me, but every week the press tried to find something negative to report. I was fortunate in having David Bell as my producer. He was wonderful throughout all this and I thanked God for him. If I had not had somebody as experienced as he was to work with, I think I would have folded under the strain.'

Eric Morecambe, an old pal of Bruce's who had performed in shows alongside him since the 1950s, sprang to his defence at this time. Asked to describe the private Bruce, he said affectionately, 'Bruce is probably the only entertainer I know who's virtually the same person off-stage as on. He is all verve, vitality, always talking, joking, quick off the mark, razor-sharp but with perfect control, always chasing round and getting the most out of every situation.'

His words of support really touched Bruce, who had reached rock bottom by this point. He was in a mess – and much of it was his own making. He knew he had screwed up his marriage to Anthea with his selfish obsession with work. And now the work that he had given up everything for was failing too.

'Looking back, I can see that much of the time when I was on a big professional "high", I was also at my lowest ebb,' Bruce explained in his autobiography. 'This was true of my Palladium days, during the huge success of *Little Me* and during *The Generation Game*. There was so much conflict in my personal life; I was never really able to enjoy the "highs" because I knew the "lows" were always lurking behind them…

'I know Ian, my business manager, would say that one of the

realities about me is that, until the latter part of my life, I was always pretty ruthless about putting my professional life first. He used to joke that if he happened to drop dead before a show, I would be very sorry, but I'd give a damn good performance to compensate.'

Bruce had been the darling of the press for most of the previous decade. But that honeymoon was well and truly over. He'd gone from being the most loved man in Britain to being the most hated. It made Bruce so angry that he decided to fight back in a very public way as the series came to end – a tactic he would repeat several times later on his career. *Big Night* always started with Bruce bantering with the audience. In the final show, he was asked how he felt about all the criticism he had been getting. Seething with anger, Bruce let rip, raging at 'press persecution', not just of him but the public in general. 'I'm not just talking about myself here. I'm talking about the ordinary man in the street,' he stormed. 'When they do something wrong – or if the newspapers think they have – they are persecuted. They're then ashamed to walk down the street, knowing that people are looking through their net curtains, pointing a finger at them.'

Then he added – long, long before the media's harassment of the Royals would become big, *big* news and result, indirectly, in the tragic death of Princess Diana after being pursued by the paparazzi – presciently, 'Members of the Royal Family are the people I really feel sorry for. They can't answer back, can't contradict any statement that's made, or picture that's taken. And I think this is very wrong in our country. I can – so I'm a very lucky person. I just had to have these few moments to put matters straight, to alert you – the viewing public – to what is going on in our country today. The only thing you can believe when you look at a newspaper is... look at the top right-hand corner – the date.'

This really was extraordinary stuff. Attacks of this kind on the press are commonplace these days in the wake of the *News of the World* phone-hacking scandal. But in the late 1970s it was unheard of for a big mainstream star such as Bruce – who needed the press to publicise his shows – to go on the attack in this way. This was a time when the newspapers were even more powerful than they are today, selling millions more copies. The strange thing is that Bruce always courted the media. He always made sure he had powerful friends in the media – particularly on two of our biggest-selling daily newspapers, the *Sun* and *Daily Mirror*. Bruce rightly concluded that these were the papers his audience were reading and, much as he loathed it when they attacked him, he still had to make sure there were journalists on both papers he could trust to talk to. So yes, Bruce had friends in the press. But he had a growing army of enemies as well. And to declare war on these enemies in front of millions on TV was a bold gamble. It won him few new friends in the press and it could have ended his career. But Bruce had bounced back from worse setbacks than this.

It wasn't just the popular papers that gave Bruce such a hard time: he also came in for a fair bit of stick from the intelligentsia. George Melly wrote a celebrated diatribe about the cult of celebrity in 1980 called *The Media Mob*, which neatly outlined why so many people relished his failure while also acknowledging why he had been so successful. Melly wrote, 'There is always a Trinder-like cocky conceit in Brucie, a patronising arrogance, a belief in his own omnipotence that makes it difficult not to be a shade pleased at his come-uppance. On the other hand, he has a real if shallow talent and thinks brilliantly on his feet.'

A year after the show ended, Bruce was vindicated by an official report from the Independent Broadcasting Authority attacking the 'cynical and bitter' press coverage of *Bruce Forsyth's Big Night*, which had 'victimised' its star. The IBA said the 'unpleasant' comments had gone 'far beyond the programme itself into areas irrelevant to what was shown on screen'. The show had 'suffered heavily' as a result. But even that didn't stop the brickbats. The legendary *Sun* columnist John Akass slammed the report, saying, 'Harsh, and perhaps undeserved, criticism is an occupational hazard of a trade in which success does not go unrewarded. I should add that I have only once seen Mr Forsyth in the flesh and in my inexpert opinion he was pretty good. He was starring in a musical called *Little Me*!'

All in all, this was a period of great turmoil in Bruce's life. And he still looked back on those days with anger and bitterness. Not just at the way he was portrayed in the press but at the opportunities he missed. He was a big star with real pulling power. He wished he had used his influence to exert more pressure on TV bosses to let him do what he really loved.

'I also regret not being pushy enough in the business,' he explained more recently. 'One newspaper headline once described me as "The most important man in television". I'd like to have used my power to do other shows.

'At one time, in the Seventies, I could have named whatever

I wanted and got it. I'd like to have stood out for something I really wanted to achieve.

'More production shows with the big stars like the one-off special I did with Sammy Davis Jr in 1980. It was the best thing I've ever done and it still stands up today. I often play it if I want a bit of a boost.'

Bruce was going through the most difficult time in his career since those early years when he was unemployed for weeks on end. But off stage, his luck was to change quite spectacularly when a second Miss World walked into his life.

CHAPTER 13

THE LOVE
OF HIS LIFE

Bruce was 52. He had just gone through an agonising split with his second wife, Anthea Redfern. The last thing on his mind was a new romance. Then he caught sight of the goddess that is Wilnelia Merced and was blown away. 'Who is she?' a stunned Bruce exclaimed when he first saw the former Miss World. She was the woman who would completely turn his life around and with whom he would finally find happiness.

It all began – as it often did with Bruce and women – at a beauty contest. More precisely, the 1980 Miss World contest at the Royal Albert Hall in London. The organisers had asked Bruce to be a judge for two days. He was busy filming *Play Your Cards Right* for ITV and had to turn them down. They quickly re-jigged the schedules so that Bruce would only be needed for one day. He happily accepted.

All the other judges were there when Bruce arrived except one: Wilnelia. She finally rushed into the room clutching a very large black bag. 'Good heavens,' Bruce thought immediately, 'she looks like a South American princess. She's absolutely gorgeous.' Bruce had never seen anyone so beautiful. To him, she was sheer perfection: flawless skin the colour of cappuccino, sensual dark eyes, lips to die for and the kind of hour-glass curves that could have been carved by the gods.

'I was absolutely besotted with her but I didn't push it,' Bruce recalled later. 'My philosophy has always been to play it cool. It's probably quite hard to think of me as a cool person in that way, but I am.'

Nevertheless, he wanted this mesmerising fellow judge to notice him. And he did that by cracking a joke. Before the pageant started, the contestants were interviewed by the judges.

Bruce got the biggest laugh of the day when he turned to Miss Turkey and said, 'Tell me, what do you eat for Christmas dinner when you are at home?'

'Turkey of course,' she replied. Bruce anxiously cast a glance along the panel and, sure enough, the girl of his dreams was giggling mischievously. She liked his jokes – that was going to be a big help!

When the actual pageant started Bruce was at the wrong end of the panel from this mysterious beauty. He had no chance of chatting her up for hours. He learned through talking to the other judges as the evening progressed that she was from Puerto Rico and had won Miss World five years earlier in 1975 when she was only 17, the youngest winner ever. Bruce had actually been watching the contest on TV that night but she barely registered with him at the time. 'I just flicked on the television at the end, saw her and thought, isn't she gorgeous, and that was it,' he said.

A veteran of countless beauty pageants, Bruce knew his chance with Wilnelia would come at the dinner dance held after each year's contest. But already there was a problem: when she arrived at the dance, she was accompanied by a smooth, good-looking Oriental man who Bruce assumed was her boyfriend. Game over, it seemed.

Ever the trier though, Bruce arranged to sit with Wilnelia anyway – at least the eye contact would be enjoyable. After dinner, Bruce signed a few autographs for fans, hoping Wilnelia would realise that he was a big star in Britain and be impressed. Then he got his lucky break. The other guests disappeared and he found himself alone at the dinner table with Wilnelia. He quickly made his move. 'Would your boyfriend mind if I asked you for a dance?' he inquired. 'No,' she replied. 'He's not my boyfriend – just a very dear friend.'

So they danced... and danced... and danced. Wilnelia, the smouldering Latin American beauty, was, of course, a natural on the dance floor. She hadn't expected Bruce to be any great shakes as a 'cold Englishman'. She was in for a very big surprise. He guided her, gliding through one step after another as the electricity coursed through both their bodies. They were inseparable for the next two hours.

Wilnelia told Bruce her life story as they melted into each other's bodies. This was only her second trip to Britain. The first had been when she won Miss World. She was 21 now and busy working as a model in New York. It had been an incredible few years for her since winning the title just out of high school. She was incredibly close to her family back in Puerto Rico. The more Bruce got to know his new companion, the more he liked her. She wasn't like so many of the girls he had met at beauty contests. Not only was she beautiful, she was also intelligent but grounded and totally unaffected by fame. Clearly, being so stunning opened doors to her but it was obvious to Bruce that she had never let those privileges go to her head.

Bruce had seen how truly eye-catching natural beauty could cause all sorts of problems for women. 'I had met many, many beautiful women – perhaps too many,' he explained. 'Some exceptionally good-looking women are ruined from the age of fifteen or sixteen, can so easily become spoiled, hard and manipulative, using their looks to get things they would probably be better off without.' From their very first meeting, Bruce knew this remarkable new girl was not like that. Not only was she one of the most attractive women he had ever met, she was also one of the nicest.

He had to see her again. He thanked Wilnelia for 'the most wonderful night of my life' and she gave him the number of the hotel she was staying at in London. Bruce was like a breath of fresh air to this exotic beauty. He was 'courteous and gentlemanly' – so unlike the pushy men she met most often while modelling in New York, who only seemed interested in her because of her Miss World fame.

They arranged to go out a few nights later to the nightclub Stringfellows, of all places. At the time, it was the place to be seen. Once again, Bruce and Wilnelia gelled on the dance floor but they were with a big group of friends and there was little chance for real intimacy. What Bruce longed for was an evening where they could be together alone. He asked her to dinner the next night but once again she had commitments with friends from Puerto Rico, though she stressed that Bruce was welcome to join them.

But in the end Wilnelia's friends couldn't join her that night and she found she had only Bruce to take her out. He, of course, was delighted. Over dinner, their full life stories finally emerged. This was a difficult conversation for Bruce. He had to explain that he had already been married twice and had five children, three of whom were grown up. Though he was separated from his second wife Anthea and there was no chance of reconciliation, the split was so recent that they were still living under the same roof in Surrey. Throw in the fact that he was 31 years older than Wilnelia, plus she had already been warned by pals that he was a 'ladies man' with a 'bit of a reputation' and his odds didn't look good. But that would be to underestimate just how besotted Bruce was. And she could see that he was genuine.

Wilnelia had a lot to tell her charming suitor. First, she had to explain to Bruce exactly where Puerto Rico was. It is a beautiful Caribbean island not far off the coast of America. Its Spanish-speaking inhabitants are actually classed as US citizens, though they cannot vote in US presidential elections. Winning Miss World had made her a huge star in Puerto Rico – she was as famous there as their head of state. She loved her new life in New York and was busy modelling for big labels like Christian Dior. She had had a strict Catholic education and had never really been in a serious relationship before. She came from a big close-knit family with lots of aunts, uncles and cousins. Her parents had split up and she was the apple of the eye of her very protective father who was very successful in construction. The same father, she added, who was two years younger than Bruce! With all this against them, would this fledgling romance ever get off the ground? They were at least going to give it a try.

They saw each other every day from then on for the remainder of her trip to Britain. They were very easy in each other's company despite Wilnelia's faltering English and Bruce's non-existent Spanish.

Bruce couldn't bear to be parted from this dazzling new girl in his life when she returned to her life in the States. He had been booked to appear at a charity gala in Florida a few weeks later and he suggested they meet up in New York afterwards. Whatever Bruce said to Wilnelia over those few days in the Big Apple made all the difference. She may have had doubts about Bruce before but they quickly dissolved as they relaxed together. As Bruce prepared to fly back to Britain, they were both determined to make this unlikely romance work – even if 3,500 miles and one very large ocean divided them.

They decided to keep things secret at first because news of the relationship would be big news in both Britain and Puerto Rico. For Bruce, it would mean more bad headlines so shortly after the bruising split with Anthea. And it wouldn't look good back home for Wilnelia to be seen with a married man more than 30 years her senior. So both their home countries were largely out of bounds for the lovebirds. Instead, they had to meet on neutral territory and do so without telling their families, who they'd decided to keep out of the loop until they both knew for sure that the relationship would last the distance.

They enjoyed their first holiday together in Antigua in the Caribbean. Wilnelia brought a male companion so they would not arouse suspicion. They went out for a romantic night together one evening, only to discover the England cricket team, accompanied by an army of nosy Fleet Street newshounds, were staying at the same place. So once again they had to pretend that they were just good friends. Nevertheless, at the end of the trip, Wilnelia was ready to make a firm commitment. As they prepared to fly home separately, she told Bruce, 'I want you to come to Puerto Rico and meet my family. I will introduce you as the man I love.' He had finally cracked it.

For the next year, the globe-trotting romance continued but not without complications. They arranged to meet in Madrid but one time contrived to book themselves into different hotels. Work kept them apart continuously and there was still the issue of Bruce's divorce to Anthea. By now she had started a new relationship herself with the hotelier Freddie Hoffman. Bruce told her about his new love and swore her to secrecy. The fact that they were both happy and settled and in new relationships made the divorce far simpler than it could have been.

Bruce found it increasingly difficult to be away from Wilnelia, or Winnie as she insisted on him calling her. He hated the name, saying it was for old ladies in Britain. But somehow it stuck. Bruce had never been particularly possessive. But gnawing away at him throughout all this time was the fear that another man would whisk his new love away from him. Winnie was continually hit on by younger men but she simply wasn't interested. She was happy with Bruce.

She found living away from her new man in New York really tough. 'Transatlantic affairs are fun and exciting to begin with but they don't last very long,' she said. 'One of you has to move eventually.'

The couple spent Christmas and New Year 1981 in Puerto Rico. Bruce finally met Wilnelia's mother Delia, who by now had been told all about the romance. Winnie had agonised about this moment for a long time. 'I didn't tell my parents because I wanted to be sure that this was the right relationship,' she explained. 'There seemed no point in upsetting them. Maybe they expected me to marry someone like Prince Charles! In the end, I said, "Mummy, I've found the man of my dreams, the man I want to spend the rest of my life with. I'm in love with him and he's really special." I then told her about all his good points – how kind and caring he is, the fact he doesn't smoke or drink very much, likes dancing and all the things I enjoy, that he's very athletic and amusing, and how much he loves me.'

Then she broke the other news. 'I said, "There's just one problem." And I told her he was older. There was a long silence and then she said, "How old?" But she knew he was the first and only man I've ever been in love with and that's what mattered.'

Any doubts Delia had were dispelled by Bruce. She was bowled over by her daughter's new man and never once mentioned the age difference even though, like her estranged husband, she was younger than Bruce – in her case, 10 years younger. 'She just seemed happy to accept that I was truly in love with her beautiful daughter,' said Bruce, beaming. 'We all had a marvellous time – it was the best New Year's Eve ever. If I could have dreamed up a perfect beginning to 1982, this would have been it.'

Bruce made two New Year's resolutions that year. The first, of course, was to propose to Winnie. The second was not to repeat the mistakes of the past that had ruined his first two marriages.

Bruce and Winnie spent the next summer together living at a flat Bruce owned in Chelsea, west London. His friends, who could have been forgiven for thinking that this foreign beauty was targeting a multi-millionaire like Bruce for his money, took to his new love immediately. 'She is just a lovely, lovely woman,' they told him.

The proposal came six weeks into her trip – at Turnberry in Scotland, where Bruce had been invited to film a golf series. He knew that this was an enormous step for a girl who was still only 22. Bruce wasn't just asking her to be his wife but to uproot her whole life to spend it with a twice-divorced man, two of whose daughters were older than her. He knew it was a huge decision and he told her she could have all the time in the world to make up her mind. He made it clear that, although his work would mean that they would spend more of their time in Britain, he was prepared also to buy them a home in Puerto Rico and spend a substantial part of the year there so she would never lose touch with her family.

Winnie just knew this was right. Spurning his offer of a pause for a few weeks to decide, she hugged Bruce and told him, 'I have never been in love before but I am now with you. I know there's a difference in our age but, even if our marriage lasts for only a few years, I'm too happy to care at the moment. I love you. The answer is yes.'

There was just one issue they needed to sort. Winnie made it clear from the start that she wanted to have children. Bruce had been in this position before with Anthea. But he was as excited as his new fiancée about the prospect of starting a family – his third. And, after five daughters, perhaps they would be lucky enough for Winnie to provide him with a son.

Winnie was then introduced to all of Bruce's daughters who, like his friends, took to his new love immediately. Bruce admitted he was worried at first about whether the girls would accept her. 'It could have been the trickiest of situations – the girls meeting a stepmother who is the same age,' he explained. 'If they hadn't got on, it would have been so destructive, however much we'd loved one another. In the end, it could have cost everything – my love and my daughters. As it is, they love her, which is wonderful, and they all get on marvellously.'

Winnie was terrified about the meeting too. 'I spent about five hours changing clothes because I wanted to look older than I was, which was so silly,' she recalled. 'In the end, I just decided to be myself. We ended up having a wonderful time and they've given me so much good advice, it's like having lots of new sisters.' The bond between Winnie and her new British family runs even deeper than that. It would be fair to say that she is the glue that has kept the whole Forsyth clan close to this day. She also forged a close relationship with his ex-wife Anthea.

Winnie admitted that emigrating to a new country was not easy for her. 'The first year I was in Britain, I was lonely,' she explained. 'I'd left everything behind. It was actually the new friendships I had forged with Bruce's daughters [that] helped me through that time. I could have been scared off when he told me he had five children but, because they are near my age, it was like having friends round all the time.'

News finally leaked out about Bruce's new girl when they were pictured together at a golf club in north London. By that stage, virtually everyone who was close to Bruce and Wilnelia knew about the romance and approved, so there was no problem as the couple found themselves continually in the newspapers and pursued by paparazzi photographers. Bruce also met Wilnelia's father at Christmas in Puerto Rico and he also gave the romance a big thumbs-up.

A wedding in Puerto Rico was never going to be an option. Winnie was such a huge name there that they would have wanted to hold a national holiday – and there wasn't a hotel in the world big enough to accommodate all of her extended family. So instead they tied the knot in New York – on a snowy day two weeks after New Year in 1983. Winnie looked stunning in a long white over-the-shoulder dress. Her great friend Jonathan Luk, who Bruce had assumed was her boyfriend when they first met at Miss World, was the best man. They honeymooned in Maui in Hawaii before work commitments took Bruce abroad to New Zealand. Winnie joined him and they went on a whistlestop two-month tour, taking in Hong Kong, Rome and Marbella.

They began married life at Bruce's old marital home in Wentworth (Winnie was shocked to discover that Anthea's coats were still in the cupboard, even though she had moved out by then and also remarried). Bruce was happy to buy a new house for them and start afresh but his new bride loved the tranquil location and they decided to stay after carrying out major renovations. 'You are the one with the memories in this house. If they do not bother you, they do not bother me,' she told him.

Bruce still cannot believe his luck in falling in love with Wilnelia. 'I'd got to the stage when I'd thought I would never fall in love again,' he said. 'I'd been through it all: marriage, divorce, the lot. The last thing I was thinking of that night at Miss World when I met Wilnelia was falling in love. I'd reached the point where I was doubtful I ever wanted to get involved again. Playboy of Wentworth, that's what I planned. I'd bought the house on the golf course.

'After two failed marriages I was happy to be on my own. My life had taken a certain road, it didn't involve a serious relationship and that was it. I'd done it before and I didn't get lonely. It didn't worry me. But when I met Wilnelia, I couldn't believe that anyone could be so nice and so unspoilt after being through what she had as Miss World. She had a very rare quality.'

For her part, Wilnelia liked the fact that Bruce was so sure of himself. He had had the confidence to make a move in the first place. Her beauty scared off most men from even trying their luck because they were convinced she would be way out of their league.

'I think, if you are attractive, most men are too scared to even come and say hello because they are afraid of rejection,' she explained. 'Older guys are so much more confident. Brucie was so sure of himself. I liked that.'

Bruce wasn't like other men she'd met, she explained. 'I'd

met so many men since I'd been Miss World, and they all just wanted to be seen with a pretty girl and say they'd been out with me. But Bruce wasn't like them. He'd made sure he was sitting at the right table but he didn't rush anything – he waited for the right moment. I was wondering if the evening would be over before he even asked me for a dance. Then, when he held me in his arms, it just felt right. When he said goodnight, he didn't even try to kiss me on the cheek, he just gently kissed my hand. Men expect so much on the first night – because they have bought you dinner, they think they can have everything. But Bruce wasn't like that; he was a gentleman. He had the sort of values you just don't find in younger men. I sense he was someone special even though I wasn't looking for a relationship. I knew I wanted to see him again.'

She liked the fact that he could dance too. 'Of course! I could never have married someone who couldn't dance! I hear the music and my feet just go; it's part of my nature. I think you suddenly know when you are in love and that you want to be with that person for ever. I was soon like a leech. I was glued to Bruce. I'm a typical Latina.'

And any worries her parents had about her marrying an older man soon passed. Winnie continued. 'On our wedding day, my mother gave [Bruce] a book called *The Fountain of Youth*. It's all about exercise and he has been exercising regularly ever since. She also gave him a letter about how to look after me. I don't know if he ever followed the advice in the letter but he has looked after me so well. I could not have been happier with any other man.'

So Bruce, at the third time of asking, had finally found

happiness with a woman. After the miserable failure that was *Bruce Forsyth's Big Night*, his career was about to take off again too.

CHAPTER 14

WHAT DO POINTS MAKE? PRIZES!

By the end of 1979 Bruce was in America trying once again to do what so few British entertainers have managed to achieve: make it big in Hollywood. He had been working away from Britain for a year with varying degrees of success and was longing to return home. The last leg of this stint in the States saw him take his one-man show to the Huntington Hartford, a major Tinseltown venue, for two nights in front of a glittering audience that included Cary Grant (amazingly, a fan of Bruce's after seeing him many years before in panto in Bristol!). The US shows were sold out but, as ever with Bruce's adventures across the pond, they didn't lead to anything concrete. However, the trip was by no means a waste of time. Relaxing in his hotel one morning in Los Angeles, he flicked on the TV. He was channel surfing when he came across a little-known 30-minute show that he just knew would be a big hit in Britain.

It was a game show – yes, one of those again – called *Card Sharks*. The format was beguilingly simple. Contestants were posed a question based on a survey of 100 people. The first competitor would guess how many of the 100 had given a specific answer to a question and the second would guess if the real number was higher or lower. Whoever was closest got control of a giant pack of cards. Pretty female dealers would then deal out the cards one by one and the winning contestant would say whether the next card was higher or lower. If they guessed a sequence of five cards correctly, they won the game and a big prize. It was stupidly simple but horribly addictive. All the drama came from the turning over of the cards. Sitting in his hotel room, Bruce found himself shouting 'higher' or 'lower' as each giant card was revealed – and realised that viewers in the UK would do just the same.

All he needed to do now was find out who owned the show and see if they wanted to sell the rights to a British audience. There was another show on American TV called *Family Feud* that Bruce also fancied exporting to Britain. If anything, he thought this would be even more successful than *Card Sharks*. As luck would have it, both shows were owned by the same organisation, Goodson-Todman Productions. Bruce was soon negotiating with Paul Talbot, who was in charge of their overseas sales.

First Bruce wanted to know about *Family Feud*. He was told the show had just been snapped up in Britain by none other than Bob Monkhouse just a week earlier. Like Bruce, Bob had a good eye for a hit format – and he was spot on with *Family Feud*. Monkhouse launched it in Britain under the new name of *Family Fortunes* in 1980.

Bruce, always a canny dealmaker, asked if Bob would swap *Family Feud* for *Card Sharks*. Monkhouse was keen to hang on to his show, so Bruce ended up doing a deal for *Card Sharks*. Michael Grade, the ITV boss whose name was to crop up in connection with Bruce's career for many years to come, loved the format and bought it immediately, just weeks after he had also bought *Family Feud* for Bob.

Perhaps as a result of the guilt he still felt at all the flak Bruce had taken for *Big Night*, Grade paid his old mate handsomely for the new show. He picked up £10,000 for each of the 30-minute episodes and he would record 30 of them in a matter of weeks.

Broadcasting started in 1980. Whereas it ran five times a week in the States in the day-time schedules, *Play Your Cards Right* – as the show was renamed by Bruce – would be weekly in Britain in a primetime slot. Four gorgeous girls were hired as Bruce's 'Dolly Dealers' along with a male assistant because, already, television was becoming politically correct and bosses were worried about appearing to be sexist.

Capitalising on the successful elements of *The Generation Game*, a string of new catchphrases were born. Bruce introduced the Dolly Dealers with a rhyme:

I'm the leader of the pack,
Which makes me such a lucky jack.
And here they are, they're so appealing,
OK, dollies, do your dealing!

Cheesy, yes, but of course it worked brilliantly – though the PC brigade ensured that it was rewritten a few times in later years because of those dreaded charges of sexism.

Bruce would begin each show by saying, 'What a lovely audience! You're so much better than last week.' The joke was that the same audience was used for the recording of more than one show – therefore it was more than likely to be the same one, with a few people rearranged in the front row so that the audiences at home didn't notice.

Other catchphrases came thick and fast. If two cards of the same number came up, Bruce would say, 'You don't get anything for a pair.' 'Not in this game,' the audience would quickly add at Bruce's invitation. There were more. 'Oh, you've cheered me up', 'What do points make? Prizes!' 'Don't touch the pack, we'll be right back' and, of course, Bruce's final line, 'Well, it could still be a big night – if you play your cards right. Goodnight!'

Disaster almost struck before the show was launched in the autumn of 1980 when Bruce broke his arm in a fall. Thankfully, he had just enough movement in his fingers to turn the giant cards, despite the plaster cast. It was a tricky show to make because it was impossible to predict how the cards would fall.

Bruce filmed long interviews with the contestants – lasting up to eight minutes and inevitably involving lots of laughs and mickey-taking. But if the cards fell unluckily and the game dragged on before a winner emerged, almost all of this banter would have to be cut from the final edit to fit in with the 30-minute running time. There were other petty rules that at the time ITV bosses had to adhere to. For instance, the maximum value of the first prize could not exceed £4,000 – so just about the only car they could give away was a Mini. These rules were gradually relaxed so that when the show was revived in the 1990s the value of the car had gone up to £16,000 and contestants could win up to £5,000 in cash. Of course, all those rules have been scrapped now and shows regularly have £1 million up for grabs.

After the first series, Bruce switched from having individual contestants and instead pitched a married couple against each other. It was a really clever change and became a key part of the show's success.

Bruce was on a huge deal for *Play Your Cards Right* – far more money than he had ever earned at the Beeb. He earned the same from one episode of *Play Your Cards Right* as he would from six one-man shows. As Bruce explained, 'I have been incredibly lucky to have found my way into a business that throws money at you for what most of the time you love doing! If I had been born a billionaire I would probably have paid those who paid me to let me perform,' adding cheekily, 'But, just in case I become a billionaire, I intend to keep that under my hat.'

Play Your Cards Right ran very successfully between 1980 and 1987 – attracting 15 million viewers at its peak. Almost all game shows have a shelf life, though, and the decision was made to rest it for a few years. Bruce was angry at the decision and felt it was popular enough to carry on for a lot longer.

* * *

Bruce's television work continued alongside his game shows. He had always loved acting and he appeared in the hugely popular American series *Magnum PI*. He was excited to be offered Leonard Rossiter's role in the ITV sitcom *Tripper's*

Day, which was renamed *Slinger's Day* when Bruce took it over in 1986, two years after Rossiter's death. He played a dour supermarket manager called Cecil Slinger in what became Bruce's one and only sitcom. The show was a moderate success. It ran for two series and Bruce was offered the option of a third but it was clear that it hadn't really worked. The trouble was, the public found it difficult to accept Bruce in a role outside of his usual game show.

Bruce by then had his eyes on another show after a tip-off from his daughter Julie. She had seen a show on TV in Holland that she reckoned would be perfect for her father. Bruce went over with his manager Ian Wilson and they both agreed *You Bet!* fitted the bill nicely. LWT quickly bought it in 1988.

A panel of celebrities had to bet on the ability of members of the public to achieve seemingly impossible challenges and stunts within a limited amount of time. The studio audience would place a bet on the outcomes – hence the name of the show. The panellists received points for each outcome they predicted correctly. If they got it wrong, they had to do a forfeit. All the points accrued were increased several times, converted into pounds and donated to a charity chosen by the celebrity panellist who had achieved the highest score.

It was one of the most ambitious game shows ever staged in Britain because, with spectacular stunts involving motorbike stunt riding and mechanical diggers, it all had to be organised on a huge scale. It lead the way for other game shows filmed in big arenas, such as *Gladiators*. Bruce hated the show, which was all about the stunts and the celebrity betting and not about the presenter. He wasn't able to ad-lib or given time to properly interact with the contestants. He felt like he was just reading an autocue. He quit after three series. He was forced to take legal action against the *News of the World*, which wrongly said that he had been axed by ITV for being too old. In fact, ITV wanted him to do a further two series but he declined. He won substantial damages. *You Bet!* prospered without him, running for six more years, first with Matthew Kelly hosting and then Darren Day.

After three disappointing years on *You Bet!* Bruce left ITV on pretty bad terms. He made no secret of the fact that he had no faith in the bosses, whom he branded 'limp wristed' in a very public attack. It was an unfortunate choice of words and it damaged his reputation. But it was born out of frustration at the direction in which his career was heading.

Bruce got into a regrettable spat with his old pal Ernie Wise at this time. We all know how easily offended Bruce could be and he took exception to a passage in Ernie's autobiography *Still on My Way to Hollywood*. Ernie claimed that Bruce was not happy as the stooge when he was a guest on the *Morecambe and Wise Show* and tried to get the better of Eric Morecambe. 'The result was two large egos, metaphorically speaking, slugging it out on stage trying to top the other,' he wrote.

'Throughout my career I have believed it is wrong for performers to publicly criticise their colleagues,' Bruce fumed in response. 'In the old days this was an unwritten rule of etiquette and I think it undignified, the way it has been broken more frequently in recent times. As far as the incident regarding myself is concerned, suffice to say that he and I remember it differently. What truly saddens me is to think of how Eric, a man for whom I had the greatest respect professionally and personally, would have felt if he had seen this.' The last word went to little Ernie, who quickly backed down, saying, 'I'm sorry I upset Bruce. I am his biggest fan.'

Bruce was starting to realise that, while game shows had pretty much defined his career in Britain in many ways, they had also killed it. He was a song-and-dance man at heart. But just as actors can get typecast in a role, so can game-show hosts. It wasn't a bad career – and the money was fantastic – but going from one new format to the next was making Bruce seriously down in the dumps. 'I do wish I had not done quite so many game shows,' he later said. 'In television terms, it's my only true career regret. To my mind, I am what I was when I first came into the business: an all-round performer. I wish I had held out for more musical entertainment shows, more "specials". I should have done this in the seventies when I was at the height of my powers to pick and choose. They would have let me then. I got carried along on the tide to do ever more similar programmes, when I should have swum against it.'

Bill Cotton, his old boss on *The Generation Game*, summed up Bruce's problem neatly. 'It's not that Bruce isn't good in variety; it's that he's so bloody marvellous at game shows.'

Bruce gave a lot of interviews at this time, reflecting on his career and the nature of his appeal. He said he was a comedian – but not one who told jokes. 'I just can't remember them,' he said. 'I don't have a computer brain containing twelve jokes on vicars. I don't think I told one joke in all those years at the Palladium.' His passport lists his occupation as 'entertainer'. 'I decided all those years ago that I wasn't going to put "comedian" because there would come a day when some customs man or immigration officer would say, "Alright – make me laugh.'"

And the secret of his success? 'Well, I switch between many elements in my act but ultimately all of it hangs on this idea of me thinking I'm much grander than I am. I'm fooling myself – and I let the audience know I'm fooling myself. I try to keep up The Forsyth Façade, this outer thing. But – although I'm really trying the best I can – everyone knows I'll crumble if something goes untoward. So I'm a superstar who crumbles.'

Bruce was a member of several double acts in the early years of his career, including one with his first wife Penny Calvert. But the second partner in all of his best work has been the audience. 'They are always my yardstick,' he explained. 'I have never found television easy. I do use the cameras at times – for close-up looks, as though they are people I can confide in, but most of the time they are an infringement. To do what I do without an audience would be virtually impossible. An audience of 200 or 300 is all you get in a television studio and anything under 500 is difficult anyway. And if you can't see them, what do you do? I'd love to do a TV show in which all these special cameras are at the back of the studio and they can just zoom in with different lenses – it would be a lovely thing of just you and the audience.'

Despite misgivings about committing to another game show, Bruce returned to the Beeb to do five more series of *The Generation Game* after *Play Your Cards Right* ended the first time in 1987. By 1994, though, Bruce was back with ITV again – any offence at his 'limp wristed' tirade long since forgotten.

He was lured back by Marcus Plantin, ITV's network scheduler who had previously been responsible for wrapping the conveyor belt prizes on *The Generation Game*; he was keen to revive *Play Your Cards Right*. Originally ITV had brought in the comedian Brian Conley as presenter but at the last minute they persuaded Bruce to return to the role after he unexpectedly quit *The Generation Game*. Bruce had been left completely washed out by the rigours of presenting the BBC show and was looking for an easier life. He had done a one-off chat and entertainment show for the Beeb called *Bruce's Guest Night*. He'd hoped that this would be made into a series, but there was no sign of a firm commitment from the Beeb. ITV definitely looked like the better deal to Bruce.

Despite signing with ITV, he was still contractually obliged to make the final series of *The Generation Game*. It was an unhappy period for Bruce and the whole of that last series became a chore. The problems that had been building up throughout the series reached their climax at the end of its run when the show was switched from Christmas Day to the less prestigious Christmas Eve. As soon as he was free from his contractual obligations to the BBC, he went on the attack. 'They call the BBC "Auntie". I think it should be called "the Wicked Uncle",' he stormed. 'I'll miss my own production team but nobody else in the building. They don't know anything about my kind of show business. The bosses there are faceless bureaucrats who know nothing about family entertainment. Middle-of-the-road entertainment is sadly lacking at the BBC. People have started treating variety as a nasty swear word in the last few years – but what is wrong with stars performing together? It's nice entertainment. I am sure the public would like to see more music, variety and middle-of-the-road comedy shows.'

Bruce believed the Beeb's treatment of some of their biggest stars had been shameful and disgusting and that he was shown zero respect. 'They haven't got a clue,' he continued. 'Family entertainment is nothing more than an embarrassment to them, a necessary evil. They just put up with it.'

He said he hadn't been upset when he left the BBC because he wanted to leave. 'It was my decision to go. I don't want to work with them any more. I axed them and it's nice for a performer to axe a corporation rather than the other way round. They're not my kind of people. I've nothing in common with them, I'm glad to say. In the days of Bill Cotton and Michael Grade it was wonderful to work there but not now. It's all indecision, indecision, indecision. They couldn't even make up their minds when the show was going to run.'

He was also disgusted at the way they treated other performers. 'Do you know how Les Dawson found out *Blankety Blank* was finished? He was at a press launch for his panto at Manchester Palace and a journalist asked, "How do you feel about your show being axed?" Les had no knowledge of this; he'd never been informed. He had to face the press there and then. He was very disillusioned with the BBC before he died. This was shameful. How can they call the BBC "Auntie" when they have no warmth, no sensitivity and no morality. Somebody should at least have told him.'

Bruce cited Roy Castle as another example. 'Nobody was better known for his courage and talent. They did a tribute show for him in which many stars he had performed with were shown. He did a wonderful drumming routine with Russ

Abbot and a dance routine with me. But because Roy did *Record Breakers*, the BBC put the tribute show on at 4.30 in the afternoon. This was an insult to him. That should have been a primetime slot. Why not show some feeling for the man? It disgusted me.'

The tribute show to celebrate Bruce's 50th year in show business was treated with similar disrespect. 'It was a wonderful night,' he explained. 'We had Sir Harry Secombe, Jimmy Tarbuck, Ronnie Corbett and Peter Alliss. But before it was shown it was cut and cut. The date for it going out was changed three times. Maybe fifty years in show business doesn't mean much to Alan Yentob [then controller of BBC One]. Maybe he has a complex about people with experience. In the end he put it on at ten past eleven on a Wednesday night. It was as if he was saying, "He is a has-been, bung it on there."'

Bruce first became aware of the BBC's cockeyed attitude to light entertainment five years earlier when he and Ronnie Corbett were recording a Christmas special. 'After a week of rehearsals the producer came into the studio with a face longer than mine,' he told the *Sun*. 'He'd just see the Christmas schedules. Our show was going out at 11pm on Boxing Night after *Lenny Henry*. Ronnie and I were staggered. We're both family entertainers. How can you put us on at 11pm after Lenny, who is aiming at a very different audience? Jonathan Powell [who was in charge of BBC One before Yentob] condemned the show before we even taped it. How unjust can you be? Throughout my time at the BBC, management indecision was staggering. It was impossible to get transmission dates until the last minute. I wrote Jonathan

Powell three letters and didn't even get an acknowledgement. Yentob was no better. He destroyed *Celebrity Golf*. He moved it from a popular slot where golfers could watch it to 5.30pm. Is this scheduling?

'The BBC think variety is dead. But when they slip on a *Morecambe and Wise* repeat it goes straight into the Top Ten. My show, *Bruce's Guest Night*, was as near to a variety show as you can get. I even won an award for it. But their attitude was, "People don't want that, they'd rather be watching performing pets."'

Explaining why he finally decided to leave, he said, 'I made up my mind to leave the BBC when nobody bothered to tell me that for the first time in twelve years they weren't going to put out *The Generation Game* on Christmas Day. Yentob didn't ring me or get one of his lesser-in-commands to call. He then scheduled us directly against *Coronation Street* on Christmas Eve. It was an insult to a show that for five years had worked very hard for that company. That is the thanks you get from Alan Yentob. And that was the day I said, "Enough is enough." Thank God I can afford not to need it any more. There are lots of good people at the BBC, but the top management are a disaster.'

The BBC refused to rise to the bait. A spokesman said, 'To the younger generation, the term "wicked" is quite a compliment. Brucie has to-ed and fro-ed between the BBC and ITV two or three times in his career and I wouldn't rule him out coming back to the Beeb.' How right they were!

Bruce's outburst didn't surprise his close friends. Lionel Blair, who had worked with him as far as back as the 1950s at the Windmill Theatre, said, 'Bruce has had such an up-and-down life and he has been hurt. He is a professional man and professional men can be difficult because they want perfection all the time. He is very quick-tempered and he bears grudges. He can keep a row going too long, which is silly, particularly when it's with good friends.'

To Bruce, all the fun was going out of show business – and he blamed 'the loony left'.

'We decided these days you have to be aware of the loony left,' he explained. 'The loony left ruined Miss World by saying you're using women like cattle. They marched around them with placards. They forgot that Miss World raises hundreds of thousands of pounds for charity.'

* * *

In February 1995 a star-studded banquet was held at London's Dorchester Hotel to honour Bruce's 50th year as an entertainer. His old pal and golfing companion Jimmy Tarbuck gave a speech that brought the house down.

'We're here tonight to honour one of the great men of show business, a man of principle, a man of love for his fellow man, a man of dignity and human decency – but enough about Harry Secombe. Tonight let's talk about this long-chinned prat over here! He's possibly one of the greatest entertainers of our generation. Now that's not only my opinion, that's Bruce's! And in celebration of his fifty years he's doing a week on Broadway... and he's very big in Hammersmith and I wish him the best of luck.

'Bruce, you started off your career as the Mighty Atom and look at you now – the Knackered Neutron! What can you say about Bruce? The first thing to go is usually your eyes; with Bruce it was the hair. But it hasn't all gone. Some of it's still in a drawer at Wentworth.'

Then he got on to his favourite subject: Bruce the golf curmudgeon. 'People ask me on many occasions, "What is he like to play golf with?" Well, I'll tell you from the heart. He is the most miserable, moaning bastard God has ever put life into on the golf course!'

With everyone – including Bruce – now crying with laughter, he ended with a touching tribute. 'I have to go back thirty years when a very nervous young man was going on at the Palladium. Bruce, you were in charge that night when I came on the show and you'll always be in charge.'

Bruce said it had been an unforgettable night. 'There were so many mates there – they all said a few words, the wine flowed and we danced the night away. The only problem was my speech – I had so much to say after fifty years in show business. I had to cut it short. There were a lot of people there from the variety world and they all agreed – we've never had a night quite like it.' Bruce was presented with a cake in the shape of the London Palladium, and a silver miniature grand piano.

Tarby's speech was detailed in Bob Monkhouse's brilliant 1998 autobiography *Over the Limit*. In it Bob also gave what is perhaps the best description of Bruce ever made. 'Tap dancing his way through life while bestowing his prestigious gifts upon us all, Bruce has had the companionship of exquisite women, three of them his wives. Penny Calvert was the sexiest of Windmill Theatres ecdysiasts, Anthea Redfern was foxy enough to make loins combust, and the current and last Mrs Forsyth, Wilnelia, has a beauty that refreshes tired eyes.

'Bruce's daughters are lovely; his ratings have always been high and his handicap low. His genes have allowed him to become a skilled pianist, tuneful singer, convincing actor and magnificent TV host; it would have been going too far to make him an intellectual too.'

Bruce has always described himself as a bit of loner – away from his family, he is happiest in his own company. But Tarby and Bob showed, in their different ways, that he also had a real talent for male friendship too.

Bruce presented *Play Your Cards Right* for a further five years on ITV between 1994 and 1999. He then brought it back again in 2002 in a slightly modified format for another year.

In 1998, he celebrated his 70th birthday by performing his one-man show for a week at the London Palladium. 'It's lovely to be back in the West End,' he told the sell-out audience on the first night, with Wilnelia watching proudly from the royal box. 'It's where I belong.' There was lots of banter with the audience. 'I know what you're wondering,' he announced. 'How long is he going to be on? If you're a good audience it will be two hours... otherwise it'll be three!' He had a lot of fun with elderly ladies in the audience, complete with jibes about their cheap dresses ('All clothes and no money') and their questionable taste in food. 'I bet McDonald's is empty tonight,' he joked to roars of laughter. 'And the Little Chef.'

The men were ridiculed more publicly, four of them being hauled onstage to make fools of themselves with top hats and canes while Bruce shuffled his way through a dance routine before demonstrating a sprightly hop on to his piano. A few songs, an impressive tap-dancing routine and some comic impressions later and Bruce was ready for his ovation. 'You've been my kind of audience,' he said with a grin. 'No taste.' He performed all week, culminating in a re-creation of his old *Sunday Night at the London Palladium* TV show with all the old favourites, such as 'Beat the Clock'.

In 1999, Bruce had the clever idea of reviving *The Price Is Right*. This had been a huge hit in the 1980s with its original host Leslie Crowther when it ran for an hour. The second half of the show was simply a repeat of the first half, so Bruce suggested just cutting it in half. It was quickly re-launched as *Bruce's Price Is Right* and ran between 1995 and 2001. Once again, it faced accusations of sexism and changes had to be made to make sure it was politically correct. Three beauties were brought in to act as hostesses, including a blonde model called Emma Noble who went on to marry former Tory Prime Minister John Major's son James. In times that Bruce described as 'PC-obsessed' there was also a male hunk showing the prizes.

The beauty of *Play Your Cards Right* and *Bruce's Price Is Right* was that they could both be filmed so quickly. It left Bruce free most of the year to relax in Puerto Rico with Winnie. When both shows were briefly on at the same time, he would record them on the same day. 'Naturally, people who see me on TV all the time think I am still working every hour that God has given me but I had more time off than ever,' Bruce explained. 'It really suited me.'

Bruce's career was on a high. And life at home with Winnie was perfect too, apart from one area. Bruce had five lovely daughters. What he had always wanted was a little boy. Winnie was about to answer his prayers.

CHAPTER 15

THE REGENERATION GAME

Bruce and Wilnelia had been married for three years when she sat him down to tell him some momentous news. 'Darling, I'm pregnant,' she told her delighted husband. 'And I am convinced that I am going to have a boy.' Bruce longed to have a son but deep down he really didn't care what the sex was, just as long as the new arrival was healthy. 'I just think it is wonderful news, darling,' he told her. 'Wonderful.'

At the four-month scan, Winnie could not bear to find out the sex of the baby. She figured, quite wrongly, that Bruce would be disappointed if he was told he was having a sixth girl. However, a slip of the tongue by the woman who was operating the scanner meant she did find out. When she pointed at an image of the baby wriggling in Winnie's womb, she said delightedly, 'Oh, look, she's turning around.' So that was it then – Bruce was having another girl. Bruce cheered himself up with the thought that, if she looked anything like her mother, she would be an absolute stunner.

Just a month before the birth, Winnie went for another scan. She told the technician how this would be her husband's sixth daughter. But that was not what the scan was showing. 'You'll be a very happy woman if I tell you what the sex of your baby really is,' Winnie was told. It was a boy after all!

Adhering to the protocols of the day, Bruce had missed the births of all his previous five children. He had sat outside the labour ward anxiously waiting for news while his two ex-wives had done all the hard work. Times had moved on and Bruce was right by his wife's side this time at London's Portland Hospital. Also there were several of Wilnelia's relatives who, keen to show their love and support, hadn't wanted to miss out on the action either!

Little Jonathan Joseph Enrique Forsyth – JJ to everyone – was born on 10 November 1986. Wilnelia explained how they arrived at the name. 'Long before I was pregnant, Bruce told me if he had a son, he'd want to call him Jonathan after his father and the brother he lost in the Second World War. I knew the name was sacred to him, so there was never any disagreement over it.'

Bruce said, 'The births of all my children are among my happiest memories, but having a little boy was special.'

JJ was the most laid back baby from day one, refusing to cry even when he had his first bath. Winnie felt that this was because he was half-Puerto Rican and was therefore an 'island boy' who would always love water.

Bruce's daughters were thrilled with the new arrival. By this time Bruce was a granddad – his eldest daughter Debbie had two children of her own, Josie and Jeremy. Everyone laughed when the two youngsters were introduced to their new 'uncle' gurgling away in his cot.

Fatherhood the sixth time was different for Bruce. Yes, he loved all his other children but he had had them at a very different time in his life when he was, by his own admission, a little selfish and only really concerned with his career. The Bruce Forsyth who lovingly cradled little JJ was a changed man – far more relaxed and easy going and, most importantly and for the first time, prepared to put the needs of his wife and his baby boy first and his career second.

Bruce explained his whole new attitude to life in his 2001 autobiography. 'There was a time when, if I'd been asked to name the most important things in my life, the word 'work' would have taken the top five places. It had to be that way if I was to stay at the top. After all, it's far too competitive, too cut-throat and too tough a business to go into half-heartedly.

'But when I met Wilnelia, I realised that my life seemed to be all work, I always seemed to be signed up for about 18 months in advance. However, when I started to take some time off, I wasn't bored. I was really enjoying myself. There were so many other things to do.'

He was enjoying spending more time at home too. 'Even before JJ was born, I was spending much more time at home and was now looking forward to even more time there in future. I no longer needed work to turn me on, no longer needed to see my name up in lights to make me feel good. I would still enjoy working but it was no longer everything – my wife and little fellow were more important.'

Bruce admitted that he had only been 'half a dad' to his five older daughters because he had been absent from so much of their childhoods through work. That wasn't going to happen with JJ.

He had also learned to cherish life more – and enjoy the simple pleasures that come with a contented family. He felt that by slowing down in this way and removing a lot of the stress from his day-to-day routine, he might still be around to be a granddad to JJ's kids as well as his daughters. He had seen so many of his show-business contemporaries die at such a young age. Leonard Rossiter had been just 57, Eric Morecambe a year older and dear old Tommy Cooper had only made it to 63. 'I didn't want people standing at my memorial service saying he was a great performer, so sad he was only fifty-eight years old,' Bruce said sadly. 'I don't have any of my real old friends here. That does upset me because I did like them so much for so many different reasons and we used to have such fun. I'm the last of that breed and that's sad.'

By 1995, Bruce had quit the BBC (he had previously returned to re-launch *The Generation Game*) and returned to ITV. The move allowed him to enjoy the perfect work–life balance. He was presenting two shows for ITV – *Play Your Cards Right* and *Bruce's Price Is Right*. Bruce was able to record several episodes of each on a single day. It meant he would be on TV for the bulk of the year – getting the kind of exposure vital to a show-business career – while only working a fraction of that time. The rest of the time could be spent relaxing with JJ and Winnie on the beach in Puerto Rico. By now, the couple had two homes there: a beautiful mansion on the coast at Dorado and a flat in the capital, San Juan.

Bruce celebrated his 70th birthday in 1998 with a whole series of parties and events including the previously mentioned five-day run of his one-man show at the Palladium to mark 40 years since his first appearance on *Sunday Night at the London Palladium*. Bruce was exhausted at the end of it and went off to Spain on holiday with his family. It was there that Winnie gave him some very unexpected news – she was pregnant with their second child. Bruce was entering his eighth decade and his wife was 40 the following year. This was going to be one major upheaval. The couple had longed for a brother or sister for the then 11-year-old JJ. They had resigned themselves to it never happening after years of trying. Now this news seemed like a 'miracle' to them.

'I was surprised and a little shocked when Winnie told me she was pregnant,' Bruce said. 'It took a couple of days to sink in. I was trying to think what it would be like going through fatherhood again after all those years. But I knew it was what Winnie really wanted – she had always wanted a little girl after JJ and I was so excited for her.'

In a series of interviews with the press, Wilnelia told of how thrilled but surprised she was. 'We had been trying for so long and nothing happened. I just forgot about it and got on with life. I hadn't been taking precautions for some time – but even so the pregnancy came as a big shock. It had been a long time since I was pregnant – I had forgotten what it was like. I can't tell you how happy I was. The news came as an enormous shock to both of us – I was so overwhelmed, I just couldn't believe it was happening. In the beginning Bruce was thinking, "Oh no, here we are starting all over again," but he knew how much I wanted it and how thrilled I was. I went to see my specialist. He explained that these things often happen when you least expect it because you've actually stopped thinking about it all the time and you're relaxed. I had a blood test and everything seemed OK. Bruce and I were so excited. It seemed that it was all just meant to be. The baby would have been born in the year Bruce celebrated his seventieth birthday.'

Sadly things started to go wrong weeks into the pregnancy. Winnie started having pains in her stomach, so was sent off for more blood tests, but nothing showed up. She wasn't concerned at first. 'I'd never been sick while pregnant with JJ so I thought it was just nausea. We were about to go to the Seychelles, where I was going to be involved in the Miss World contest and Bruce put his foot down, saying, "No way are you going." Then the pains got worse and I found it hard to digest food. My doctor was worried. I went to the Portland Hospital for a scan. Though the tests showed I was pregnant, they couldn't see the baby. Clearly it was an ectopic pregnancy.'

Wilnelia was rushed back to the Portland for an emergency operation. 'My right fallopian tube had to be removed. I was in hospital for five days and it was the saddest experience of my life. I had really wanted it so much and to me it was a huge loss.'

Bruce stayed by her side. 'I couldn't have got through it without him,' she said. 'The physical pain was awful but much harder to deal with was the emotional aftermath. We didn't even know what sex our child was. I have learned since that a great many women have undergone this operation so it has helped to talk to them. Though at the time no one except close friends and family knew what we'd been through. I was so lucky to have Bruce to support me. A great many men wouldn't understand what a woman goes through at a time like this but Bruce was wonderful. He was as heartbroken as me. He knows how women tick and he feels comfortable with them. It helps that he has five beautiful daughters.'

Bruce stayed with her at the hospital and Wilnelia's mother came from Puerto Rico to look after JJ. 'Mummy was marvellous,' she recalled. 'I really am very lucky to have such support. Once I got home I had to recuperate for a month and was desperately down but Bruce was there the whole time giving constant support. He was so caring, thoughtful and understanding.

'We didn't want to tell JJ too much because we didn't want to worry him,' she said. 'I look at him and feel so grateful that we have a healthy and happy son – so many don't get to have a child. I am always grateful that I had that chance.'

The family went to Puerto Rico on holiday to get over the grief. 'I was fine until New Year's Eve, then I admit I did cry,' recalled Wilnelia sadly. 'How can I ever forget my baby? I have a scar to remind me all the time. On New Year you reflect on what has gone by in the previous year. And it was part of my life that I will never ever forget. But the operation did not mean that I am unable to become pregnant again. We've put it on the backburner for now. But someday, maybe. In the meantime I'm just so happy to have Bruce and JJ.'

Sadly, that second child never came for Wilnelia and Bruce.

Bruce had been accused by his second wife Anthea of not being there for her when she suffered several miscarriages before they started a family. Bruce wasn't going to make that mistake again after Winnie's miscarriage. 'I was desperately upset for her,' he explained. 'It was such a tragic thing to happen. It was awful to see someone you love going through something so painful and difficult. Thank heavens I was able to give her the help and support she needed.'

* * *

Bruce stayed young with a healthy diet and exercise regime involving early morning stretches, which he followed for years. He never felt tempted to go under the knife to stay young. His famous hairpiece was the one concession he made to halt the ageing process. He had several different types over the years with his fringe going up and down more times than an elevator. It's a subject he barely ever talked about publicly and there is no mention of it in his autobiography. It's the same with Terry Wogan. We all know he also had a hairpiece but, like Bruce, he never mentioned it. And Bruce, of course, was never pictured without his toupée.

In all the interviews Bruce did over more than 50 years in show business, only one interviewer was brave enough bring up the toupée in print. That was *Tatler* – the *nom de plume* of a waspish celebrity writer who used to interview celebrities over lunch for the *Sunday Express* magazine and met Brucie way back in 1989. 'Why do you wear a toupée?' Bruce was asked. His eyes swivelled perilously and he drummed his fingers on the table. 'Boring!' he exclaimed. 'Talk about comedians not having new jokes. How about old questions? Do people really want to know about that? I do it for me but it doesn't mean anything. It's old hat.'

In fact, Bruce had been having help with his hair from as far back as the 1960s. A Doctor Lebon told the *News of the*

World how he had given Bruce a hair transplant after he came to him for help. 'He came to me around 1965 with a badly receding hairline and I knew what was needed,' he recalled. 'With this procedure you take tiny plugs of hairy scalp and put them on the parts that don't have any hair. It's intricate and Bruce made me realise just how painful. Following the first session, which cost £75, he telephoned me to say he wouldn't be coming back because it hurt too much. Bruce will never know how much I appreciated him having the guts to tell the truth. Really, he was the perfect patient. Most never complain even if they're hurting a little and a surgeon needs to know. So thanks to Bruce, the pain was reduced considerably and word got round that it was a successful op with the minimum of discomfort. That particular line of business boomed.'

As for other stimulants to keep the magic alive in his marriage, Bruce was proud to say that he had never needed Viagra. 'What you can't take away from an older man is experience,' he said, smiling. 'And an older man knows it's not just about making love but how to treat a woman. There's a wonderful song by Richard Harris called "How To Handle A Woman". Young men should take some tips from that.'

Bruce described Winnie as the 'sexiest woman alive'. 'She is still so beautiful. I look at her and think, "My God, how did you get hooked up with someone like me."'

Winnie giggled when asked about Viagra and confirmed her hubby was as sizzling in the bedroom as he was on the dance floor. 'That is true,' she said with a smile. 'I have to tell you. Lucky me, hey?'

She said their marriage had endured when so many showbiz couples split because he made her laugh. 'He's funny but not in a jokey way,' she explained. 'He doesn't tell me jokes because he doesn't know any.'

Wilnelia was thrilled that they had proved the doubters wrong. She described Bruce as her 'mentor, teacher, lover, my life'. They boasted that they celebrated their wedding anniversary monthly – with a special meal on the 15th of every month.

'People didn't give us a year,' she said. 'Mainly because of the age difference but also because they didn't really know me. They misjudged me. But I never had any doubts that it could work. Age is just a number. Besides, you can't worry about what might happen because bad things can happen to anyone, at any age.'

She admitted she had worked hard at their marriage, even taking up Bruce's favourite game so she did not become a golf widow like Anthea. 'When I met Bruce, I thought he was a professional golfer because he loves it so much,' she said. 'Now it's something we play as a family. I learned because it's something we can do together. If he loved fishing, I'd be doing that! I'm good enough at golf that I can play it with him when we're on holiday.

'Wherever we are, we have to be near a golf course, even on our honeymoon! Before I met Bruce I didn't know there were so many golf courses in the world.'

She said that Bruce loved the anonymity he enjoyed when they were in Puerto Rico. 'Coming from a small island, we celebrate anyone who's had international success, like Ricky Martin or Jennifer Lopez, so I'm still a big celebrity there,' she explained. 'Bruce loves the attention being on me because he just likes to be a beach bum when he's in Puerto Rico. But because he has one of those faces everyone recognises, people now say, "Oh, you're Wilnelia's husband!"'

Even in London, where he had always been the more famous one, Wilnelia noticed a huge increase in Brucie's public profile in recent years. 'He gets all the attention!' she joked. 'Sometimes I have to look at myself twice before I leave the house because no one looks at me. I find myself thinking, "Do I look OK?"'

Despite all the attention, she never worried about him straying. 'I don't get jealous,' she insisted. 'And he's not the jealous type either; that's what I liked about him from the beginning. You have to trust the person you're with.'

She explained how JJ had inherited his dad's love of entertaining – and his mother's looks. He could have been in trouble if it had been the other way round! 'Many people say JJ looks more like me and he's four inches taller than his dad, at six feet and three inches. But he's very English and like Bruce in every other way.' JJ had been working as a musician since leaving posh Charterhouse School in Surrey.

JJ also appears to have inherited his father's eye for beauty queens. After Bruce's 80th birthday celebrations in 2008, JJ left London's Dorchester Hotel with the reigning Miss Puerto Rico – Jennifer Guevara Campos. Wilnelia had, of course, won the same title 33 years earlier before going on to take the Miss World crown.

JJ wasn't the only member of the family bitten by the entertainment bug, Wilnelia said. 'Bruce's daughter Julie sings in a country band with her husband Dominic – they're very famous in Holland – and his grandson, Nicky, has an amazing voice too. Show business is in their blood. JJ has his own band

and plays the bass guitar. I think he'll be very successful one day because he puts his heart into what he does.

'He'll make the most amazing husband one day too! I'm excited about getting some grandchildren, especially a girl.'

Reflecting on what had been the key to her successful marriage, Wilnelia's conclusion was that it worked naturally, so why dwell too much on the reasons. 'Time has gone so quickly. If we didn't have such a strapping young son, I'd have thought we got married yesterday.

'We renewed our vows in Las Vegas. Sometimes relationships don't work even if you're the same age. No one knows what's inside that relationship and personally, I couldn't be luckier.'

She and Bruce agreed an extraordinary pact when they were first together – that if the love ever went from the marriage or another person came along on either side, they would part as friends. 'We have this thing that at the moment the relationship has to end, it is better to talk and part,' she explained. 'I don't want me to be with him if the love is not there. If somebody can make him [happier], he should go. We always talk about this, that if somebody else came into our lives, we would part as friends. But that has never happened over thirty years.'

Despite two messy marriage break-ups, there was never any danger of Bruce cheating. He felt lucky that he still had a wife he desired so much. He and Wilnelia fell in love over their mutual love of dancing – and they still smouldered on the dance floor even then. 'All dancing is very sexy, especially ballroom, because you get so close to your partner,' he said. 'There's a dance my wife and I do called the Merengue, where you get really close to your partner and just wiggle your hips. It's very simple but very sexy.'

JJ kept him young too – and was a crucial showbiz sounding board. 'I'm quite scared of him – he towers over me,' said his proud dad. 'I used to worry that having a son when I was in my sixties would mean I wouldn't be the kind of dad who could romp with him and chuck him over my shoulder. But I've always been here for him. And he's my yardstick. If I can come out with something that makes him laugh, I know I've got it right.'

He admitted he could have been more help to his wife when JJ was young. 'I'm not very good with young children and I'm certainly no good at changing nappies,' he revealed.

Talking about being an older dad, he said, 'I would love to be twenty years younger so that I can enjoy seeing what happens to him and to my younger daughters in later years. It saddens me that I might not be able to help JJ at a time when he might need me a lot. But if I can give him a good start in life, which so many children don't have, and if he knows he comes from a loving couple, that can influence him for the rest of his life.

'I was very lucky to have a loving mother and father who did everything they could to get me into this business. Without their help and encouragement I couldn't have made it. I just want him to know how much love we have for him. Because he was born into an affluent background, I do try not to spoil him but it is hard.'

Bruce said the marriage worked because he was completely different at home to how he was at work. 'I leave him behind when I come home,' he said, referring to the more uptight

Bruce who appears on stage. 'No wife could live with that maniac going at 120mph for a day, let alone a lifetime. I wouldn't have him as a lodger.'

He said they kept the romance alive by going on date nights and relaxing for at least six months of the year. 'We're pretty much inseparable,' he said. 'We make an effort to organise weekends away to keep the romance alive. We have a wonderful time at places like Lake Como in Italy. The spark is still there, absolutely.'

In many ways as people he and Wilnelia were opposites and that's what made them gel. 'We have our disagreements but not often,' said Bruce. 'I'm organised and meticulous. Winnie's not. She and JJ will leave the house lit up like a Christmas tree. I turn the lights out. Years of show-business discipline have made me pernickety.'

And he loved the fact that she was so independent, unlike his first two wives. He said she could have easily pursued a career as an interior designer if she had not devoted so much of life to looking after JJ and him. 'She paints, sculpts, designs swimwear and runs a foundation in Puerto Rico,' he said. 'She has recently completed a degree in humanities. Winnie's a cordon-bleu cook. She says she is proud of me but it's the other way round. I think she's brilliant.'

Bruce was proud of his huge family – and the crucial role Winnie played in making them all stay in touch. 'We're our own soap opera,' explained Bruce. 'It's Winnie who keeps us all together.'

His favourite day of the year was Father's Day, when his five daughters would come over to visit. 'I love it because I can sit around all day being waited on by my lovely girls and they spoil me rotten,' Bruce said. It's much better than Christmas because it's my day. It's probably unusual to have three different families that are so united. But there are no funny feelings between us. My daughters all love my wife. They come over to see her as much as they do me and the love they bring into this house is unbelievable. You can feel it all around you.'

So we've heard how Bruce viewed his daughters but what was he like as a father to them? His second eldest daughter Julie, now in her fifties and a successful songwriter and singer, gave a valuable insight into what it was like growing up with Bruce in the 'Relative Values' feature in the *Sunday Times* magazine in 2000.

She told how Bruce 'wasn't at home very much' when she was a girl after he had broken away from the double act with her mum Penny Calvert, Bruce's first wife, to go solo.

'I suppose I am in awe of him,' Julie said. 'Before he comes on stage, my stomach churns and I'm so nervous for him. Then he walks on and it's wonderful.

'To me, he's a legend. *The Generation Game* was such a lovely interaction between the man in the street and the performer, and Dad respects the man in the street. OK, he was rude to them but there was so much fun going on as well, nobody minded.'

She was never embarrassed by him, though she understood he wasn't everybody's cup of tea. 'The thing I didn't like was the Roller – I used to get him to park it round the corner from school. There were kids who would try to make me angry but I would get hurt more than anything. I think if you're the son or daughter of a famous person, you grow up very quickly and you have this wall around you that protects you.

'We had a lot of love at home. Mum gave up a lot and I think it was hard because she was a very gifted entertainer. She was terrific on stage and she loved it but they couldn't both work and have us. In this business, if people are apart, the marriage isn't going to work. Mum was at home, writing little plays for us, doing arty things. Dad was out building his career.'

Julie was aware of his weakness for beautiful women. 'It's no secret that Dad liked women. When you're touring, you're surrounded by beautiful women and the temptation to have fun is very great. When Anthea came along, Mummy said, "Look, I think there's going to be something in the press." It wasn't a shock to us because Daddy had left and we knew he was with Anthea.

'Of course I missed him but he'd phone us. Looking back, Mum was probably still in love with him. It's hard to be the wife of someone in the entertainment business. Dad would have this amazing day where so much was happening and, when he did come home, it would be to this person who had been doing the washing and dealing with kids. It must have been hard for him to be enthusiastic about that.'

Talking about her own life in entertainment, Julie said, 'My husband Dominic and I are a double act. I never thought about doing anything else. My sisters can take the business or leave it. You have to be naïve and blinded by belief to really get there and I think Dad and I are probably both those things. We both have a kind of inner drive – you can be tired, ill, feeling at death's door but you walk out on that stage and you're somebody else.'

She revealed that her dad had always been careful with money. 'I think anyone who's come from a poor background is controlled. I really wish my mother had had an easier time but I don't blame Daddy and I don't begrudge him his happiness.'

Bruce said he was relieved that, despite all the turmoil in his private life, all his girls still got on. 'I consider myself terrible lucky because the situation could have been horrible. My first three girls could resent Anthea's two girls because they took me away from them; they could all hate my boy because they might think that he's getting privileges they weren't allowed. And I've finally slowed down enough to actually be a father and spend some time with him, which they undoubtedly missed out on.'

Bruce said he was amazed that they all still wanted to be around him. 'I hope it's because I may have walked out on marriages but I never did walk out on them. And the lovely thing is that they're there for me as well.

'I couldn't say I love one more than the other because they're all so lovely. And the marvellous thing is that, as they've grown up, we've grown closer. The trouble is that I don't have any strong memories of them as babies because I wasn't there very much.'

He did recall one incident. 'I do remember coming home one time to find that Julie's long hair had been cut short. She must have been about three and she wanted long hair so badly that she'd tied a ribbon to the back of her head just so she could feel something flowing down her back. I issued an ultimatum. I said, "If this child's hair is ever cut again without consulting me, there'll be big, big trouble." Julie was so grateful, bless her heart. I've always loved long hair on a woman.

'Julie is the only one in the family who has inherited my musical ear. She's a great songwriter. She has combined motherhood with looking fantastic on stage every night. You've got to admire her.'

In his day, Bruce said, you were in a different town every week and marriage and family had to take second place. 'I do regret it,' he said. 'But I've been able to do far more for my kids financially than if I had spent my life playing clubs and pubs. I'm a pretty stable guy: I don't drink much, I don't gamble and I've been able to offer them stability too. If I wasn't there for Julie when she was younger, I am now. I'd far rather it was this way round and I think she agrees.'

So it all ended happily for Bruce. The key to that contentment – and the stable and loving relationships he had with his daughters – was his wife Wilnelia.

'She is the most wonderful woman: clever, inspirational and extremely hard working,' he said. 'The reason it's lasted longer with Winnie than my previous marriages is simple – I'm with the right woman.'

Bruce was happy at home for the last 30 years of his career. But his show-business career had lots more ups and downs. The most spectacular bust-up came with ITV.

CHAPTER 16

LIED TO AND STRIPPED OF HIS DIGNITY

By 1999 Bruce was enjoying the life of Reilly. He had not one but two hit shows running on ITV at the same time: *Bruce's Price Is Right* and *Play Your Cards Right*. Both were relatively straightforward to make. He could record three or four episodes a day and not feel exhausted in the same way as he had when he was presenting and co-producing *The Generation Game* a few years earlier. It meant he was only working 17 weeks a year, yet appearing on TV for more than 30 as both series played out. And he was being paid an absolute fortune: £1 million a year – the best money of his career. To put that into perspective, he was on less than half that sum working on *Strictly*, more than 13 years later.

This cushy new schedule allowed Bruce to enjoy a blissful life of semi-retirement with Wilnelia and JJ, who was by now at boarding school but home most weekends. Bruce could also escape the British winters by jetting to Puerto Rico where he and Wilnelia were spending as much as six months of the year at the home they had built next to a golf course. All good things come to an end though. And when they did for Bruce, he ended up throwing the biggest tantrum of his career.

It is surprising that Bruce's relationship with ITV should have ended so messily because he really seemed to have reached a new serenity during this period of his career. He was so relaxed and contented with his lot that, for the first time – the only time really – he was seriously talking about retirement. He was 70. He had been working tirelessly for more than 50 years. 'It depends on what happens but my plan is to give it another two or three years and then I'll make a clean break,' he said. 'I won't return to guest spots. It's sad when performers make comebacks. I hated to see Fred Astaire, who I idolised all my life, doing "bit" parts and looking so old and past it. I wanted to remember him as he was. I love being on stage and enjoy the applause and laughter but, fortunately, I'm not one of those who need it to make life worthwhile.'

It was perfectly possible to take what Bruce was saying here with a large pinch of salt. We all now know how much longer he carried on working. And he was very dismissive of any talk of retirement. But it is worth remembering that this was the first time in his career that Bruce had properly slowed down. He had been terrified that he would become bored and restless but he had loved being relieved of the pressure of holding together a big show like *The Generation Game*. He really did have things easy now he was back on ITV. With game shows, the format was everything. Bruce just filled in the gaps, in his own inimitable fashion.

Bruce was very proud of the success – and the wealth – he enjoyed. 'I always like it when they say, "He's one of the top earners,"' he explained. 'I've never had the luxury of a fixed-format show before – *The Generation Game* was much more difficult because there are five games every time and you're always trying to find a different way of doing them.'

Bruce could do both ITV shows almost effortlessly. 'I'm lucky enough to get away with being semi-rude because the contestants accept it as a bit of fun,' he said. 'At the end, they'd put their head in a gas oven if I asked. You're on a knife-edge though and it's hit and miss. Those who look as if they're going to be good sometimes freeze. I love something to go wrong because I can play off it. The worse thing for me is when it goes smoothly.'

Bruce's Price Is Right was an unashamed celebration of greed. It came in for a fair bit of flak at the time and was seen as a vulgar symbol of the 'loadsamoney' consumerism that marked the final years of Thatcherism. Bruce was happy to defend the show. Most of the contestants were not rich, he pointed out, and badly needed the money. 'Greed has always come into it but the contestants are usually lovely people,' he said. 'There wasn't a greedy one in the whole of the first series. Some miss a showcase of £25,000 and accept it graciously. You don't see anyone getting into a temper about it. I'm honestly disappointed when they lose and elated when they win. The British like to see someone win, even if it's not them. I won't say we're always good losers. But accepting defeat graciously is a national trait.'

What Bruce was probably slow to pick up on was how fast TV was changing towards the end of the 1990s. He was still consistently delivering big ratings and audience shares in excess of 40 per cent. But the viewers who enjoyed his shows – mostly older and with lower incomes – weren't those coveted by advertisers. Game shows were seen as very old hat. To make matters worse, ITV had a thrusting new boss in David Liddiment – who had made his name working on *Coronation Street* in Manchester, before becoming a successful head of entertainment at the BBC. Now he was back at ITV and he was keen to freshen things up. Central to that strategy was to air the farming soap *Emmerdale* five times a week at 7pm – the same slot occupied by *Play Your Cards Right*. Liddiment didn't want to sack Bruce – he knew he was dealing with a legend who still had a huge fan base. Bruce was still part of his plans; he just wasn't a very big part of those plans. Bruce, prone to conspiracy theories at the best of times, sensed that he was falling out of favour. And he was not the type to accept being moved from centre stage without kicking up a fuss.

The first signs that all was not well came in the early summer of 1999 when ITV cancelled some filming dates for *Play Your Cards Right* – the show Liddiment was most keen to get rid of. There had been talks about a new series almost a year earlier but these had stalled and Bruce sensed that ITV had lost faith in the show, despite ratings holding up well. The press sensed that these cancellations meant the show was doomed, even though no announcement had been made by ITV. Nevertheless, the headlines could not have been more brutal: BRUCIE AXED! HE'S TOO OLD SAYS ITV. What hurt Bruce was that he had not been told directly by ITV but found out instead through the newspapers. ITV initially denied the reports but no one really believed the company.

Bruce had a meeting scheduled with Liddiment the day after these hugely damaging headlines appeared. Inevitably, there were fireworks but Bruce emerged from it all rather well. Although it was clear that *Play Your Cards Right* was doomed, Liddiment was keen to stick with *Bruce's Price Is Right* and he also offered Bruce the chance to front six one-hour variety specials. For a period, there was an uneasy peace between Bruce and ITV. The old stager was still wary of his new boss and admitted he felt 'frustrated and hurt' that a much-loved format such as *Play Your Card Rights*, which had served ITV so well over two decades, could be so casually discarded.

This seething resentment grew as he filmed the new variety shows that Liddiment had promised. They didn't pan out in the way Bruce had hoped: it was difficult to get the calibre of star he wanted at such short notice but even more upsetting was how the new shows were scheduled. Bruce wanted the shows to largely be a remake of his 1960s hit, *Sunday Night at the London Palladium*. There was one problem with this: the new show was due to go out on Friday nights and would be called *Tonight at the London Palladium*. It just didn't quite have the same ring to it, and it all seemed a bit of a damp squib to an angry and dejected Bruce.

There was more disappointment for him over the scheduling of his other game show, *Bruce's Price Is Right*. This didn't appear to be valued by Liddiment either. In the previous year, only 11 of the 17 shows Bruce had recorded had been screened. Bruce wrote to Liddiment to ask why six of the shows had been axed. He was furious at the arrogance of the reply. Liddiment did apologise but he explained that the missing shows 'fell through the crack'. The phrase enraged Bruce: it was as though his whole career at ITV was falling through that same crack.

ITV now had 23 further episodes of *Price Is Right* to screen – a new 17-part series and the 6 episodes that had been discarded in the crack. To cram them all in, the new series started in August, when ratings are at their worst because of the holidays. Bruce was furious. 'It was the first time in my long career that a series of mine had ever been shown in the summer month,' he sniped. The final indignity came when *Bruce's Price Is Right* was rescheduled out of primetime after the first few shows to 5.20pm on Saturday nights – what Bruce described as a 'death slot' when viewers were busy either shopping or returning from football and certainly weren't watching television. The ratings reflected the change, dropping quickly from eight million to three million.

This was the final straw for Bruce. He called a press conference for Fleet Street's finest and, with a spectacular fanfare, announced, 'I will axe myself from ITV.' He vented all the anger that had been building up for months against Liddiment and the network. Even by Bruce's standards – and at this stage of his career he was a diva to rival Sir Elton John – this was an unprecedented rant. He declared emphatically that he would not work for ITV again if Liddiment was still in charge. 'He has lied to me, stripped me of my dignity and humiliated me,' he stormed. 'Even *Who Wants to be a Millionaire* (then the big game show of day) would have no chance at that time. In all the forty years I have been in the business, I have never been treated so badly.'

Bruce had come prepared. He had devised cards for the waiting journalists to show that he was no has-been and was still delivering good audiences for ITV. The cards explained how *Bruce's Price Is Right* was still getting the all-important 40 per cent share. Indeed he was still contracted to film another series of *Price Is Right* in the coming months. But that didn't stop him from again attacking Liddiment. 'I would much rather someone had the guts to say to me, "It's time to call it a day." I've always said that I would retire when I no longer get enjoyment from walking on to the studio floor, or the stage, or when the ratings go. That hasn't happened, so I'm simply axing myself from ITV and this man. What he's done to me, I cannot forgive him for,' he said furiously, clearly referring to his new boss.

Obviously hurt, he continued, 'When you feel as though you can still perform and you have what it takes to get out there and do what you've done all your life, and all of a sudden the door's shut, what do you do? How do you face that? It is a terrible feeling.

'I'd always said to my agent, "If ever you know that the door is closing, let me know and I'll retire gracefully." But people were coming up to me in the street, saying, "We haven't seen you in such a long while. Aren't you doing any more television?"'

Bruce was realistic enough to acknowledge that you always get highs and lows in show business. 'I have always been very resilient,' he said. 'When you're a variety performer, you go from town to town. You'd have Monday-night audiences that were so bad, you'd go out there and some guy would be reading the newspaper. So rejection is part of being a variety performer. It brings out the feeling that next week will be better. That becomes ingrained in you.'

To declare war on ITV so publicly had been enormously stressful, even for an old trouper like Bruce, but also wonderfully cathartic. The press took Bruce's side and gave ITV, and David Liddiment in particular, a big kicking. 'To be completely honest,' Bruce said, 'like having a troublesome tooth extracted, I felt much better afterwards, relieved that I had got all this off my chest – and had little or no concern for the consequent hurt and discomfort I had caused David. I honestly didn't care how many bridges I had burned.'

Liddiment could not have been more diplomatic in the face of such a sustained attack. Far from rising to the bait, he cleverly soothed Bruce's battered ego. He quickly put out a statement saying, 'Bruce Forsyth is probably the greatest all-round entertainer British television has ever known and ITV is immensely proud of its long and successful relationship with him. It has been a delight for me to work with him over the past three years and I am very sorry he feels the way he does.'

Bruce's pals rallied to his defence. His mate, the veteran comedian Barry Cryer, wrote in the *Daily Mail*, 'Bruce is not one to be broken on any wheel. He's no angel. He can be difficult to work with – brilliant people often are. He's a perfectionist and can spot somebody not doing their job a mile off. But the atmosphere he creates is phenomenal. Bruce was always the virtuoso of the catchphrase. May I present him with a new one from the unlikely lips of Arnold Schwarzenegger in *The Terminator* – "I'll be back." And he will.'

Bruce and Liddiment did patch things up to a certain extent but they had both been badly wounded by the row. By 2001,

Bruce parted company with ITV when the final series of *Price Is Right* finished. A year later, Liddiment was gone too.

But this time, there were no new shows to fill the void. The BBC did not come calling for its old King of Saturday Nights. There was no way back with ITV even with Liddiment gone – Bruce's face simply didn't fit a network targeting the 18 to 30-year-olds beloved of advertisers. The phone simply stopped ringing. And Bruce faced up to the grim prospect that he might have to retire whether he liked it or not. For the first time in his career, there seemed no obvious route back to the Big Time.

Bruce was hit by other setbacks at this time too. In 2002, while he was away in Scotland watching the British Open golf tournament, armed robbers broke into his mansion in Wentworth and left his wife Wilnelia fearing for her life. The gang burst into her bedroom at midnight shortly after she had undressed, yelling, 'Where is the safe?' Then they held a knife to her throat as they ripped off her jewellery.

'I was lying on the bed and suddenly saw a face at the bedroom door and thought it was my son who had come to see me,' Wilnelia recalled. 'But then this figure suddenly burst in and screamed, "Put the telephone down." I said, "Please don't hurt me. Don't hurt me, don't hurt my baby."'

Believing they were going to kill her, she offered them everything. 'I gave them my engagement ring and my watch and they kept asking, "Where is the safe?" I said we didn't have a safe but I offered them my handbag and said there was money in it. I grabbed the handbag and gave it to them just to get them out of the room. I offered to give them my wedding ring but it was difficult to remove. They just ripped it off anyway. It all lasted about fifteen minutes but it seemed longer.'

At the time Wilnelia had no idea that the robbers had already seized her then 15-year-old son JJ, who had been playing on his computer downstairs, and brutally attacked the family's housekeeper, tiny Cora Gumerang.

'After the robbers left I went downstairs and found my son,' Wilnelia continued. 'There was no answer from Cora's room so I went into the kitchen and dialled 999. I armed myself with a golf club and then went upstairs and knocked on Cora's bedroom door. But she was so frightened she had climbed on to the roof of the house to escape the robbers.'

Terrified Cora, then 48, had already been savagely beaten by the thugs, who broke her jaw in two places when she tried to hide a mobile phone behind her back as they tied her up. She needed specialist surgery for her injuries. Dramatic pictures of Bruce comforting a black and blue Cora were published in the press several days later, capturing the full horror of the raid.

'It amazes me how anybody could inflict such horrific injuries on such a tiny person,' Bruce said. 'They behaved like animals. Words can't describe what I think of them. I don't like to swear but if I try to use a word to describe them, I'll end up swearing. Cora's jaw was fractured twice during the attack. How could anyone treat someone so brutally? She is like one of our family and we love her very much. I am so upset something like this could happen to such a dear person.'

Bruce promised to turn his home into a fortress to ensure it would never happen again. Sadly, the raiders were never caught.

All in all, it had been a miserable start to the new decade for

Bruce. Having well and truly burnt his bridges with both of his main employers, ITV and the BBC, his career appeared to be over. And then there was the trauma of that awful raid. But there was to be one final, glorious hurrah for our favourite showman. And the spark for this unexpected revival would come from a most unlikely source… a TV show that was the antithesis of everything Bruce stood for.

CHAPTER 17

HAVE I GOT BRUCE FOR YOU

It really did seem to be the beginning of the end for Brucie. By the early noughties, his career had hit a brick wall. He had spectacularly walked out on ITV, branded the boss a liar and put his career there well and truly in the 'graveyard' – the same slot that his show *Bruce's Price Is Right* had been shifted to when it was moved to Saturday afternoons where it haemorrhaged viewers. For the first time in more than 50 years, the phone wasn't ringing. It really did seem that Bruce was heading from our TV screens to spend more time with his golf clubs. Yet Bruce himself wasn't ready to call it a day. And he turned things around by 'hustling' for work for the first time in his life – and making the most extraordinary comeback of his career.

No one knew more about the ups and downs of show business than Brucie. And this, for him, was the longest low that he had ever endured. He would admit later that he had been rash in walking out of ITV with such petulance. If you want to carry on working in TV – which Bruce very much did – it is not a good idea to attack the chief of ITV and one of the most powerful men in television with such vehemence. Bruce had worked for ITV for more than 30 years. It was inconceivable – certainly in the short-term – that he could ever go back there. In fact, his only slots on ITV during these bleak years were during the adverts. Bruce had been the face of the Courts furnishing firm for several years, starring in ads that may have been as cheesy as a warehouse full of Edam but that did very good business. Sales leaped by a third when Bruce first signed up with the firm in 1996. And the work was so lucrative for Bruce that he could earn a year's money in just a couple of days. Even so, it wasn't where he wanted to be. He had always been the star of the show – not the ads during the breaks.

It had got to the stage where it is no exaggeration to say that Bruce's wife Wilnelia was bigger than him. With no work commitments in Britain, he was spending as much as six months of the year in Puerto Rico with Winnie. Obviously over there she is the star – her Miss World success has never been forgotten. Bruce, to the Puerto Ricans, is Mr World, her other half.

So how was the great man going to turn it around? It was Winnie who came up with idea. She and Bruce were at home watching *Have I Got News For You* – the BBC's leading satirical show. For years it had been presented by Angus Deayton but he had been sacked by the BBC after being caught snorting cocaine with a prostitute. After that, a series of guest presenters had been used, with varying degrees of success. Some had died horribly (the former Labour leader Neil Kinnock) while others have been naturals and have gone on to present the show many times (Alexander Armstrong, Jeremy Clarkson).

Winnie turned to Bruce and said, 'You know, you could do that.'

'I was thinking the same thing, darling,' Bruce replied.

But how was he going to get the booking? He was going to have to hustle for it. The opportunity to hustle came just a few weeks later when he was at a charity jazz night and bumped into one of the show's team captains, Paul Merton. 'He didn't realise I could play the piano,' explained Bruce. 'He's into jazz and we got talking. There was some mutual admiration there. I asked him what he thought about me hosting the show.' Paul replied, "Well, you've obviously got comic timing." I said, "Oh, thanks very much, thanks for noticing." He said, "I'll put your name forward but they're probably all booked." And that was it, bang.'

A few days later, Hat Trick Productions, which makes the show, rang and said they thought it was a wonderful idea. 'It was amazing the way it happened,' Bruce said. 'That was the first time I've hustled. People have always come to me. But people weren't coming to me any more. That was the first time I tried to get a job.'

Bruce really was entering the lion's den. *Have I Got News For You* – which grew out of the move towards alternative comedy in the 1980s – was a direct antidote to the cosy middle-of-the-road entertainment that he personified. And in Merton and the other team captain, *Private Eye* editor Ian

Hislop, it had two stars that could make or break you. The pair could be merciless if they wanted to. They had humiliated Piers Morgan when he tried to trade comic blows with them. And they had effectively got Deayton the sack after he was exposed in the *News of the World*. Merton and Hislop had spent their career lampooning pillars of the establishment like Brucie. What were they going to make of him when he arrived to take charge of their show?

Bruce didn't really care. He was just thrilled to be back. And with all those years of experience, he had a few tricks up his sleeve to cope with Merton and Hislop. If all failed, surely his charisma would pull him through? That's what he figured.

'I felt reborn,' he told the *Daily Mirror*. 'I can't tell you how rejuvenating it all was. I had always loved the show. My son Jay thought it was a bit odd me agreeing to host it. He looked at me for a while but then said, "Yeah, OK, Dad."'

It was measure of just how far Bruce had fallen that he had not been asked before. His career really was in the doldrums. He had spent too long doing game shows that were well past their best. His name was no longer on anyone's lips. One time, it would have seemed unthinkable to have a British television industry that did not include Bruce Forsyth. Not any more. In truth, many people had sided with Liddiment when Bruce was sacked. It was felt that the old showman had horribly overstepped the mark in flouncing out. Liddiment, despite feeling that Bruce was past his sell-by date, acknowledged that he was 'probably the greatest all-round entertainer British television has ever known'. But did he really have it in him to show the viewers that this was still the case?

Bruce admitted he had missed being in the spotlight for

the first time in his life. 'So many people have come up to me commenting on how they haven't seen me on the TV for a while,' he told the *Daily Mirror*. 'People do notice when you are not and, to be honest, it feels nice that they have noticed. I've had a lot of letters too, asking where I have gone. It was nice to show viewers that I haven't gone anywhere.'

Bruce had spent his time away 'going back to my roots', by taking part in big-band events. But it was clear that the lack of a primetime TV platform had made him more nervous when he did have to take to the stage. 'Oh, yes, I get much more nervous than I ever did when I was in my thirties or forties,' he said. 'Then, there wasn't anything to prove. I went to the Cambridge Union to give a talk and I got really nervous about it. They were all fifty years younger than me. What if they didn't laugh? What if they thought, "Who is this silly old fool coming and wasting an hour of our time?" But they did laugh, which was wonderful. It doesn't half give you a boost to prove that you still have it, that you can still given an audience a good time.'

So Bruce knew that he still had it – but would Merton and Hislop? And perhaps more importantly, how would the show's six million fans take to their new host?

On the night, Bruce – with the help of some of the cleverest scriptwriters in the business – never put a foot wrong. He had everyone – Hislop and Merton included – rooting for him from the moment he bounded on to the set, done up as if it were a game show, and revived one of his best-loved catchphrases to kick things off.

'Welcome to *Have I Got News For You*,' he boomed. 'For you, have I got...' 'News!' the audience cheered.

The other guests that night were the newsreader Natasha Kaplinsky and the comedian Marcus Brigstocke. They were largely bit part players as Brucie, Merton and Hislop dominated proceedings. Hislop's tactic all night was to appear bemused by the whole thing. Merton, meanwhile, enthusiastically joined in. 'I've wanted the show to be like this for years,' he cried at one point. 'I'm having the time of my life here.' So, of course, was Bruce.

The producers had written the show around their host – so all the regular rounds had a Brucie theme. Round two, for instance, was 'Play Your Iraqi Cards Right' in homage to Bruce's 1980s ITV game show. Hislop, unbelievably, had never seen it – so Brigstocke had to explain the rules to him. That round ended with the second gag based on an old catchphrase. Bruce joked that supposedly there were weapons of mass destruction in Iraq. 'Still, it would be nice to see them – to see them nice!'

The cards showed wanted Iraqi war criminals. Just as in the game show, Bruce would shout 'Higher or lower?' as each one was turned over. Hislop – by now warming to things – replied, 'I don't think this programme can get much lower.'

Other Forsyth career highlights were revisited – later on they had to pick the odd one out from a *Generation Game*-style conveyor belt of objects. Each gag worked brilliantly and, at the end of the show, it wasn't just the audience at home who were left thinking, 'There is definitely life in this old dog.'

Bruce admitted later it had been one of the best experiences of his life. 'I walked on and within five minutes they were like a game-show audience,' he said. 'It was beautifully written around me and I had such fun with them.'

Ian Hislop was asked by the *Guardian* if they were laughing with Bruce or at him. 'Oh, with him,' he replied. 'The Iraqi Play Your Cards Right was a new low in terms of bad taste on television and, actually, I'm not sure anyone else would have got away with it. But he knows how to make an audience laugh. And you know what it's like in Britain – at a certain age people just like you. What's the Alan Bennett quote? "If you can boil an egg when you're eighty, you're a national institution." By the end, I thought it was a hoot.'

Paul Merton reckoned it was one of the best shows they had ever done. Unlike Hislop – whose humour is very political – Merton much prefers it when the show is looser and the gags a bit more madcap. 'On *Have I Got News For You*, when they talk about the Home Office, I can't move on fast enough,' he explained. 'I like stories like the goldfish that burns the house down. I was in my element when Bruce was the guest presenter.'

As for Bruce, he never looked back. Jane Lush – then head of entertainment at the BBC – was watching that night. She knew immediately that Bruce could still be huge.

Bruce was aware he'd been taking a gamble in agreeing to the show but it was a gamble which had come off spectacularly. A career that was heading for the graveyard had suddenly been reborn.

'I wouldn't have believed you if you had told me how it became such a game changer for me,' he explained. 'It all came down to *Have I Got News For You*. A lot of people thought I was mad to do it and told me, "You're asking for trouble." But I am so pleased I took the gamble. Who knows where I would have been without it. Probably sat at home watching TV with

Winnie. There is that saying, "Nothing ventured, nothing gained." Throughout my career I have never been afraid to take a risk, never been afraid to push things. I have always hated standing still. So yes, it was a gamble. But it wasn't like I haven't gambled with my career before. It all gets very dull and routine if you don't take a few risks.'

Bruce worked so effortlessly on *Have I Got News For You* because he was never afraid of laughing at himself. And while he always treated his career with deadly seriousness, he was never slow to play up his own perceived failings for laughs.

'One time somebody threw his fish and chips at me from the gods at the Wood Green Empire and it hurt very much because that and the Finsbury Park Empire were where my parents used to take me every week,' he recalled. 'I think there was another comedian on the bill who didn't like me very much and he threw them.' But he did manage to get a joke out of it. 'I walked over and opened them up and – the audience didn't know whether to laugh or what – I just got one of the chips and put it in my mouth and I said, "No salt and vinegar? For goodness' sake, what class have you got?" And the audience was on my side.' And what happened to his nameless rival, the chip chucker? 'Well he's still fairly nameless,' said Bruce with a grin. 'He did actually do a warm-up for me three or four years ago in a television show. So he didn't get much further. There was some satisfaction for me in that.'

Bruce and Paul Merton became friends after *Have I Got News For You*. Paul later invited him on to his other show, *Room 101*, where stars have to list their pet hates. For Bruce, these were the rules of golf, female presenters who shout at the end of sentences, and poor quality food and drink. 'Paul is fascinated by old comedians and he took me for a drink to ask me all about the ones I've known and studied,' Bruce said. 'We've been friends ever since.'

Bruce was asked at this time about the dreaded word: retirement. He explained that he had only thought about stepping down once – after that desperate week in Leeds years before when he was the second-spot warm-up comic that we detailed earlier in the book.

'That was a thankless job,' Bruce said. 'You came on after the dancing act and yours was the first voice the audience heard. It was your job to warm them up before the main act came on. It was awful. I vowed back then that, if I couldn't get out of that slot, I would give up. I saw what that sort of frustration did to people. I didn't want to finish up a bitter old pro, like so many did.'

Have I Got News For You emphatically ended any thoughts of retirement. It may never have crossed Bruce's mind but, until that show, there was no doubt the TV industry was thinking of retiring Bruce. He was gradually slipping away from view, like so many old showmen before. But now things had changed. He had shown, once again, he had universal appeal – spanning all ages and both sexes. You could build a show around him and be sure that people would tune in. And perhaps most importantly, as he approached his late seventies, he was still physically fit and sharp as a tack. No one would be taking a risk in hiring Bruce.

So it was no surprise that, when Jane Lush gave the go ahead for a major Saturday-night family show, there was only one person she wanted as her main presenter.

CHAPTER 18

STRICTLY BACK ON TOP

By 2004, Saturday nights had become a real headache for bosses at the BBC. The shows were tired, the ratings were dire and what should have been the most important night of the week was, frankly, a bit of an embarrassment. It was time for a radical change. Bosses badly needed a new hit – something that tapped into the new vogue of reality television, involved celebrities yet was distinctive to the Beeb. They simply couldn't mimic their commercial rivals. The solution was quite brilliant and also quite radical. The radical element was not to create something new but to do the opposite: revive an old favourite. And who better to front this new extravaganza than the former King of Saturday Nights – even if he was 76?

Few people missed *Come Dancing* when it quietly disappeared from the BBC schedules in 1998. Amazingly it had been running since 1949 and was one of the BBC's – if not the world's – longest-running shows. Even its fans had to admit that it was a little fusty and dated. It had been shunted out to a late-night slot with barely a murmur of protest. Which is what made the decision to repackage the old ballroom competition – while keeping the professional dancers – such a stroke of genius. In the new format, celebrities would be brought in, with one being knocked out each week, based on a viewer vote and marks by four judges.

To signal to viewers that this was something different from *Come Dancing*, the word 'Strictly' was added to the title. This was a change from the name it was originally given – *Pro Celebrity Come Dancing* – which was eventually ruled out for being old-fashioned. It was a very clever piece of re-branding and, of course, no one to this day bothers with its full name. To fans, Saturday nights mean just one word: *Strictly*. All that was needed now was a charismatic host. It had been 30 years since the Beeb had dominated Saturday-night television with the unforgettable line-up of *The Generation Game*, *The Duchess of Duke Street*, *Morecambe and Wise*, *Michael Parkinson* and *Match of the Day*.

Bruce's name had been at the top of the thoughts of Jane Lush – the BBC's head of entertainment – since his show-stopping performance on *Have I Got News For You* less than a year earlier. She felt that the old entertainer had got a raw deal when he was sidelined by ITV and that he still had the presence and the fan base to front one last big show. 'Jane wrote me a letter after the ITV thing and said she'd like to talk to me in the future,' Bruce said. 'I wrote back saying I hadn't even thought about more television. I just wanted a little period to relax and feel what was going on.'

To Lush, *Strictly* was the perfect vehicle for Bruce. He was a trained dancer so he could talk knowledgably about the different dance steps. And his song-and-dance roots on stage gave the modern version of the show an indelible link with its *Come Dancing* tradition.

He was paired with a much younger female co-host, Tess Daly, an attractive blonde who had enjoyed a relatively successful career in television before getting her big break alongside Bruce. The pair established an immediate rapport – with Tess a willing foil for Bruce's gags. It was clear from the outset that this would always be Bruce's show – he was unquestionably the main star, with Tess a likeable and highly able second string.

A key element of the show would be the interaction between Bruce and the judges, who were chosen very carefully. Len Goodman, old sage and king of the British ballroom dancers, would be head judge. Wise and always prepared to see the best in people, he would give the show its heart. Bruno Tonioli, Italian choreographer and camp little firecracker, was brought in to add some pizazz. There had to be a female element and who better than Arlene Phillips, the brilliant choreographer and creator of *Hot Gossip*, famed for their risqué routines on TV in the 1970s. Bitchy Australian Craig Revel Horwood took on the role pioneered by Simon Cowell on *The X Factor* – he was the tough one, not afraid to really let rip when a celebrity couldn't hack it. Bosses wanted real fireworks between Bruce and the judges – stealing a trick from shows such as *The X Factor*. Its phenomenal success had allowed ITV to wrestle back control of Saturday nights and attract record audiences. Bruce had shown over the years that he was a master of thinking on his feet. He could slap one of the judges down if it was needed but also be the butt of their jokes.

Bruce was just thrilled to be back in the limelight. He declared, 'I've been forced to make another comeback. It's better than going around with a begging bowl. It's wonderful to be back on television and I feel blessed to still be here.

'I thought I'd reached my sell-by date when I got to sixty-five and it did go a bit quiet around that time. Then along came this big revival. I've made enough money not to have to work any more but I enjoy it, I'm an entertainer. I can honestly say the last part of my life has been the best. There's no doubt about it. And that's down to my home life, my love life and my career.'

He'd been in the business for so long, he explained, because every generation had grown up with him since the 1950s so they didn't think of him as being particularly old. 'TV bosses forget that most people who watch the television are people post-40 or 50. They're the people who stay at home in front of the box when the youngsters are out at a club. I love the idea of a new generation of kids and their parents watching me on Saturday nights and getting back to good old-fashioned family entertainment.

'I love Saturday nights. The audiences are kinder, perhaps because they are drunk. Children who have only ever seen dancing on *Top of the Pops* will like it. And older people who have been missing ballroom dancing on telly for the past ten years will love it. We're going out with all guns blazing.'

The first series ran for just eight weeks. The celebrities included the opera singer Lesley Garrett, antiques expert David Dickinson and eventual winner, newsreader Natasha Kaplinsky. They had to master one of the great dance steps each week – the waltz, foxtrot, or faster numbers like the quickstep or Latin American favourites such as the salsa. Each week a star was voted off.

Bruce denied that it was a reality show, a format he hated because he felt it was too slow paced and lacked any intelligent content (maybe he was thinking of *Big Brother*!). He reckoned *Strictly* would be a hit precisely because it was so old-fashioned – and was so unlike many primetime shows that were often crude and pandered slavishly to the under-30s who were so coveted by advertisers. In Bruce's view, the new show harked back to a simpler, purer age, whereas so much current TV output was too smutty.

'I still don't like a lot of the dirty humour that's on at the moment. I have a yardstick,' he told the *Guardian*. 'I grew up in the days when where there was a risqué line in the script you'd say, "Ooh, we'd better go upstairs about that, it's a bit strong." And then they'd say, "No, you can't say that." Although I'm a lot cheekier now than I was forty years ago, I'm not downright dirty. It's the lavatorial and sexual humour I can't stand – where there isn't even a double entendre. It's just dirtiness for the sake of it. I don't do that and I think a lot of people respect that.'

Bruce reckoned those in charge pander too much to the young audience. 'There aren't that many younger presenters I can say that I like,' he said. 'But I do like Patrick Kielty. He's a good presenter and a good stand-up comedian. I also like

Jonathan Ross, although I'm not sure you'd call him young! I think he is marvellous.

'People like Des O'Connor and Michael Parkinson proved that older presenters could still bring in the ratings.'

Series one was a slow-burning hit – building its audience every week. It went from attracting to just over 5 million for the first show to having more than 10 million for the final, which was won by Kaplinsky. A big part of her success was down to the sizzling sexual chemistry she shared with her professional dance partner, the fiery Kiwi Brendan Cole. It was suggested that the couple had become lovers in real life. Speculation reached fever pitch when Natasha split up with her then boyfriend Michael Barnard during the show and Brendan called off his engagement with Danish beauty Camilla Dallerup, also a *Strictly* dance professional. Natasha and Brendan have always denied that they shared a romance, though few people connected with the show believed them. Whether they were or weren't sharing a bed as well as the dance floor certainly played well to the TV viewers at home, who lapped up all the intrigue.

Bruce said the show worked because viewers could see the celebrities improve each week, egged on all the time by the professionals, who were fiercely competitive.

'It didn't take me very long to realise that professional ballroom dancers are every bit as competitive as racing drivers or professional footballers or top-class athletes,' he explained. 'And this rubs off on the celebrities. There is always a wonderful camaraderie among all the competitors. But, underneath all that, they each want to be the best. Otherwise, why take part? And that's the very heartbeat of the show.'

There was inaccurate speculation that Bruce had been left so exhausted by the first series that he would have to quit. Of course, it was nonsense. Bruce was thrilled to be back for the second series, which took the show to even greater heights. He admitted that his career revival had made him so busy he had barely had time to play golf. For Bruce to give up golf meant that *Strictly* must really have got under his skin.

It all just got better and better. And Bruce suddenly discovered that he was considered trendy by the hot stars of the moment. 'I love being thought of as cool,' he said. 'Even the young comedians I meet at BBC parties, like Matt Lucas and David Walliams from *Little Britain*, have said they are fans. Of course, I don't appeal to everybody but in each generation there's a good number who will put up with me.'

Each new series was an even bigger success than the last – and the ratings continued to climb. It even overtook its big rival *The X Factor*. *Strictly* was seen as having an innocence that the brash and rather more cynical ITV singing show lacked. It also meant it got far more favourable press coverage than *The X Factor* – much of it focused around its evergreen host. The longer the show went on, the more Bruce loved it.

In an interview in the *Daily Mirror* with Sue Carroll, he said, 'They'll have to drag me off with my heels drumming the boards. Those rumours about me packing it all in because I was exhausted were absolute rubbish. When you do a big live show like that, it's bound to be tiring but you keep going on the sheer excitement. There was never a moment when I felt so exhausted I thought I couldn't carry on.

'I tell you, when I walk on to the studio floor, I feel 37, not 77. Something takes over. I've felt like that for the past 40 years, although I must admit sometimes in the morning I do feel my age.

'I always get edgy before a show. I don't like people coming up and talking to me. I like to get in my own little meditation. I have a bit of a glazed look in the eye, wondering whether it's going to be all right and thinking about what I'm going to do. Then I do a little hop before I walk on and the other me takes over.'

He maintained his energy levels by following the same healthy routines he had kept up for decades. 'I lead a safe life,' he said. 'I'm not a drinker. The most I'll have is one or two a week. And I don't overeat but I make sure I have plenty of fruit and vegetables. I also make sure I get plenty of rest. If I've had a hard day, I'll come in, lie down for a couple of hours, then get up for dinner. We always eat early, so my meal is digested properly. It's a performer's discipline, but it seems to pay off because people do marvel at me.'

For a man who at the time was fast approaching his eighties, his work schedule and stamina levels were nothing short of remarkable. 'From Wednesday I'll work with the script editor and, when I get to the studios on the Friday, there'll be a script meeting to go through the whole show,' he told the *Mail on Sunday*. 'Then we'll all vote on which jokes we like and try out the best in the dress rehearsal.'

Bruce was completely out of his comfort zone on *Strictly*. 'It's the hardest thing I've ever done because I am not working to an audience. People are behind me and at the side of me. I can't see them,' he explained. 'But it's so good. It works for me, in spite of all the things about it that are against me. People seem to like me in it.'

STRICTLY BACK ON TOP

Although his corny gags became as much a part of the fabric of the show as Craig Revel Horwood's acid put-downs or Bruno Tonioli's exuberance, he didn't read too much into the reaction of the audience. 'You've got six hundred people in the audience being the yardstick for nine million at home so you never know how it's all going by the response from the people in the studio, plus I'm aware I'm working to a family audience.'

And how different was the laugh-a-minute showman we saw on Saturday nights to the real Bruce Forsyth? 'He's not that different but he's an extension. He is much more gregarious, much more over the top than I am normally. I couldn't stand to be him all the time; he'd drive me crazy. I have to put him in a little box to get rid of him.'

Bruce largely ignored the rivalry with *The X Factor*. He saw them as two very different shows. That may well have been true but both their ratings suffered when they were pitched against each other in the schedules. This happened during a period when the BBC declared all-out war on its ITV rival by putting *Strictly* on slightly later so they were both on at the same time. It didn't work and *Strictly* was soon moved back to an earlier slot so that any clash was minimal.

'It doesn't bother me because we have a completely different audience,' Bruce explained. 'I think the forties-up are our crowd while *The X Factor* caters for the bulk of the teenagers. There's no rivalry as far as I'm concerned. Simon Cowell came up to me at the *Pride Of Britain Awards* last year, when we were all being presented to Prince Charles, and said, "It's all banter, isn't it?" and I said, "Of course it is."

'He was meant to have said that *Strictly* is only for the old people and it should be put on in the afternoon so the viewers can watch it and then have a little rest afterwards before watching their show. I couldn't agree with Simon because we have a more varied audience than that of *The X Factor*. I know this for a fact because Simon's mother came up to my wife and me in Selfridges. She said, "I love your show Mr Forsyth and I watch it every Saturday." I said it would be a terrible thing if Simon's mother couldn't go out on a Saturday afternoon and do her weekend's shopping. So I suggested Simon worked out the schedules with his mother. It was never right that the two shows clashed.'

Strictly became a huge money-spinner for the Beeb. The format has been sold to more than 30 counties. It is a big hit in the States where it goes under the name of *Dancing with the Stars*. Len and Bruno are judges on the American version too – jetting across the Atlantic each week while the two shows run simultaneously.

So everything seemed perfect for Bruce. *Strictly* was a smash-hit, it had toppled *The X Factor* in the ratings and the show looked to set to run and run. But then the BBC, suicidally, decided to change things. The changes prompted a huge backlash from the audience and left Bruce looking highly vulnerable as the show's host, with accusations flying that he was too old – too 'doddery' – to carry on.

CHAPTER 19

DODDERY I AM NOT!

It had all been going so swimmingly. From its launch in 2004, each series of *Strictly Come Dancing* was even more successful than the last. It was a show adored by everyone: the stars, the critics, the dancers, the celebrities, the hosts and, most importantly, the viewers – who, by 2007, were numbering more than 12 million every week. It was all going so well that something just had to go wrong. And when it did, Bruce was left fighting for his show-business life.

The first signs of trouble came in the autumn of 2007. *Strictly* was well into its fourth series and all seemed to be well. Alesha Dixon was already fast emerging as the runaway winner. Kate Garraway from *GMTV*, on the other hand, was showing that she was Alesha's polar opposite – she had the lightness of foot of an elephant and was unquestionably the worst dancer in the entire history of the competition. It all added to the fun and ensured that the show had the perfect mix of serious dancing and laughs. It was just at this point that Craig Revel Horwood, the acerbic Australian judge, decided to declare war on just about everyone on the show – including Bruce.

The source of all the trouble was an interview Craig gave to the *News of the World*. Craig had always enjoyed a bit of controversy. In fairness, he had been hired for the judging panel specifically as the pantomime villain, to pour a bucket-load of vitriol over everyone. He was to *Strictly* what Simon Cowell was to *The X Factor*: his job was to tell it straight and not worry if anyone was offended. And that is exactly what he did in his interview with the *News of the World*.

In typically combative style, he said that the singer Rod Stewart's wife Penny Lancaster dressed like she was going to a 'swinger's party'. The former *EastEnders* star Letitia Dean – heartbroken after splitting with her husband during the show – was a 'fat porker' who could cheer herself up by losing a few pounds. The rugby player Kenny Logan looked like a 'gorilla' while the pint-sized TV presenter Dominic Littlewood resembled a 'dancing bullfrog'.

No one was spared but it was his remarks about Brucie that were to cause the most controversy. If anything, they were the mildest of the lot. But, as we know from the past, Bruce didn't take kindly to criticism. And when he was attacked, he tended to fight back – very publicly.

It all revolved around one word: 'doddery'. It had not even been said by Craig in the interview but his words could certainly have been construed to mean he thought Bruce was indeed doddery. He had been talking about Bruce's difficulties reading the autocue. 'There's only three words to each autocue page now so he can see them,' Craig revealed. Quickly aware that he was making mild criticism of a prickly national institution, he qualified his comments by adding, 'If Bruce didn't do the screw-ups, it wouldn't be the same. People wait to see what he does wrong next.' Craig added, 'I can't bear him interrupting me. It makes me look bloody stupid and the biggest bitch. But I'm there to criticise the dances.'

What really set the cat among the pigeons was the headline BRUCIE IS AN OLD DUFFER and one little word – 'doddery' – buried in the text. The *News of the World* had introduced the quotes about Bruce showing his age by saying, 'Craig even had a pop at doddery host and TV icon Bruce, 79, for stumbling over his words.' Somehow the only two words anyone remembered from the whole interview were 'duffer' and 'doddery'. Bruce demanded an immediate apology from Craig. He got one because, though he had been critical, Craig could argue that his comments had been sensationalised.

There the whole matter may have ended if not for Bruce's battered ego. Far from forgetting about the doddery description, he decided to turn it into a catchphrase. He adapted one of his old catchphrases – 'Nice to see you, to see you nice' – updating it to 'I'm not doddery, doddery I am NOT!'

It was mildly amusing and, as with almost all of Bruce's jokes in front of such a forgiving audience as *Strictly*'s, always got a laugh. But it was perhaps not the wisest move. Because from then on, every little mishap Bruce made was picked up and used to illustrate the point that he *was* doddery. In a quick-moving live show like *Strictly*, a presenter is always going to make the odd mistake. For one fast approaching his

80th birthday, inevitably there would be a few more than average. Soon the whole question of Bruce's age and possible retirement became an issue – one that was almost entirely of his own making.

In February of 2008, Bruce celebrated his 80th birthday. The BBC did him proud with a TV special highlighting more than 60 years in show business. But what should have been a joyous occasion was completely overshadowed by continued speculation over whether he would quit the show or – unthinkable just months before – be sacked. They were compounded by an inaccurate report at the time saying that he would leave *Strictly* at the end of the year because he wanted to 'bow out with dignity'. Bruce was forced to take legal action to correct that lie.

He was decidedly grouchy at a party at the Dorchester Hotel in London to mark his birthday. And he used the opportunity to dismiss suggestions that he is too old to front *Strictly*. 'I am not that doddery,' he said. 'You try to do live television for two hours on a Saturday night without making a mistake.

'If I make a fluff, I try to get out of it and say something funny. It's only one a show. I am not doddery. Senile, yes. But not doddery.'

He admitted, however, that TV presenting was becoming very tiring. 'Adrenalin is a marvellous thing,' he said. 'Whenever I do a show for two hours, afterwards I am still in that frame of mind. Then I start to fade and go downhill and then I have to shut the eyes.' Forsyth said that having a younger wife had helped to hold back the years. She does keep me young. She is the most wonderful lady,' he said.

Loyal Wilnelia jumped to his defence too. 'I don't know why there has been so much criticism,' she said. 'It is very easy to make mistakes because it's a live show but he doesn't make that many. I'd like to see anyone, even someone younger, work from 8am till midnight – which they do on filming day – and not get tired. It needs so much adrenaline.

'I've presented a live television show myself in Puerto Rico and I was petrified, and I wasn't doing it every Saturday. Brucie doesn't even wear glasses – but I do. What people don't realise either is that he has someone in his ear all the time saying, "Hurry up, move along." I think what he does is amazing. I'm so proud of him.'

There was a brief respite from the criticism in the April of that year when Bruce was awarded a BAFTA fellowship – the lifetime-achievement award that is the highest honour in British show business. Bruce highlighted his age in talking about the honour – and how his wife Winnie was the first to get the news. 'I heard it had been mooted but confirmation came in an email to Winnie,' explained Bruce. 'I don't have a computer – no idea how to work the damn things – and anyway, as I always say, I haven't got email because I'm too famous. *Strictly Come Dancing* is what clinched it. If that hadn't come along when it did, I don't think the BAFTA would have happened. In fact, I'd probably have faded into the sunset, never to be heard from again.'

The whole fuss over Bruce's age may just have been a storm in a teacup if the BBC hadn't then made the disastrous decision to sack 66-year-old judge Arlene Phillips months before the 2008 series started. BBC One controller, Jay Hunt, said the format needed 'freshening up'. Arlene was replaced by

31-year-old Alesha Dixon, who had easily won the 2007 series, as everyone predicted.

The BBC had been badly stung by accusations that the show was too white and too middle class. Bosses wrongly believed that the show was such a ratings blockbuster that viewers would happily go along with the changes. Only they didn't. Much as they loved Alesha as a dancer, they didn't feel she was qualified to step up as a judge. It was felt, rightly or wrongly, that as a mixed-race woman she had just been promoted for reasons of politically correct tokenism. Arlene was a victim of ageism and should be reinstated immediately, they screamed in increasing numbers. The row – which broke during a slow summer for news – ran for months and months, and the BBC was hit with more than 4,000 complaints.

It completely overshadowed the launch of the 2008 series and the ratings suffered a two-million drop. Alesha got off to a very uncertain start and was blasted in the media. The calls to bring back Arlene grew ever louder. The BBC refused to back down and the show never really recovered throughout the whole of that year's run.

Bruce admitted the decision to sack Arlene was wrong. 'It should never have happened,' he stressed. 'Arlene should have stayed and we should have had five judges. To sack her was crazy; it did us a lot of harm.'

Alesha found switching to the judging panel really difficult. It was only in her last year, with three series under her belt, that she seemed truly confident and assured in judgements. It had taken all this time for her to have the self-belief to contradict the other more experienced judges and really tell it how she sees it. Having finally cracked the new role, she promptly quit *Strictly* at the start of 2012 to appear as a judge on Simon Cowell's hit ITV show *Britain's Got Talent*. Cowell had cleverly waited for Alesha to learn the ropes as a judge before swooping.

The whole Arlene-Alesha row made *Strictly* a target to be shot at – and increasingly that negative focus turned away from Alesha and on to Bruce. Some early mistakes in the 2008 run – referring to the *EastEnders* star as 'Jelly' and not Jessie Wallace – just added to the impression that he was indeed 'doddery' and that he should make way for a new host: Graham Norton, Paul O'Grady or possibly the dance professional Anton Du Beke.

Bruce couldn't put a foot right. At the time, the Beeb was also coming under fire over the huge salaries earned by its leading stars – particularly Jonathan Ross and his notorious £16 million contract. Bruce's name was also dragged into this row. Was he really worth £500,000 a year for simply reading an autocue?

Suddenly, what had all seemed like effortless fun a little over a year earlier, started to seem like very hard work to Bruce. He started talking about some of the difficulties he faced in interviews. 'I don't like working with autocue as much as I have to but I do have to because it's a very regimented show,' he moaned to the *Daily Express*. 'When the show goes on and I do a reasonable job, it looks nice and easy, which is what light entertainment's all about – as though we're just having fun. But I hate the phrase "light entertainment". I call it heavy entertainment. It's a damn sight harder to get a laugh than to do a straight line.'

He was forced on to the back foot again after being asked

about retirement. For only the second time in his career – no doubt in response to all this pressure – he admitted it could be a possibility.

'That's got to be around the corner,' he admitted. 'It could be next week, next month, next year – who knows? I've always said, if I become past it, if I've gone over the top, I think I'll know. If I don't, I'll rely on my agent, my manager and my wife to tell me it's time to turn in. But, looking at my tapes myself, I know I'm working pretty well.

'I don't want to do a Tommy Cooper and die on the stage. Of course I don't. If I'd like to die anywhere, it would be on a golf course, having just got a birdie... that's a one under par – not a girl!'

He admitted, though, that he was totally drained after the show. 'By the time Sunday comes round, I have to spend the entire day in bed because I'm that exhausted,' he said.

People weren't slow in coming forward to demand that the Beeb sack Bruce. 'All this fuss about Alesha Dixon on *Strictly Come Dancing* and not a word about doddery old Bruce Forsyth,' wrote one critic. 'Does anyone else find themselves humming or muting the television when he is talking, or is it only me? HE is the one sending the ratings down.' Another wrote, 'The people who criticise Alesha Dixon need to remember that it is just an entertainment show. The most embarrassing thing is to see Bruce Forsyth fumbling his way through the show. How much do they pay Tess to laugh at his feeble jokes?'

Some big hitters rallied to Bruce's defence. Judy Finnigan, of *Richard & Judy* fame, wrote of how privileged she was to witness 'how totally on top of his game this extraordinarily talented man still is. Calm when things went wrong, unfailingly polite and, of course, always very funny, he was perfect.'

'Should the producers of *Strictly Come Dancing* ditch our Brucie?' Vanessa Feltz wrote in the *Daily Express*. She continued, 'Carping voices on spiteful websites are decrying his "shakiness". Vituperative viewers are calling for him to be replaced by a younger model...

'When Mr Forsyth does his legendary hot-shoe shuffle into my living room, I respond like any other member of the viewing public with a handle on history and a respect for professionalism. I am suffused with the overwhelming feeling that it's nice to see him, to see him nice.

'More than any other human being, Bruce Forsyth embodies the very essence of popular TV. Just one glimpse of his perennially long, lean silhouette propels us back to more wholesome times when he asked Anthea Redfern to give us a twirl and we bloomed with youthful innocence as we watched dads and daughters failing to shape sausage meat into sausages, all for the sake of a cuddly toy and a decanter and six matching glasses.

'He reminds us of the days when Saturday-night television united the entire viewing public. Bruce alone, of all British presenters, takes us straight to the roots of light entertainment and our role – laughing at it.

'Brucie's gaffes and the sprightly, adroit way he claws himself back from the brink and extricates an even bigger laugh from adversity give what would otherwise be a fairly standard dance competition a vital dollop of heart, soul and wit.

'The rigours of hosting a highly complex live show would tax the resilience of presenters decades his junior. Unbelievably for an octogenarian, this is one gentleman still truly at the peak of his talent. He deserves his place centre stage. Long may Brucie reign.'

Bruce decided to slow down a little at the beginning of the 2009 series. The BBC decided to split *Strictly* into two – with a separate results show on the Sunday night. It was actually filmed on the Saturday but it meant that Bruce could knock off a little earlier and leave his co-hosts Tess Daly and Claudia Winkleman to take over presenting duties for the extra show when one of the celebrities was eliminated. There was no doubt that there were many in the BBC who had hoped Bruce would make 2009 his last. After the disastrous sacking of Arlene, there was a feeling that the show needed a complete overhaul. But BBC bosses knew it would be impossible to sack Bruce – he could only go at his time of choosing. They were not going to have a repeat of the Arlene fiasco. The irony was that, in sacking Arlene, they had made Bruce unsackable.

But it all turned around in 2009. The whole series – won by the likeable BBC sports presenter Chris Hollins – gelled and the ratings picked up. Bruce's gaffes were seen simply as the understandable odd lapse of a brilliant professional, rather than a reason for pensioning him off. Suddenly, all talk of his retirement once again seemed absurd.

* * *

Bruce was busy in the early part of 2010 making three big TV shows before the start of *Strictly*. The first came in March when he appeared on *Piers Morgan's Life Stories*. Piers is well known for making his guests cry by recalling tragedies from their past and eliciting sensational revelations. In truth, his interview with Bruce was not that eventful – the best line was Bruce moaning about missing out on a knighthood – which, of course, was rectified a year later. 'It's not a popularity contest when these people grant these privileges, shall we say,' he said. He then repeated an argument he had made before about how entertainment greats such as Morecambe and Wise and Les Dawson never received the ultimate honour: 'Why is that? Is it because we are all comedic people. Do they think that we haven't got a proper job?' he asked.

In the previous series of *Strictly*, there had been a race row after the professional dancer Anton Du Beke had jokingly called his dance partner, actress Laila Rouass, the 'P word' after she had a spray tan. There had been calls for the popular Du Beke to be sacked but producers stood by him after he apologised for his comments and insisted he was not a racist. Bruce rallied to his defence, saying, 'Anton is one of nicest guys I've ever met and wouldn't say anything malicious to anyone. It was a ridiculous situation and all I said was that I think at times political correctness does go over the top, and I think it does.'

Bruce played his own generation game when he took part in the BBC One's popular genealogy series *Who Do You think You Are?* a few months before the start of the eighth series of *Strictly* in 2010. When he first agreed to take part in the series, Bruce already knew his paternal great-grandfather was something of a character. Joseph Forsyth Johnson was an eminent landscape gardener who had written several books about gardening. That he looked vaguely like his forebear – they share an impeccably groomed air, not to mention a penchant for moustaches – seemed to please him. And as Bruce trooped around parks and botanic gardens in such diverse places as Belfast and New York's Brooklyn, he basked in the reflected glory of what Joseph had started. He also travelled to the southern US state of Georgia, where Joseph created something of an empire, with the great and the good flocking to have their gardens and parks designed by him.

But there was a darker side to Bruce's discoveries. It transpired that green fingers and a liking for sharp suits may not have been the only legacy passed down from Joseph. His great-grandfather, like Bruce, was something of a ladies' man. But even Bruce was horrified at how much of a ladies' man he was.

Bruce discovered that Joseph was almost certainly a bigamist and may have even faked his own death in an attempt to rid himself of domestic shackles. In fact, he walked out on two wives and families – one in England and one in the US. Neither branch even knew of the other's existence, until they turned amateur genealogists and started unearthing records.

Bruce didn't shy away from these painful truths in the show. He even drew parallels with how he has behaved in his own life. And he asked whether the tendency to cheat and desert could be inherited.

Bruce's research showed that Joseph's first marriage failed because of his roving eye – just as Bruce's had. Joseph married for the first time in 1861. He was a 21-year-old apprentice gardener and his wife, Elizabeth, was eight years older and working for a grand Yorkshire family. They had six children, the eldest of whom, John, was Bruce's grandfather.

Until recently, the Forsyth family in the UK assumed that they were the only branch of this particular clan. Then Bruce got a surprising letter from a woman in Georgia who claimed to be a descendant of Joseph. Was it possible, the letter asked, that he had two families? 'Was he a bigamist?' asked Bruce on the show. 'That was what we wanted to find out.'

And the news was shocking. On his return from a very successful eight-year stint working in Belfast, helping establish the city's Botanic Gardens, Joseph's star was on the rise. London was booming and the ambitious Joseph opened a shop in Bond Street, where he sold exotic plants and seeds, and undertook landscaping commissions. 'He really did well for himself,' said Bruce, quite taken with this idea of his great-grandfather's life.

At some point in the early 1880s, Joseph met a young woman named Frances, who worked as draper's assistant near his shop. On 28 December 1885, they are both listed as passengers on a liner heading for New York. Joseph was 46 and Frances 26, pregnant and listed as his wife.

Bruce was shocked to discover that his great-grandfather had effectively run out on Elizabeth and their children – although they may not have been aware of this at the time – leaving them in dire financial straits as a result. His wife was forced to take a job in service, as were their children.

There was an awkward moment during filming when the clerk charged with helping Bruce trawl public records offered her conclusion on what happened. It was, she said, a 'classic story of a very successful man who leaves his first wife – the one who has stood by him'. Bruce immediately offered a parallel with his own life. 'I can sympathise with him a bit,' he said. 'He suddenly finds himself in affluent surroundings after being a very simple young man. It is similar to my life. When I married my first wife, we were a double act. Then, all of a sudden, I went to the top of the business.

'In just six weeks I was one of the biggest names on TV. When you finally get the big break, it is difficult to still be a family man. I think that is what happened to me. It is very similar to Joseph in a way. He just had to leave all that and go to where he thought his destiny was.'

When Bruce came across a birth certificate for Joseph Jnr – Joseph's seventh child – he again made a comparison with his own life. Laughing, he said, 'I have six. He's already better than me.' A further two children were born; then, in the late 1880s, something strange happened. At first, it seemed that Joseph died. Public records start listing Frances as a widow and an obituary suggested Joseph had died at sea.

But this did not tally with Bruce's own records – primarily based on a diary kept by Joseph's youngest daughter from his English family. It mentioned him returning to the port of Liverpool in 1894, which was confirmed by passenger records.

The next year, he returned to New York. In fact, he kept popping up on passenger records, flitting between the two countries, with his last voyage recorded as 1903. 'What was he playing at?' asked Bruce, puzzled. When it emerged that Joseph had abandoned both families, Bruce was aghast. 'He left one lot in Tottenham and now he has ditched her [Frances] and their three children. For the second time he has let his family down.'

Bruce was horrified. 'He's been so devious. So many lies must have been needed to cover up his tracks. It doesn't look too good that he deserted two families.'

Particularly sad for Bruce was how it all ended for his great-grandfather. He was shocked to find that Joseph actually died in 1906, alone and living in a hotel in New York. He didn't leave a will. 'Two families and he never left a will,' said Bruce. 'What a strange character.' He also died virtually penniless, with less than $400 to his name. 'That's all he had after all the work he did,' Bruce said sadly.

That Joseph was buried in an unmarked grave was something his great-grandson found particularly difficult. Visiting the cemetery to lay a bunch of flowers, Bruce drove past lavish monuments and thought he was heading for the section where gravestones were more modest. Alas, no. There was not even a gravestone. 'I can't believe it has come to this,' he said. Moved by what he discovered, Bruce commissioned a memorial to honour his great-grandfather's work.

At the same time, Bruce also gave an insight into his home life with Wilnelia in an hour-long fly-on-the-wall *Cutting Edge* documentary for Channel 4 called *Living With Brucie*. It showed that Bruce had more energy and enthusiasm than many men half his age. Bruce talked in detail for the first time about the secret of his success – an ancient exercise regime favoured by Tibetan monks. As we've seen earlier, the veteran entertainer religiously followed the strict programme, which was laid out in a book his mother-in-law had given him on his wedding day almost 30 years before.

He showed off his bizarre exercise routine on the show. Viewers saw Bruce complete 25 twirls, wriggle his toes, do press-ups and stretch in a bid to stay young and in shape. The moves were similar to gentle yoga and were said to help followers look younger, sleep more soundly, wake up fresh and offer relief from chronic pain.

'I'm doing this for me,' Bruce said on the documentary. 'I don't want to grow old gracefully. I want to put up a bit of a fight. I want to keep as young as I can and as mobile as I can because one day it's all going to stop – I'm not going to be able to do this.'

The regime was based on five rites – energy, fire, water, earth and air – laid out by the monks more than 2,500 years ago and promising rejuvenation and 'everlasting youth'. They were first made public by Peter Kelder in his book *The Eye of Revelation* – the basis for Bruce's bible, *The Fountain of Youth*. The book, which is still in print, claimed the exercises were so potent that they could turn back time – turning grey hair black, improving eyesight and memory and banishing wrinkles.

Cameras followed Bruce and his wife for several months and revealed him to be a superstitious creature of habit. He washes his own socks and shirts and has porridge every day with blueberries on top, meticulously placed an equal distance apart. The star believes the colour green is unlucky and, if he sees a single magpie, he will say, 'Good morning, General,' to dispel its curse.

The fact that Bruce was giving a crew from a Channel 4 show such an intimate glimpse into his private life showed just how much television had changed in the previous two decades. For many years, Bruce based his career around two channels, BBC1 and ITV – switching for years between the two. But as TV moved to a multi-channel format, all performers needed to diversify and explore new avenues for their talents.

With so many channels to pick from, audiences on both the BBC and ITV dropped and that inevitably drove down the wages of the big stars. The recession that was blighting the British economy was forcing all the major broadcasters to make savings. And the BBC was under pressure from the new Coalition government to make major economies so that the licence fee could be frozen. Bruce took a £50,000 pay cut for the 2010 series of *Strictly* as the BBC slashed the salaries of all its top earners. He did so without complaint – well aware he had to make sacrifices like everyone else. Again the series was a triumph, with soap actress Kara Tointon a very popular winner.

And as Bruce celebrated finishing the ninth series at the end of 2011, his position was even more unassailable, with the *Daily Mail* – that crucial arbiter of the tastes of 'Middle England' – hailing it as *Strictly*'s greatest ever series. The show, won by McFly drummer Harry Judd, had comprehensively trounced *The X Factor* in the ratings war for the first time in years, consistently winning one million more viewers every Saturday. For Bruce, who has always considered TV ratings to be the ultimate gauge of his success, there was a real sense of satisfaction that the old-fashioned values epitomised by *Strictly* at its best had triumphed over its flashy and far more brash ITV rival. In a series of interviews with the press, Bruce made his feelings known.

'I am thrilled with the figures,' he said. '*Strictly* is doing better now than it has ever done. I don't watch *The X Factor* because it is not my cup of tea. It is one singer after another singer after another singer. They say they miss Simon Cowell, which I can imagine, but I think they should put different judges in it, like they do in America.' And, accusing the likes of judges Gary Barlow and Tulisa Contostavlos of practising their apparently spontaneous lines, he added, 'Their judges are doing what they call rehearsed ad-libs.

'People forget we are a live show. When I am out there, I am doing live jokes I haven't tried before. I am not doing the type of show where you can cut it out or say you would like to do it again.

'TV these days is too sanitised. Everything is too perfect. I would like to see more things live, a few more mistakes. I would love *Strictly* to be full of mistakes so I can ad-lib my way out of a problem. That is part of what I do. I love to get in among upheaval and try to straighten it all out.'

Bruce said that *Strictly* focused on the talent while *The X Factor* bosses spent their time chasing publicity. 'When we started, it was all about pairing people off. They are off having a coffee or lying down in the park together. Then a story would be leaked. All that kind of nonsense. I didn't think that added to the show and made it very tacky. So I'm glad we got rid of that.'

Speaking about the contestants, he said, 'We had a great group of people this year and the show is all about them. What I love is when they have been dancing for four or five weeks. By then about four have shown such improvement. Some came in and couldn't even walk properly, let alone dance. That is what I love, the improvement – and the occasional mistake.'

Bruce said that he had the most laughs over the years with the older contestants. 'They make it fun, of course they do,' he smiled. 'Edwina Currie was marvellous this year. She went out with no inhibitions and had a go, and I admire that. The year before, Ann Widdecombe was amazing – she really got the joke of it. John Sergeant didn't, sadly, and I thought it was a shame he resigned from the show because he put our semi-final right out of sync. Dear Ann knew when it was time to go, the public knew when it was time to go and it worked out fine.'

The question was: would Sir Bruce ever know when the time was right for him to hang up his dancing shoes? Yes, it was the dreaded 'R' word again.

'I often wonder how long I will go on for,' he patiently explained for the umpteenth time. 'Each week, I do a fifteen-minute warm-up before the show starts. I'll do a couple of gags and a song to get the feeling of the band. That's what a performer is; that's the fodder that performers feed off – getting up there, doing your bit.

'I could not be happier finishing my career on such a high. I really don't care what happens now. *Sunday Night At The London Palladium* was the biggest show on TV in the Sixties. *The Generation Game* was the biggest show in the Seventies. *Play Your Cards Right* was a huge, huge show in the Eighties. And now *Strictly* is the biggest show – or thereabouts when you consider the rivalry with *The X Factor* – at the start of this century. That's four really big shows in a lifetime.'

With the tenth anniversary of *Strictly* coming up, he was

enjoying it as much as ever. 'It's a lot different from shows I have done before,' he said. 'I am essentially just a presenter on this. I am pretty much a full-time stand-up comic, which I wasn't on other shows like *The Generation Game*, where I was joining in all the games.

'What has been so wonderful for me is that years ago, when performers got to their sixties, they naturally retired and a new generation of younger comics took over. It seemed to happen almost seamlessly. Performers would simply disappear to the great theatre in the stratosphere. Of course, I assumed that this would happen to me. When I was getting to fifty and fifty-five, I thought I would be retiring in five or ten years and I was ready for that. But somehow I have managed to keep going and no one has wanted me to retire.'

So with a hit show in the Sixties, Seventies, Eighties and noughties, what were the chances of Bruce doing it again in another ten years? He laughed at the suggestion. 'I am just grateful every time I wake up in the morning! I'll still be singing and dancing when I'm a hundred – I just hope my wife can keep up.

'I plan to book the London Palladium to celebrate my hundredth birthday. The American comedian George Burns booked it for his hundredth birthday but sadly he didn't make it, so I've taken over the date.

'I'm still enjoying doing *Strictly*, I'll keep on going. It gives you a certain feeling – the feeling of being really in the show business that you've loved all your life. If that is still there, why shouldn't I keeeeeeep dancing.'

CHAPTER 20

NICE TO
SIR YOU

It was the final missing piece of the jigsaw. By 2007 – at the age of 79 – Bruce Forsyth was the man who truly had it all. There was the beautiful wife of 24 years. He had six well-adjusted children who all adored their irrepressible dad. Then there was the career dating back an astonishing seven decades, to the time when Adolf Hitler was still ruling Germany. He had a beautiful home overlooking one of the greatest golf courses in the world and he had earned enough money to last him several life times. In *Strictly Come Dancing*, he was starring in the BBC's most popular TV show and, fit as a fiddle, showed no signs of ill-health or slowing down. Retirement was still out of the question. But one thing eluded him. The one thing he craved above all else – the Queen saying, 'Arise, Sir Bruce.'

Brucie wasn't the only person who wondered why he had been overlooked for a knighthood. His sense of injustice was shared not just by his millions of fans but by the wider celebrity community. His case was taken up by our most powerful newspaper, the *Sun*, which launched a campaign to get the 'King of Show Business' the gong he so richly deserved. The response was instantaneous. Within days, an Internet grass-roots campaign had raised more than 15,000 signatures on a petition to Downing Street calling on the then Prime Minister Gordon Brown to knight Bruce. A parliamentary early-day motion signed by 73 MPs reiterated the call. Stars rallied to the cause. And with the help of social media, the fervour grew. A Facebook page – entitled simply Give Bruce Forsyth a Knighthood – soon attracted 25,000 supporters. Surely the government would finally take notice.

But nothing happened. Bruce was ignored in the 2007 honours, despite all the hard work of his fans. Why? Bruce's old pal Michael Grade had his own typically forthright views. It was simply down to 'innate snobbery'. Lord Grade, who privately wrote to the government on behalf of Bruce, told the *Radio Times*, 'It's shocking that he and other variety performers are never knighted. There's an innate snobbery in Whitehall that music hall is vulgar. It's the same with television. I've lost count of the number of dinner-party conversations where someone says, "Television is dreadful." I ask if they've seen a particular programme. "Oh, yes, that was good." Their arguments fall apart within seconds. Television hasn't got worse. It's different.'

So snobbery was possibly one reason. But was there another? Was Bruce harbouring some dark secret in his private life that the honours committee was keeping from his fans? Certainly there was plenty of completely unfounded speculation suggesting so. It was all nonsense, of course. The true reason was rather more prosaic. Officials say that there is an informal convention within the honours system that individuals who have received an award in the past will not be considered for another honour for five years. Bruce had been given a CBE in 2005 in recognition of his work in show business and charity. That meant the knighthood would have to wait until 2011 to fit in with the prevailing protocol. He had also been given an OBE in 1998, so it wasn't as if his work hadn't been recognised by the Queen.

The rules didn't stop a huge betting coup on Brucie waltzing off with a knighthood in the New Year Honours in 2008. Odds plummeted after a tidal wave of bets. He was 2/1 odds-on favourite – down from 33/1 at the start of the year – to be given the coveted accolade for his services to entertainment. It was the shortest price on a knighthood in betting history. Bookies feared a huge sting by punters with inside information on the honours list. William Hill refused to take any more bets on Sir Brucie, with spokesman Graham Sharpe admitting, 'We already face a substantial liability. We've had a surge. We fear some people in the know are trying to sting us. But if he gets the knighthood, we will be first to say, "Didn't he do well?"' David Williams, of Ladbrokes, said, 'A knighthood would be a rich reward for his incredible career but the sight of Sir Brucie at Buckingham Palace would make us wince.'

Alas, as they often do, the betting coup failed and the bookies were the only winners. Another year passed with Bruce once more overlooked.

Bruce gave the impression publicly that he wasn't hurt by the snub. 'I'm in very good company. It's not a popularity contest when these people grant these privileges,' he explained. 'Eric Morecambe, Ernie Wise, Tommy Cooper, the Two Ronnies and Frankie Howerd all missed out despite their popularity. I have a CBE, which I was very pleased to accept and, if that's as far as it goes, that's as far as it goes.'

But deep down he was bitterly upset. He had twice been honoured before and knew exactly how the system worked. Recipients receive a letter from the honours committee around a month before the official announcement. They are all sworn to secrecy.

'Brucie absolutely knew the pack drill – the letters go out twice a year. A few weeks before Christmas for the New Years Honours and towards the end of spring for the Queen's Birthday Honours,' a friend said. 'When he knew it was time for the letters to arrive, he would be anxious every time the postman arrived. He'd always feel a little deflated when the envelope wasn't there.'

The lack of progress didn't stop more big names joining the campaign, including the one man who could rival Brucie as our ultimate showbiz national treasure – Elton John. Sir Elton, who was knighted in 1998, revealed that he was so angry at Bruce's lack of a knighthood that he had written to the honours committee. He said the star had become part of the fabric of British society. 'It's an outrage that Bruce Forsyth hasn't been knighted,' he told the *Radio Times*.

Two more years passed and still nothing. The campaign continued. And Bruce's celebrity pals remained baffled, particularly as he continued to defy the gods by staying right at the top of show business by presenting *Strictly Come Dancing* well into his eighties. Where else in the world was there a star whose career had enjoyed such amazing longevity?

Bruce's long wait finally ended in June 2011 when he was knighted in the Queen's Birthday Honours. He celebrated with a glass of champagne but admitted, 'I thought it would never happen. I had said to my wife earlier in the year that it is just something that will never ever happen and that is just the way it is. The only stars from light entertainment to be knighted were Norman Wisdom – and he was 90 – and Harry Secombe. But people who make people laugh, why should they be ignored?'

He said that, when he received the letter telling him about the honour, he wondered if it was a wind-up. 'We were doubtful because it's been going on so long, the speculation,' he said. 'We thought it might be a hoax so we did check all the way down the line that it was real.'

Then came the really tricky bit – keeping schtum. 'Being sworn to secrecy was the hardest part,' he said. 'I was able to say to my wife, "Darling, you're going to be a Lady but you can't tell a soul."'

Bruce said that the award was the pinnacle of his long career in show business. 'When you are keeping a thing like that secret, you don't know whether it is real or not. But it has finally become real now. I'm so grateful to the people who have supported me for so long and helped make this possible.

'It makes me feel as though my life has been worthwhile. To have got this, it makes [you] feel as if you have achieved something [in life]. You have got something near the end of the journey that comes from so many people.'

Proud Lady Forsyth, Wilnelia, was flying back to Britain from Puerto Rico as her hubby celebrated. Bruce said, 'I am going to the airport to meet her as she has been doing a show in Puerto Rico. I am going to say, "Welcome back, m'lady." That will be such a pleasure as I'm just as thrilled for her as I am for myself.'

But Sir Brucie said the honour would not force him to retire. 'I am doing the next series of *Strictly Come Dancing* and looking forward to it,' he stressed.

The Cabinet Office, which manages the honours system, finally confirmed what fans had suspected for a long time: the delay was simply down to protocol due to his 2005 CBE. A spokesman said, 'Committees like to see four or five years' further service before they start to consider another award. They will take into account a number of factors or achievements.'

Celebrities rushed to congratulate Sir Brucie. His *Strictly* co-presenter Tess Daly said, 'Arise, Sir Brucie! What wonderful news. It couldn't happen to a nicer bloke. Our parents, grandparents and now through *Strictly*, our children, all love him too. Bruce is a national treasure we should all be proud of. But does this mean I'll have to curtsey at the start of each show?'

Former BBC chairman Michael Grade, whose work on his old pal's behalf had at last been recognised, said, 'About time. Nobody deserves it more than him.' BBC One controller Danny Cohen said, 'Bruce Forsyth is a TV legend and a true gentleman.' Bruce was also inundated by emails and messages from the public. 'It's been hectic,' he explained. 'So many calls to make and people to thank.'

Not everyone joined in the national celebration. Take this curmudgeon – a reader, who wrote to the *Daily Express* to express his disappointment. 'OK, let's get the Bruce Forsyth knighthood into proper perspective. The man is a game-show host – and not a particularly good one at that. His past efforts at stand-up comedy were nothing less than cringeworthy – and that just about sums him up.' And that wasn't all. He continued, 'But he has an ego the size of Buckingham Palace and is already talking about his next move into the House of Lords. Describing him as a "national treasure", which I have heard said, borders on the hysterical and reflects more on the people who say it than the man they are talking about. However, given that nowadays they give knighthoods to just about anybody, he is probably as qualified as the rest of them for this honour.'

However, the negative reaction was completely out of synch with the rest of the nation. It was best summed up by a witty and hugely affectionate leader in *The Times*, published the day after the announcement.

Bruce, ever the perfectionist, pored over every review, good or bad. So barbs like that would have hurt.

'Sir Bruce Forsyth, at the age of 83, with almost 70 of his years spent entertaining audiences with his singing, dancing, wisecracking and gurning, finding time in between to wed a string of beautiful women who were seduced by his wit, his waltzing feet and by a hairdo so hypnotic it must occasionally make even Donald Trump envious.

'The knighthood brings to a happy end a campaign waged by his show-business friends, by the media, in Parliament, and by admirers on Facebook and Twitter. It is a battle for recognition that has been fought for so long that you might be forgiven for wondering if the first people to express outrage at Forsyth's omission from the Honours List included Tacitus and Pliny the Younger.

'Gags about Forsyth's venerable age have become traditional among his fellow comics and presenters. But the jokes are accented by admiration for his professional longevity in an industry so fickle that today's TV star can, as early as next Tuesday, be as popular as a Spanish cucumber in Hamburg.

'Having started work at 14, touring Britain as Boy Bruce, the Mighty Atom, his big break came with *Sunday Night at the London Palladium* in 1958. *The Generation Game* cemented his fame. *Play Your Cards Right* prolonged it. A guest presenter slot on *Have I Got News for You* in 2003 revived it. *Strictly Come Dancing* has crowned it.

'Forsyth is the last survivor of a generation of performers who learned how to warm up an audience from playing to a cold crowd in Cleethorpes. He comes from a time when TV presenters grew out of musical hall rather than reality TV. He is the closest Britain has today to a Sammy Davis Jr. A knighthood is a fitting capstone to his career.'

Bruce described that long wait for his final gong as 'five years of torment' in an interview with the *Mail on Sunday*. 'It has done wonders for my confidence,' he explained. 'I'm a pretty confident person. But after 83 years you need a boost now and again. The knighthood has definitely given me a boost.

'Since I got the CBE in 2006, people have been coming up to me from all different walks of life and asking, "Why haven't you got a knighthood?" The more people kept asking me, the more I wondered why it was. I asked myself whether

I had done something wrong,' he said, looking genuinely perplexed. 'I wondered what the reason might be. Now it's actually happened it's a relief to me.

'It's also a relief to be part of the British nation. A lot of people feel they were part of it, that they helped make it happen.'

Bruce spoke in more detail about his joy with his old pal, the late Sue Carroll, in the *Daily Mirror*. Sue had interviewed Bruce countless times over the years. She had been battling cancer but stepped off her sick bed to celebrate and reminisce with her old pal.

Bruce explained to Sue how he had asked each of his five daughters by two previous marriages to the house separately to tell them about the knighthood face-to-face. 'Which meant I got a hug too,' he said with a smile.

He was as pleased for Wilnelia as he was for himself. 'I'm hoping this will make her the first woman to be the first lady of a knight in Puerto Rico. She was, after all, their first Miss World. We continued celebrating with breakfast and champagne at home, which turned into family brunch organised by our fabulous housekeeper Cora, who now – get this – wants me to be a Lord. "Steady on," I told her.'

Bruce, while grateful for the support, was keen to distance himself from the public campaigns on his behalf. 'I've never been one for pushing myself into things,' he admitted. 'I can be quite shy – the polar opposite of my TV personality. It's the other side of me. I often think I'd have got a lot further a lot quicker if I'd made those calls or buttered up the right person – it's just not my way. It worked out in the end. There's absolutely nothing like the British people, who are so very loyal and stick by you.

'In other places audiences can be fickle but here they are fiercely loyal and a hundred per cent behind you. Truly the best in the world. If I've learned anything from this honour, it's that I am one extremely lucky man.'

He also paid tribute to his parents. 'For the first 72 hours after the news was made official, I thought a lot about my parents and how proud they'd have been. My mum and dad had such ambition for me. My brother, sister and I wanted for nothing when we were kids. We were never a rich family. So a lot of sacrifices were made on our behalf.'

Barely able to stifle the tears, he paid a special tribute to his beloved late brother John – killed in the Second World War. 'My brother was only 20 when he died,' said Bruce. 'I've lived 63 years more than he ever had a chance to. It doesn't seem right. Perhaps he might have become a Sir before me, who knows?

'I have tried to make the most of the years I've been given. I have a wonderful family, a beautiful wife, a job I love and which I still have the energy for. It seems to me I'm the luckiest man in the world – except on the golf course, obviously.'

Bruce's big day at the palace came on 12 October 2011. He was accompanied by his beloved Wilnelia, daughters Laura and Charlotte, and son JJ.

There may have been a long, long wait for his day of pure majesty, but Bruce showed no signs of bitterness. In fact, he even managed to surprise the Queen in the process.

He said, 'The Queen told me, "Thank you for entertaining the country for so long." I told her that I will have been in the business for 70 years next year. She looked at me in astonishment and said, "Seventy! Goodness, how old were you when you started?"

'"I was 14, Ma'am," I told her. "Been in the business since the war." I think she was rather taken aback, to be honest.'

But there were no other shocks as the 85-year-old monarch – a fan of *Strictly Come Dancing* – awarded him the title of Sir Bruce Forsyth-Johnson, Knight Bachelor, for services to entertainment and charity.

And Sir Bruce looked only ever so slightly creaky as he got down on one knee while the Queen touched him on each shoulder with her father's sword and placed the insignia around his neck. Afterwards, he blew a kiss in the direction of Winnie. Lady Forsyth, who turned 54 the day before the ceremony, said, 'I could not be more proud of him.'

Sir Bruce said his knighthood felt 'completely marvellous'. It was the perfect end to a brilliant career. And didn't he do well!

BIBLIOGRAPHY

BOOKS

Bruce: The Autobiography by Bruce Forsyth
Golf...Is It Only A Game? by Bruce Forsyth
Nice To See You! The Bruce Forsyth Story by Stephanie Pinder
Crying With Laughter: My Life Story by Bob Monkhouse
Over The Limit: My Secret Diaries 1993-98 by Bob Monkhouse
A Fart In A Colander: The Autobiography by Roy Hudd
Bananas Can't Fly: The Autobiography by Des O'Connor
Better Late Than Never: From Barrow Boy to Ballroom by Len Goodman
All Balls And Glitter: My Life by Craig Revel Horwood
My Turn: An Autobiography by Norman Wisdom
Tommy Cooper: Always Leave Them Laughing: The Definitive Biography Of A Comedy Legend by John Fisher

Ken Dodd: The Biography by Stephen Griffin

It's Not What You Think by Chris Evans

High Hopes: My Autobiography by Ronnie Corbett

And It's Goodnight From Him...: The Autobiography of the Two Ronnies by Ronnie Corbett

The Chronicles Of Hernia by Barry Cryer

You Won't Believe This But... An Autobiography Of Sorts by Barry Cryer and Michael Palin.

Windmill Theatre by Ronald Cohn and Jesse Russell

London's Theatres: A Guide To London's Most Famous And Historic Theatres by Zoe Wanamaker, Mike Kilburn and Alberto Arzoz

We Never Closed – The Windmill Story by Sheila Van Damm

An Introductory History Of British Broadcasting by Andrew Crisell

A History Of Modern Britain by Andrew Marr

The Eye Of Revelation by Peter Kelder

Morecambe And Wise by Graham McCann

Eric & Ernie: The Autobiography of Morecambe & Wise by Eric Morecombe and Ernie Wise

Strictly Come Dancing: The Official 2011 Annual by Bruce Forsyth and Tess Daly

Double Bill 80 Years of Entertainment by Bill Cotton

Stage Struck by Lionel Blair

The London Palladium: The Story Of The Theatre And Its Stars by Christopher Woodward

Tarbuck On Showbiz by Jimmy Tarbuck

Tarbuck On Golf by Jimmy Tarbuck

Now And Then: An Autobiography by Roy Castle

Twice Brightly by Harry Secombe

NEWSPAPERS
The Sun
Daily Mirror
Sunday People
Daily Express
Sunday Express
Sunday Times
The Times
Sunday Times
Daily Star
Daily Telegraph
Sunday Telegraph
Daily Mail
Mail On Sunday
The Guardian
The Observer
News of the World
Daily Sketch
London Evening News
New York Times
New York Post
New York Daily News
The Stage

MAGAZINES
Radio Times
TV Times
Hello!
OK!

TV SHOWS

Celebrity Come Dine With Me Channel 4 (2010)
Living With Brucie Channel 4 (2010)
Who Do You Think You Are? BBC1 (2010)
Have I Got News For You BBC1 (2003, 2010, 2011)
Room 101 BBC2 (2008)
An Audience With Bruce Forsyth ITV (1997)

AUDIO CD

These Are My Favourites by Bruce Forsyth